ASTON MARTIN
Model by Model

ASTON MARTIN
Model by Model

ANDREW NOAKES

THE CROWOOD PRESS

First published in 2012 by

The Crowood Press Ltd

Ramsbury, Marlborough

Wiltshire SN8 2HR

enquiries@crowood.com

www.crowood.com

This impression 2020

British Library Cataloguing-in-Publication Data

A catalogue record for this book is available from the British Library.

ISBN 978 1 84797 322 1

Frontispiece: Aston Martin's modern ethos of 'Power, Beauty and Soul' is typified by the 189mph V8 Vantage S of 2011.

Typeset by Shane O'Dwyer, Swindon, Wiltshire

Printed and bound in India by Parksons Graphics

CONTENTS

ACKNOWLEDGEMENTS

THE PRESS OFFICE staffs of Aston Martin, Aston Martin Racing, Jaguar, Ford and Prodrive, past and present, have provided a multitude of facts and many photographs, and have given me opportunities to photograph Aston Martins in many different settings. Two excellent car museums, Coventry Transport Museum and the Heritage Motor Centre at Gaydon (just down the road from Aston Martin's current headquarters) also allowed me to photograph Aston Martins they had on display. The Aston Martin Heritage Trust, which safeguards Aston Martin's history, proved an invaluable source for checking facts and provided pictures from its archives. The Aston Martin Owners Club welcomed me to club events such as the Windsor parade in 2005 and the Club concours at Blenheim in 2010, where I was able to meet owners and to photograph some rare Astons and Lagondas.

Pictures and details of the very rare Ogle Aston Martin V8 were kindly supplied from the archives section of www.allastonmartin.com owned by Philip Jones of Byron International Automotive Brokerage. Ian Callum generously gave up his time to talk to me about the DB7 for a previous Crowood book, and some of that information has gone into the chapter on the Bloxham cars. David Richards, chairman of Aston Martin and Prodrive, gave an insight into the company's future plans. Neill Bruce, Harry Calton and the late Roger Stowers have all provided useful information during my researches into Aston Martin history over the years. Aston enthusiast Tim Cottingham's amazingly comprehensive and well informed website www.astonmartins.com was another very useful source. It includes numerous photographs of rare Aston Martins taken by Tim himself, as well as information on all eras of Aston Martins.

Finally, a 'thank-you' is due to the dozens of automotive journalists and historians whose books and articles I have consulted while piecing together the stories of well over 100 Aston Martin and Lagonda models. Without their diligent reporting and fact checking, my task would have been a great deal harder.

INTRODUCTION

IT WAS ALMOST 100 years ago that Lionel Martin and Robert Bamford got together to run an agency for Singer cars in a London back street. The fledgling Bamford & Martin company was soon making its own car – the Aston-Martin – but right from the start the company struggled to maintain any kind of financial stability. In the years that followed, stable, successful eras were punctuated by crisis and, more than once, financial meltdown that appeared to be terminal.

Through it all Aston Martin, and Lagonda with which it has been associated for more than six decades, has survived to

One of the earliest surviving Aston Martins, chassis S26 was owned by Mort Morris-Goodall, the first honorary secretary of the Aston Martin Owners Club.

**The Aston Martin V12 Vantage Zagato is the latest in
a series of collaborations with the Italian styling house.**

produce some extraordinary cars and become accepted as the epitome of automotive 'cool'. From the earliest days of Aston Martin the focus was on quality, style and performance. The sports cars which come from Gaydon today have all the panache of their forebears from London, Feltham, Newport Pagnell and Bloxham, along with ever greater performance, and each model is more comprehensively developed than ever before.

This book attempts to describe every significant Aston Martin and Lagonda model – perhaps for the first time, at least outside the Aston Martin Owners Club's multi-volume model register, which is excellent, but only usually available to members. From the earliest cars built in tiny numbers by Lionel Martin, through the high-profile David Brown cars and the long-running V8s, to the Bloxham and Gaydon cars of recent years, every type and era of Aston Martin and Lagonda are represented.

Broadly this book follows a chronological order, with each significant model given an entry of its own. But history rarely runs in straight lines, and Aston Martin's history is no exception, so in a few cases the entries have been moved around in the timeline in an attempt to make the underlying story easier to assimilate. The sharp-eyed will also note that the eras described by the chapter headings in some cases overlap: most notably, the DB7 and its derivatives have been given a chapter of

their own, as their story runs parallel to, and largely separate from, that of the successive generations of 'traditional' Astons hand built at Newport Pagnell – a strictly chronological approach would have mashed the two parallel tales confusingly together. The Lagonda Vignale concept also finds a home in this chapter: had it gone into production, which sadly was never to be, it would have been built at Bloxham alongside the DB7.

In some cases similar models have been dealt with in a single entry to avoid repetition of details. There are also entries for a handful of cars that are not strictly speaking Aston Martins or Lagondas, but which have strong connections to these marques – such as the Lola-Aston Le Mans cars (of two different eras) and the Nimrod-Astons of the 1980s.

Every major Aston Martin model is covered here, together with many more which may have been less successful or had a less lasting impact, but which are, nevertheless, still of interest to an enthusiast of the marque. Inevitably with a bespoke manufacturer such as Aston Martin, numerous 'one-offs' have been built over the years as development projects or for wealthy customers, and there is not space here to cover every single one of them. But some of the most interesting rarities – such as the Ogle V8, the Atom, the DB4GT 'Jet', the 1969 Lagonda and the mysterious DB GT – are described and illustrated in the pages that follow.

THE EARLY YEARS

The 15/98 was introduced in 1936.
This car has an Abbott drophead body.

1912–1945

ROBERT BAMFORD AND Lionel Martin formed a partnership in 1912 to run a motor sales and repair business just off the Fulham Road in Chelsea. Bamford and Martin were the local agents for Singer, and were soon modifying Singer cars for competition – Martin's modified Singer, registered LH3019, becoming a familiar sight in pre-war speed events. But the ambitious Martin wanted more, and by 1914 he was ready to build a car of his own – a fast, quality car for touring or competition use, built for what he called the 'discerning owner driver'. It was launched in October of that year as the 'Aston-Martin', linking Martin's name with that of Aston Hill, a famous hillclimb venue near Aylesbury; it was registered for road use in 1915.

A second car was not built until after World War I, and shortly after Bamford resigned from the company. In 1920 Martin moved the business to larger premises in Abingdon Road, Kensington, a couple of miles from the original garage premises in Chelsea. He also moved his family home from Sloane Square to Pembroke Villas, just around the corner from the new workshop. But he concentrated on racing instead of setting up car production, designing completely new 16-valve engines and entering two cars into the 'voiturettes' class of the 1922 French Grand Prix. A short-chassis car known as 'Bunny' set a gaggle of endurance speed records at Brooklands. But despite some creditable sporting performances the company was not generating enough revenue to remain afloat.

In 1924 Martin realized his own resources were not enough to keep the business alive, and sold it to the Charnwood family. The Hon. John Benson, later Lord Charnwood, designed a new 8-valve, twin-cam engine to replace the 16-valve unit. Though Aston-Martins appeared at the Motor Show at Olympia in 1925, it was a short-lived revival: the company ran out of money, production ceased, and the receivers were called in. It was the end of the company that Bamford and Martin had founded, and it would be the end of the cars that Martin had masterminded – but the Aston Martin marque would survive.

In 1926 the Charnwoods set up a new company, Aston Martin Motors, at new premises in Feltham, Middlesex. They were joined in the new venture by W.S. Renwick and A.C. 'Bert' Bertelli of the Birmingham engine company Renwick and Bertelli. Italian-born engineer Bertelli ran Enfield-Allday Motors until its parent company failed in 1922, then worked for Woolf Barnato before entering the partnership with Renwick. Claude Hill was engaged to design a single overhead cam 1½-litre 4-cylinder engine, which Bertelli hoped he could sell to car manufacturers and use in his own car, to be called the R&B. Instead that engine went into a new generation of Aston Martins with chassis drawn up by Bertelli and bodywork by Bertelli's brother Enrico, who set up shop next door to Aston Martin in Feltham.

ABOVE: **The first 'Aston-Martin' (the hyphen was dropped later) was nicknamed 'Coal Scuttle'. It hit the road in 1915.**

LEFT: **Aston Martin earned its reputation in motor sport: this is one of two 'voiturettes' built for the 1922 French GP. Note the 'AM' logo on the windows of the works van in the background.**

BELOW: **Aston Martin first raced at Le Mans in 1928, but without success: both works cars broke axles on the way to the event, and neither finished the race.**

LEFT: **Aston Martin's first factory was in this side street, just off the Fulham Road in Chelsea. In 2010 this was a private gated mews.**
RIGHT: **Keen cyclist Lionel Martin was the driving force behind the Bamford and Martin partnership that evolved into Aston Martin, but he was always more interested in racing than in making his company profitable.**

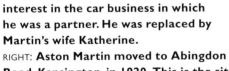

ABOVE: **Robert Bamford quickly lost interest in the car business in which he was a partner. He was replaced by Martin's wife Katherine.**
RIGHT: **Aston Martin moved to Abingdon Road, Kensington, in 1920. This is the site in 2010.**

Like Martin, Bertelli was convinced of the value motor racing had in improving and promoting his cars, and in 1928 he sent two Aston 'team cars' to compete in the 24-hour race at Le Mans. Both broke axles during the race. Racing continued, but sales were slow in the depression and once again Aston Martin descended into financial turmoil. The Charnwoods, and then Renwick, left the company. Bertelli sought outside investment to keep Aston Martin going, first from H. J. Aldington of AFN Ltd, and then from Lance Prideaux-Brune of Winter Garden Garages, a London dealer. The cars were modified to reduce costs, swapping Aston Martin-built gearboxes and axles for bought-in units, and prices were slashed.

Aston Martin returned to Le Mans in 1931, winning their class and finishing fifth overall. A year later the Aston team cars again finished fifth overall, and they took the first two places in their class – also winning the Le Mans Biennial Cup for the best aggregate result over two years. To celebrate, a high-performance 'Le Mans' production model was introduced.

The Le Mans success attracted the attention of Sir Arthur Sutherland, a Newcastle shipping magnate, who injected much needed capital. Sutherland's son Gordon had worked for Alvis and had technical training, but he joined Aston Martin to look after sales and service, while Bertelli continued to perfect the road and racing cars. But while Bertelli was keen to continue racing, the Sutherlands were more inclined to spend Aston Martin's money developing road cars. In 1936 Bertelli resigned, leaving Gordon Sutherland in sole charge of Aston Martin, and his erstwhile assistant Claude Hill took over as chief designer.

Sutherland and Hill soon started work on an all-new car, the Atom, and had built a prototype by the middle of 1939.

Then war intervened, and like the rest of the motor industry, Aston Martin swapped peacetime production for war work, in Feltham's case on aircraft components.

After the war Sutherland realized that Aston Martin needed outside investment in order to put a version of the Atom into production, and he offered the company for sale. His advertisement in *The Times* caught the eye of industrialist David Brown, who was immediately impressed when he drove the Atom. Brown bought Aston Martin, and added Lagonda a few months later – and a whole new era began.

LIONEL MARTIN SERIES

THE FIRST ASTON-MARTIN was built at the Bamford and Martin workshops in Henniker Place, Chelsea, in 1914. Power came from a sidevalve Coventry Simplex engine of 1389cc, which Martin installed in an Isotta Fraschini chassis and clothed in new bodywork – the shape of which gave rise to the car's works' nickname, 'Coal Scuttle'. The new car clocked up 15,000 miles (24,000km) during the war, both on the road and in competition, but it remained the only Aston-Martin for some years, as Lionel Martin spent the war working for the Admiralty, and Bamford joined the Army Service Corps.

A second prototype was built in 1920. The following year it acquired a heavily revised engine, still with an integral head and block but now equipped with three main bearings and improved lubrication. A 107mm stroke expanded the capacity

to 1486cc, in which form it was road-tested by *Motor* and *Autocar*. Production models were similar, but with the addition of front wheel brakes – which were still something of a novelty on cars of the time. A rolling chassis was listed at £500, and complete cars started at £650.

A new 16-valve overhead cam engine was designed for racing, but it was no more powerful than the existing sidevalve unit. A twin overhead cam 16-valve unit was built in 1922, with support from Count Louis Zborowski, and powered two cars in the 'voiturettes' class of the French Grand Prix in 1922. But the sidevalve engine also had its greatest achievement that year when a short-chassis car known as 'Rabbit' – and later, more famously, as 'Bunny' – set twenty-five 'light car' records and ten outright world speed records at Brooklands.

▌1924 SPORTS 'LIONEL MARTIN SERIES'

Engine	In-line 4-cylinder, single carburettor
Valvegear	Pushrod overhead valve
Bore and stroke	66.5 × 107mm
Capacity	1487cc
Power	45bhp @ 4,000rpm
Transmission	Four-speed manual gearbox, rear-wheel drive
Chassis/body	Steel channel chassis, aluminium alloy body
Suspension	Beam axles and semi-elliptic leaf springs front and rear
Brakes	Four-wheel drums, mechanically operated
Performance	Top speed 72mph (116km/h), 0–50mph in 25sec

A3, the fourth Aston Martin built by the fledgling firm. Its restoration by the Aston Martin Heritage Trust was completed in 2009.

1½-LITRE (including INTERNATIONAL, LE MANS)

IN 1926 THE newly formed Aston Martin Motors company created a brand new Aston Martin. The 1494cc, 56bhp engine, which Claude Hill had designed for Renwick and Bertelli, was installed in an old Enfield-Allday chassis for testing, while A.C. Bertelli drew up a new chassis, which would be clothed in Enrico Bertelli bodywork. Two new models were announced at the London Motor Show in 1927: the S-type short chassis at £495, and the T-type long chassis tourer at £575, together with a mock-up of a new competition car.

Two Aston 'team cars' – designated LM1 and LM2 – were built to compete in the 24-hour race at Le Mans in 1928. They were built on a chassis 6in (152mm) shorter than the S-type and fitted with lightweight aluminium-sleeved axles, with the rear axle passing over the chassis rails. The 63bhp engine employed dry-sump lubrication to reduce its height and allow easier oil cooling. Sadly their Le Mans appearance was inauspicious. Both cars broke axles driving to the circuit, LM1 broke its axle again during the race and LM2 retired with a broken gearlever. But Aston Martin did win the Rudge-Whitworth prize for being the fastest 1½-litre cars over the first twenty laps.

The dry-sump engine was offered in a production sports model, the International, which was announced at the 1928 Motor Show. In 1930 70bhp team cars proved fast at the Ulster Tourist Trophy, and a high-compression Ulster road car was offered at a £50 premium. But sales of all the cars were slow, thanks to the effects of the depression.

In 1931 the International was modified to reduce costs by replacing the Aston Martin-built gearbox with a proprietary

ABOVE: **Early International with special fixed-head bodywork by E. Bertelli, taking part in a parade of Astons in front of the Queen in 2005.**
RIGHT: **The oldest surviving T-type tourer, from 1928, was restored by David Hawkins in the 1970s.**

Laycock unit, and swapping the worm-drive rear axle for an ENV spiral-bevel. The chassis was also redesigned for ease of manufacture. On the plus side there were cable-operated front brakes in place of the Perrot-shaft system on earlier cars, and slightly more power. The 'New International' model, which went on sale in 1932, cost £475 – a considerable £120 less than the previous car – but only twelve were made before the model was superseded.

Gordon Sutherland's own Le Mans 2/4-seater, which was road-tested by *Motor Sport* and *Autocar* in 1933, seen at Blenheim in 2010.

■ 1929 INTERNATIONAL

Engine	In-line 4-cylinder, dry-sump, twin SU carburettors
Valvegear	Single overhead cam
Bore and stroke	69.3 × 99mm
Capacity	1494cc
Power	56bhp @ 4,250rpm
Transmission	Four-speed manual gearbox, rear-wheel drive
Chassis/body	Steel channel chassis, aluminium alloy body
Suspension	Beam axles, semi-elliptic leaf springs front and rear
Brakes	Four-wheel drum brakes, mechanically operated
Performance	Top speed 78mph (126km/h), 0–50mph in 20sec

Aston Martin's class-winning performances at Le Mans in 1931/32 won them the ninth Le Mans Biennial Cup and, to celebrate, a 'Le Mans' production model was introduced. A much lower radiator gave the new Aston Martin a distinctive appearance, and with a still higher compression ratio of 7.5:1, it had performance to match the looks. In its 1933 road test *Autocar* said it was the closest thing to a racing car available for road use, and it proved to be highly popular. With the factory at full capacity, Aston Martin could not build new team cars for racing, and Bertelli cobbled together a team by buying back one of the 1932 cars, borrowing another, and entering 'Mort' Morris-Goodall in his 1931 car. The two 1932 cars (LM9 and LM10) finished a creditable fifth and seventh, respectively.

■ 1933 LE MANS

Engine	In-line 4-cylinder, dry-sump, twin SU carburettors
Valvegear	Single overhead cam
Bore and stroke	69.3 × 99mm
Capacity	1494cc
Power	70bhp @ 4,750rpm
Transmission	Four-speed manual gearbox, rear-wheel drive
Chassis/body	Steel channel chassis, aluminium alloy body
Suspension	Beam axles, semi-elliptic leaf springs front and rear
Brakes	Four-wheel drum brakes, cable front, mechanically operated rear
Performance	Top speed 82mph (132km/h), 0–50mph in 16sec

MARK II AND ULSTER

A FLAT-TOPPED SCUTTLE and thermostatically controlled radiator shutters were the obvious changes on 1934 'Mark II' cars. Under the skin the chassis was stiffer, and relocated Hartford friction dampers improved refinement. The engine was given a stiffer, fully counter-balanced crankshaft and improved cylinder head, which raised the power output to 73bhp.

For 1934's team cars, Mark II chassis were drilled to save weight and designated LM11, LM12 and LM14. LM13 was omitted because Bertelli was superstitious – but all three Astons were unlucky that year, retiring with mechanical trouble. All three were rebuilt for the Ards TT using standard, undrilled chassis, and at Bertelli's insistence they were painted Italian racing red rather than the traditional green, to try to change Aston's luck. At the TT they finished third, sixth and seventh and won the team prize.

To capitalize on the TT success an 'Ulster' production model was introduced. Its narrow body had a horizontal spare wheel kept in the tail, and there was a fold-flat windscreen. The 1½-litre engine was tuned to give 80bhp, and Aston Martin guaranteed that each one would exceed 100mph (161km/h). It cost £750, £140 more than the 'standard' Mark II two/four-seater. Just twenty-one Ulsters were built, and today they are renowned as one of the finest pre-war production Aston Martins.

■ 1935 ULSTER

Engine	In-line 4-cylinder, dry-sump, twin SU carburettors
Valvegear	Single overhead cam
Bore and stroke	69.3 × 99mm
Capacity	1494cc
Power	85bhp @ 5,250rpm
Transmission	Four-speed manual gearbox, rear-wheel drive
Chassis/body	Steel channel chassis, aluminium alloy body
Suspension	Beam axles, semi-elliptic leaf springs front and rear
Brakes	Four-wheel drum brakes, cable front, mechanically operated rear
Performance	Top speed 100mph (161km/h), 0–50mph in 12sec

This Ulster was bequeathed to the Aston Martin Owners Club by Lewis Treece in 1974.

15/98, SPEED MODEL, TYPE C

ASTON MARTIN BEGAN testing larger versions of the Bertelli/Hill engine in 1934. After tests with a 1.7-litre engine, the 4-cylinder engine was expanded both in bore and stroke to displace almost 2 litres. Both 1½-litre and 2-litre cars were entered at Le Mans in 1936, but that year's race was cancelled at the last minute due to a national strike, and the unraced 2-litre team cars were sold. Production 2-litre cars – known as the 15/98 – were available later that year using 98bhp wet-sump engines and a similar chassis to the 1½-litre Ulster, but fitted with Lockheed hydraulic brakes and extra cable location on the front axle to prevent the leaf springs deforming under heavy braking.

RIGHT: **The Type C was built to drum up sales in 1938. Despite its aerodynamic body it proved little quicker than the regular 2-litre Speed Model.**
ASTON MARTIN HERITAGE TRUST

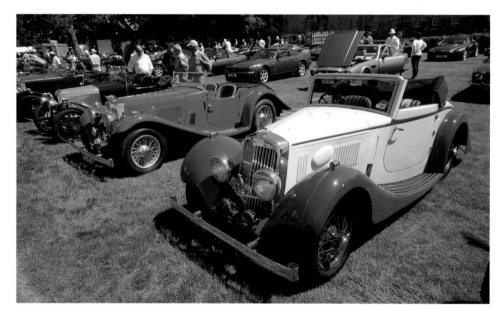

The 2-litre models were often fitted with more sophisticated bodywork than earlier cars, as these Abbott-bodied cars demonstrate.

While A.C. Bertelli had been at Aston Martin the cars' bodywork had been built by his brother Enrico, but with Bertelli's departure both Abbotts and Abbey built bodies for Aston Martin. The standard bodies for the 15/98 departed from previous Aston practice by incorporating flowing, chassis-mounted wings instead of cycle wings attached to the brake backplates.

A 'Speed Model', essentially a replica of the Le Mans racers, was also offered, but it proved to be a slow seller. In an effort to clear a stock of unsold Speed Model chassis in 1938 Aston Martin offered the 'Type C', with radical aerodynamic bodywork including headlamps set close together behind a wire mesh radiator grille. Unfortunately the Type C proved little quicker than the normal Speed Model, and it did little to speed up sales.

■ 1938 15/98

Engine	In-line 4-cylinder, twin SU carburettors
Valvegear	Single overhead cam
Bore and stroke	78 × 102mm
Capacity	1950cc
Power	98bhp @ 5,000rpm
Transmission	Four-speed manual gearbox, rear-wheel drive
Chassis/body	Steel channel chassis, aluminium alloy body
Suspension	Beam axles, semi-elliptic leaf springs front and rear
Brakes	Four-wheel drum brakes, hydraulically operated
Performance	Top speed 85mph (137km/h), 0–50mph in 14sec

ATOM

THE ATOM WAS the prototype for future Astons, with which Gordon Sutherland and Claude Hill planned to replace the Bertelli cars. Previous Aston Martins had been based on a traditional ladder-type chassis, but the Atom's was made from square and rectangular section tubes, welded to which was a lighter tubular body frame. The body tubes contributed some stiffness to the chassis, allowing the main chassis members to be lighter without compromising the stiffness of the whole car. The body frame was clothed in aluminium alloy body panels.

The styling was futuristic. In 1938 Aston Martin had built a one-off 15/98 clothed in aerodynamic saloon coachwork – a car known at Feltham as 'Donald Duck' – and the unsuccessful Type C had continued the theme. The Atom shape was clearly a development of these cars, with bulbous wings integrated into the main body and no running boards. Unlike the Type C, which had its headlights mounted behind an oval wire mesh grille, the Atom's lamps were flush-mounted in the wings. There was no conventional radiator grille, just a series of twenty-four slots arranged in a pair of triangles either side of a thin chrome strip, which continued on to the bonnet. Sutherland favoured closed cars, so there was a fixed roof and four doors, both doors on each side being hinged from the central pillar.

For the first time Aston Martin moved away from a conventional beam axle. Instead, the front suspension was independent, with a cast trailing arm and coil spring on each side, together with a hydraulic lever-arm damper, arranged so that the damper arm was parallel to the suspension arm. The steering incorporated a divided track rod to reduce bump-steer. The beam axle used at the rear incorporated Salisbury's new hypoid bevel final drive, which allowed the propshaft line to be lower. The axle was conventionally mounted on leaf springs. The Atom was fitted with a Cotal electric gearbox, a four-speed epicyclic geartrain controlled by solenoids, which were operated using a tiny gearlever mounted on the dashboard.

Gordon Sutherland ran the Atom during the war, powered by a 15/98 engine, and it proved to have good performance and excellent ride quality. The new engine, which had always been planned for the Atom, was ready in 1944. The overhead camshaft sophistication of the earlier engine was gone, replaced by the simplicity and low cost of pushrods and rockers, with a low-mounted camshaft driven by a chain from the (five-bearing) crank. It had vertical inlet valves and offset exhaust valves – the idea being to improve exhaust efficiency and increase power.

The new engine was considerably less 'under-square' than the previous unit – in other words, the bore was wider and the stroke shorter, making it smoother and freer-revving than before. Despite the poor quality of wartime 'pool' petrol, which demanded the use of a lower compression ratio, the new engine still produced 90bhp and gave the Atom a top speed in excess of 100mph (161km/h).

Gordon Sutherland and Claude Hill masterminded the construction of this prototype, the Atom, just before World War II. Though it never went into production in this form, the Atom would impress David Brown enough for him to invest in the company.

■ 1944 ATOM PROTOTYPE

Engine	In-line 4-cylinder, twin SU carburettors
Valvegear	Pushrod overhead valve
Bore and stroke	82.55 × 92mm
Capacity	1970cc
Power	90bhp @ 4,750rpm
Transmission	Four-speed Cotal electric gearbox, rear-wheel drive
Chassis/body	Tubular steel frame, aluminium alloy body
Suspension	Trailing arms with coil springs front; live axle, semi-elliptic leaf springs rear
Brakes	Four-wheel drum brakes, hydraulically operated
Performance	Top speed 105mph (169km/h), 0–50mph in 18sec

EARLY LAGONDAS

THE LAGONDA MARQUE is older than Aston Martin. It was founded in 1899 in Staines, just a few miles away from Aston Martin's Bertelli-era home of Feltham.

Wilbur Adams Gunn moved to Britain from Springfield, Ohio, towards the end of the nineteenth century. As a consulting engineer he worked on a variety of machinery, including hydraulic equipment and marine steam engines. He started building motorcycles after mating an engine to a bicycle for his own use, selling them under the name 'Lagonda' – the name of a creek running through his home town. Later Gunn moved on to three-wheelers, and in 1909 he began selling the first Lagonda cars.

Gunn's first cars were small 10hp machines, but Lagondas quickly grew in size and power, using a Coventry-Simplex engine (just as Aston Martin would a few years later). This model was developed into a more powerful 16/18hp car, which raced at

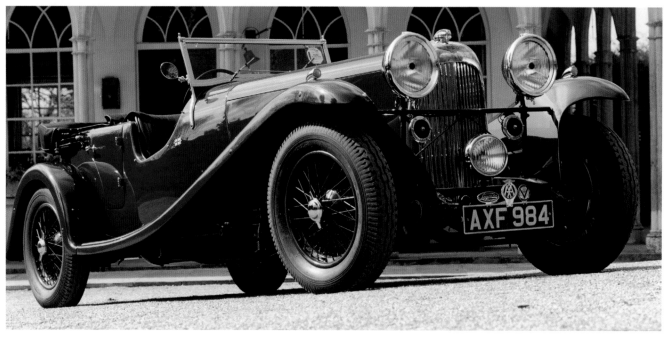

Lagonda built its early fame on fast, suave sporting cars like the Meadows-engined M45.

Brooklands and won the 1910 Moscow-St Petersburg Reliability Trial. As a result Lagonda won a number of export orders, and developed even more powerful 20hp and 30hp cars.

A chassis-less 11.1hp 'Lagonda Light Car' was added to the range in 1913, and after World War I – during which Lagonda's factory was turned over to armaments production – the car reappeared in slightly modified form. It also spawned longer and heavier 11.9hp and 12/24 derivatives. Gunn died in 1920, but the last of the cars he designed continued until 1925, and the Lagondas that followed them were much more conservative.

The first of the new range were the 14/60 and 16/65 of 1925. The former was powered by a 2-litre 4-cylinder engine with twin camshafts and hemispherical combustion chambers, while the later used a 2.7-litre in-line six. The 4-cylinder range was augmented with a lighter Speed model and a thirsty supercharged version, while the unpopular sixes were bored out to become the Lagonda 3-Litre. In 1932 Lagonda's latest 'low chassis' configuration was mated with a Crossley 2-litre 6-cylinder engine for the 16/80 model, while the Lagonda six was enlarged again to produce a 3½-litre model.

In 1933 Lagonda introduced the M45, fitted with a Meadows 4½-litre 6-cylinder engine with coil/magneto dual ignition. It was followed in 1934 by a high-performance M45R Rapide with a shorter, stiffer chassis and powerful Girling brakes.

Six different models were on offer in 1935, from the high-revving 1104cc Rapier up to the fast and beautiful 4½-litre cars – but Lagonda simply didn't have the resources to cope. The receivers were called in, and the company was put up for sale. Meanwhile, Lagonda specialists Fox and Nichol took a specially

■ 1935 M45 RAPIDE

Engine	In-line 6-cylinder, twin SU carburettors
Valvegear	Pushrod overhead valve
Bore and stroke	88.5 × 120.6mm
Capacity	4453cc
Power	140bhp @ 3,100rpm
Transmission	Four-speed manual gearbox, rear-wheel drive
Chassis/body	Steel chassis, aluminium alloy body
Suspension	Beam axles and semi-elliptic leaf springs front and rear
Brakes	Four-wheel drum brakes
Performance	Top speed 101mph (163km/h), 0–50mph in 9.4sec

The Rapide, introduced in 1934, had a shorter and stiffer chassis than the standard M45. A specially prepared car won the 1935 Le Mans race.

**After Lagonda has been rescued by Alan Good, W.O. Bentley was brought in as chief designer. His crowning
achievement was the Lagonda V12, a magnificent machine of which just 185 were built between the wars.**

prepared Rapide to Le Mans, and in the hands of Johnny Hind-
march and Luis Fontès the Lagonda won the race narrowly from
an Alfa Romeo 8C, with an Aston Martin Ulster in third place.

For a while it looked as if Lagonda would be swallowed up
by Rolls-Royce, just as Bentley had been in 1930. But instead
Lagonda was rescued by London solicitor Alan Good, who
reformed the company as LG Motors and brought in W.O.
Bentley as chief designer. Good cleared away the whole of the
extensive, excessive Lagonda range (though the Rapier was
taken on by an independent company, and lived a few more
years), while Bentley revised the M45 to produce the LG45,
then set about designing a pair of genuinely new Lagondas –
the 6-cylinder LG6 and the magnificent 4½-litre V12.

The LG6 was built on a new chassis with cruciform bracing
and independent front suspension using double wishbones and
torsion bars. It also had hydraulic brakes with a dual master
cylinder, which ensured that some braking was available even
in the event of a fluid leak. The engine was a rework of the
previous 4½-litre six, with a new cylinder head and twin mag-
neto ignition.

The V12 was intended to be nothing less than the best car
in the world. It was based on a similar chassis to the LG6, but
in slightly different lengths and fitted with a hypoid bevel rear
axle. The big news, of course, was the engine: a 4480cc V12

with a single overhead camshaft on each cylinder bank, producing 175bhp and making these elegant cars capable of 100mph
(161km/h) with almost unparalleled refinement. The V12 was
first seen in 1936, but really got under way at the 1937 Motor
Show, and 185 were built before production was called to a
halt just after the start of World War II. The prospects for
sales of this expensive and complex machine in the post-war
austerity era were dire so it did not reappear, and instead W.O.
Bentley started work on a new, smaller Lagonda.

■ 1937 V12

Engine	V12, twin SU carburettors
Valvegear	Single overhead cam per bank
Bore and stroke	82.55 × 92mm
Capacity	4480cc
Power	175bhp @ 5,500rpm
Transmission	Four-speed manual gearbox, rear-wheel drive
Chassis/body	Steel chassis, aluminium alloy body
Suspension	Double wishbones with torsion bars front; live axle, semi-elliptic leaf springs rear
Brakes	Four-wheel drum brakes, hydraulically operated
Performance	Top speed 105mph (169km/h), 0–50mph in 9sec

THE FELTHAM
YEARS

Aston Martin became Britain's answer to Ferrari in sports
car racing with machines such as the DBR1 and DB3S.

1945–1958

ASTON MARTIN EMERGED from the war with a promising prototype, the Atom, but without the financial resources needed to develop it for production. Gordon Sutherland realized that the company needed a new investor, and placed an advert in the personal columns of *The Times* newspaper offering Aston Martin for sale.

The advertisement caught the eye of David Brown, chairman of the industrial engineering group founded by his grandfather in 1860. Brown came to Feltham, drove the Atom prototype, and recognized its potential immediately. In February 1947 he bought Aston Martin for £20,000, retaining the services of Gordon Sutherland and engineer Claude Hill to develop the new car for production.

Soon after, Brown was urged to invest in Lagonda by R.A. Scratchard, who ran the company's distributor in Bradford. Brown met W.O. Bentley at Staines and examined the twin-cam, 6-cylinder engine Lagonda was developing for a range of smaller postwar cars, though he baulked at the £250,000 being offered for the company by rival investors. But the big bids evaporated, and Brown was able to pick up Lagonda's assets for just £52,500. The factory itself was sold to diesel engine manufacturer Petters, so Brown moved all the machinery into some rented hangars at Hanworth airfield, near Aston Martin's base at Feltham.

Lagonda stylist Frank Feeley was soon working on the shape of the new Aston Martin sports car – later known as the DB1 – but David Brown's plans for integration between the two companies went much further than that. The DB2 of 1949 saw the first use of the Lagonda LB6 2.6-litre 6-cylinder engine in an Aston, and all the company's products would be powered by variations of that engine for years to come. But it would also lead to the departure of Claude Hill, who had been working on a 6-cylinder version of his 4-cylinder DB1 engine.

Although Aston Martin had achieved a notable, and unexpected, win in the 1948 Spa 24-hours with a racing car based on the DB1 chassis, serious racing efforts began the following year with prototype DB2s and then a purpose-built racing machine, the DB3, designed by Professor Robert Eberan von Eberhorst of pre-war Auto Union fame. Running the team was John Wyer, whom Brown had met at Spa in 1948 when he was managing a private team running a pre-war Aston Martin. By 1949 Wyer was at a loose end, and Brown invited him to spend a year at Aston Martin running the racing activities while he decided what he wanted to do next – but Wyer was to remain at Aston Martin for thirteen years.

The DB3 proved to be too big and too heavy, and even when the Lagonda/Bentley engine was expanded to 2.9 litres, Aston Martin could not compete with the lighter, spaceframe Jaguar C-types with their 3.4-litre engines. The DB3 was replaced by the smaller, lighter DB3S, designed by Willie Watson, which proved to be much more competitive. In the second half of 1953 it won everything it entered, giving Aston Martin great optimism for the following season. But 1954 was a disaster: Feltham spread its engineering resources too thin, tackling a

The DB2 was Aston Martin's first really successful postwar car. It combined a chassis derived from the Atom with a 6-cylinder engine from Lagonda.

supercharged engine for the DB3S, a pair of DB3S coupés for Le Mans and a sport-racing Lagonda with a new V12 engine, on top of its road-car work.

Aston Martin's road cars were selling better than ever, and the DB2's appeal was strengthened when a minor rework of the chassis and body resulted in two extra seats and considerably better luggage space, a model known as the DB2/4. Further refinements produced the DB2/4 Mark II and then the DB Mark III, with DB3S-inspired styling.

The racing V12 Lagonda had been born from David Brown's desire to win overall victories at the major races such as Le Mans, but the engine proved to be fundamentally flawed. Development of the car did not continue beyond 1955, though the spaceframe chassis it used that year would live again.

Instead, attention switched to the DBR1, an all-new racing car designed by Ted Cutting. With a spaceframe chassis and a brand new engine, the DBR1 was lighter and more powerful than the DB3S. When, in the wake of the dreadful 1955 Le Mans accident, the sports car racing regulations were redrawn to limit engine sizes to 3 litres, the 2.9-litre DBR1 was the ideal car. But initially Aston Martin failed to capitalize on this piece of good fortune, with numerous retirements in 1957 and 1958, which were often caused by transmission failures.

In 1959 the team entered Grand Prix racing, but sadly for Aston Martin that venture came at just the wrong time. The DBR4 Formula 1 car, derived from the DBR1's chassis and engine, had been ready in 1958, but Aston Martin had chosen

ABOVE: **Industrialist David Brown bought Aston Martin in 1947, almost as a hobby, and added Lagonda a few months later.**
BELOW: **The DB Mark III was the ultimate expression of the DB2 family, with improvements to the body and a heavily revised engine.**

Aston Martin dallied with Formula 1 racing with the DBR4 (*pictured*) and DBR5, but by the time they appeared they were already obsolete thanks to a new era of rear-engined cars.

The DBR1 won the Le Mans 24-hour race and the World Sports Car Championship for Aston Martin in 1959.

to concentrate on sports car racing that year. By 1959, when the DBR4 was campaigned seriously, front-engined cars were on the way out, with Cooper and then Lotus showing that future success in F1 would lie with rear-engined cars. Aston Martin did not have the resources to start again with a new car, and instead the team went back to what it knew best – sports car racing.

For 1959 Aston Martin concentrated on Le Mans, attacking the Ferraris with a three-car team led by Stirling Moss. Moss set a blistering early pace in the race, and although his DBR1 did not last the distance, it did its job by breaking the Ferraris.

As the Maranello machines dropped out with engine and transmission problems, the DBR1 of Roy Salvadori and Carroll Shelby circulated without any major dramas, and at their tenth attempt Aston Martin won at Le Mans.

That win gave Aston Martin second place in the World Sports Car Championship – to take the title they needed an outright win in the final round, the Tourist Trophy at Goodwood. A team of three DBR1s was sent to battle the Ferraris and Porsches, and despite setting their pits alight (as they had done in 1952), Aston Martin won the race and with it the world title. It was the zenith of Aston Martin's achievements on the race track.

LAGONDA 2.6

LAGONDA'S PRE-WAR PRODUCTS were aimed at a wealthy clientèle, but in the aftermath of war it seemed likely that there would be few customers for expensive cars powered by vast V12 engines, so chief engineer W.O. Bentley initiated work on a smaller Lagonda. Under his supervision Willie Watson drew up a new 6-cylinder in-line engine, the LB6, giving it twin overhead camshafts, hemispherical combustion chambers and opposed valves set at 30 degrees to the vertical. At first the capacity was 2.3 litres, though that later became 2.6. The crankcase extended well below crankshaft level, and carried the main bearings in split circular carriers called 'cheeses'.

The new engine went into an entirely new car with a cruciform-braced chassis, all-independent suspension and Cotal electric transmission (which Sutherland and Hill had employed in the Aston Martin Atom). A handful of prototypes was built, but Lagonda did not have the resources to put the car into production until David Brown bought the company in 1947.

Detail improvements were made for the production Lagonda 2.6, including a reinforced chassis and a switch to a conventional manual gearbox supplied by the David Brown corporation. The initial four-door saloon was followed by a Tickford-bodied drophead. A Mark II version with more power was introduced in 1952.

▌ 1949 LAGONDA 2.6

W.O. Bentley produced a brand new family of Lagondas for the immediate postwar years, with a cruciform chassis and new 2.6-litre straight six engine.

Engine	In-line 6-cylinder, twin SU carburettors
Valvegear	Twin overhead cam
Bore and stroke	78 × 90mm
Capacity	2580cc
Power	105bhp @ 5,000rpm
Transmission	Four-speed David Brown manual gearbox, rear-wheel drive
Chassis/body	Cruciform platform chassis, aluminium alloy body
Suspension	Double wishbones and coil springs front, independent wishbones and torsion bars rear
Brakes	Four-wheel drum brakes, hydraulically operated
Performance	98mph (158km/h), 0–60mph in 16sec

2-LITRE SPORTS (DB1)

The Atom prototype was developed into this, the 2-Litre Sports – later known as the DB1.

DAVID BROWN HAD been impressed by the Atom prototype, but wanted the first postwar Aston to be a drophead. Claude Hill reworked the chassis using twin side tubes to put back some of the stiffness lost by removing the fixed roof. Though the Atom's roadholding and ride had been impressive, the suspension was modified for the production car: an anti-roll bar was added at the front, and at the rear the Atom's conventional leaf-sprung live axle was replaced by coil springs, trailing arms and a Panhard rod. The Cotal electric gearbox was swapped for a conventional manual gearbox supplied by one of Brown's companies. Test driver St John 'Jock' Horsfall was keen to enter a race-prepared version of this chassis into the Spa 24-hour race, and although Brown had misgivings, he sanctioned the construction of a single car with a simple lightweight body. Amazingly, Horsfall and co-driver Leslie Johnson won the event outright.

Lagonda stylist Frank Feeley was responsible for the blousy curves of the road-going Aston, which managed to incorporate a traditional, upright grille into a full-width modern body. It was launched at the London Motor Show of 1948 as the Aston Martin 2-Litre Sports. Alongside it on Aston Martin's show stand was a 'Spa Replica', actually the Spa-winning car rebuilt with a tidier body.

The new Aston Martins generated a good deal of interest – but that same London show also saw the debut of the Jaguar XK120. Like the Aston, it boasted excellent handling and ride, but the Jaguar had better straight-line performance and cost

just £998 before tax, when the 2-Litre Sports was listed at £1,498 and the Spa Replica was a heady £1,998 (which rose to over £3,000 once purchase tax was added). Aston Martin received no orders for the Spa Replica, and just fourteen production 2-Litre Sports were built between 1948 and 1950. All but one carried the standard drophead bodywork, the odd one out being given an Atom-like saloon body.

During its short production life the 2-Litre Sports was never known as the 'DB1' – it acquired that name retrospectively, after the DB2 appeared in 1949.

■ 1948 2-LITRE SPORTS 'DB1'

Engine	In-line 4-cylinder, twin SU carburettors
Valvegear	Pushrod overhead valve
Bore and stroke	82.55 × 92mm
Capacity	1970cc
Power	90bhp @ 4,750rpm
Transmission	Four-speed David Brown manual gearbox, rear-wheel drive
Chassis/body	Tubular steel frame, aluminium alloy body
Suspension	Trailing arms with coil springs and anti-roll bar front, coil-sprung live axle located by trailing arms and Panhard rod rear
Brakes	Four-wheel drum brakes, hydraulically operated
Performance	Top speed 93mph (150km/h), 0–60mph in 14sec

DB2

CLAUDE HILL WAS keen to build a 6-cylinder version of the pushrod in-line four that he had designed for the DB1, but David Brown had other ideas. Brown's interest in Lagonda was largely because the Staines concern had the very new, and very exciting, LB6 6-cylinder engine which W. O. Bentley's team had been developing since 1943, and which had been unveiled to the public in 1945. With the fully tested Lagonda engine available there was no need to spend time and money developing Hill's 6-cylinder motor, which existed only in drawings. Hill, annoyed that his engine was not going to be built, left the company.

The new car was called the DB2, so the 2-Litre Sports – the first car of the David Brown era – inevitably became known as the DB1. Three prototypes were built and entered into the 1949 Le Mans race, two of them powered by 2-litre DB1 engines and one fitted with a 2.6-litre LB6. The chassis was similar to that of the DB1, but with 9in (229mm) taken out of that car's rather long wheelbase. Despite Brown's preference

for open cars, the DB2 was to start life as a fixed-head coupé. Frank Feeley again penned the body shape, but in contrast to the rather overblown curves of the DB1, the new car had clean and understated lines with hints of Italian influence. To answer the common criticism that engine access was restricted in the then-new 'full-width' body styles, Feeley arranged for the whole front end of the DB2 to fold forwards for easy maintenance.

However, Le Mans 1949 was not to be a fairytale debut for the 6-cylinder engine, as Aston Martin must have hoped. The prototype DB2 had to retire just six laps into the race after a faulty water pump caused it to lose its coolant. One of the 2-litre cars finished seventh overall, a creditable performance, but the other crashed at White House on Sunday morning, and driver Pierre Maréchal sustained injuries from which he died the following day – the only fatal accident ever suffered by Aston's works team. The following month Leslie Johnson and Charles Brackenbury brought the 2.6-litre car home third in the Spa 24-hours, with Lance Macklin and Nick Haines fifth

ABOVE: **The tradition of proving new Aston Martins in competition continued with the DB2. Prototypes appeared at Le Mans in 1949, followed by tuned, lightened works racing machines in 1950 and 1951. XMC77 finished fifth overall in 1951.**
RIGHT: **The strikingly pretty shape of the DB2, with its sweeping wings and curving roof, was shaped by Lagonda stylist Frank Feeley.**

in a 2-litre DB2. Jock Horsfall was fourth in a pre-war Aston Martin Speed Model after driving the whole race single-handed. A DB2 was also taken to Montlhéry in 1950 to attack the 24-hour, 3-litre class record, but the team was forced to abandon the attempt due to fog.

Two more prototype DB2s were built, with their roof lines raised by 4in (102mm) and the front wings reprofiled, the aim being to make the production cars more practical than the early prototypes. The new model was announced early in April 1950, and made its public debut at the New York Motor Show later that month. Road-going versions were given a well appointed interior with a wide, split bench seat and a choice of floor or column gearchanges. A drophead DB2 was available from later that year, David Brown's own example later starring in the Googie Withers film *The Devil on Horseback*.

Three new DB2 team cars – registered VMF63, VMF64 and VMF65 – were built for the Le Mans 24-hour race in June. They were very close to the standard production specification, with just a few essential race modifications: the engines were given free-flow exhausts and higher compression, 40gal (182ltr) fuel tanks were fitted, and the interiors stripped out. As was the norm in those days, Aston Martin drove its cars to the circuit, and VMF65 never made it: it left the road near Rouen while Jack Fairman was driving, at night and in heavy rain. Its place was taken by the prototype 2.6-litre DB2 that had raced at Le Mans and Spa the previous year, a car the team nicknamed 'Sweatbox', which had been accompanying the three race cars on the journey to Le Mans. It lasted eight laps – only two laps more than the previous year – before it broke its crankshaft. The two new cars faired better: Lance Macklin and George Abecassis drove VMF64 to fifth overall, winning the 3-litre class and the Index of Performance, while Charles Brackenbury and Reg Parnell brought VMF63 home sixth overall and second in class.

The DB2 team reappeared in August for the Silverstone sports car race, where the cars were tried with aluminium cylinder heads. Lance Macklin had injured his foot, so regular Aston drivers Reg Parnell and Eric Thompson were joined by French ace Raymond Sommer, who led the Astons home second in class. Aston Martin ended their season with another good race at the Tourist Trophy, where Parnell, Abecassis and Macklin finished first, second and third in their class.

Experience with high-compression racing engines fed back into the road cars early in 1951. The standard engine, with a 6.5:1 compression ratio and two SU H4 carburettors, gave 105bhp, but from January 1951 a 125bhp 'Vantage' engine was offered, with bigger HV6 carburettors and 8.16:1 compression. By then Aston Martin was also offering a neat drophead coupé version of the DB2, and all the cars were benefiting from tidier front-end styling, with the three separate grilles blended into a single aperture. That grille shape would become a fixture in

Aston Martin styling, and the same basic shape is still in use on today's Astons.

Late in 1950 Aston Martin had hired Robert Eberan von Eberhorst as chief engineer. A purpose-built racing car, the DB3, was planned for the 1951 season, but team manager John Wyer could see that development of the new car would take time and was worried that only one of the new cars would be available for Le Mans, and that in untested form. As a stopgap he ordered the construction of two lightweight DB2s, which had bodies built from thinner-gauge aluminium alloy, drilled chassis members and plastic in place of glass for the side and rear windows. Registered XMC76 and XMC77, they were around 450lb (204kg) lighter than standard, and that, together with 138bhp engines with triple Weber carburettors, made them significantly more competitive.

In the event, the DB3 wasn't ready in time for Le Mans and Wyer was forced to turn to VMF64, the 1950 DB2 team car that was now enjoying retirement as one of David Brown's own road cars – though Brown had lent it to Tommy Wisdom for the Mille Miglia, where it won the GT class and finished eleventh overall. In the limited time available VMF was given a crash weight-loss programme, and an updated engine. Lance Macklin and Eric Thompson drove it in the race, thinking they had drawn the short straw because they did not have one of the full lightweights, but came home a magnificent third overall. The two lightweights were fifth and seventh, and two private DB2s tenth and thirteenth. It was the DB2's finest hour, but not quite its last gasp: works DB2s went to the Dundrod TT (where their class was won by a Ferrari) and to the Mille Miglia in May 1952 where Tommy Wisdom won the GT class in VMF64 for the second year in a row.

The DB2 proved popular and 411 were built, more than double the number of any previous Aston Martin model, in the three years before it was replaced by the DB2/4.

■ 1950 DB2

Engine	In-line 6-cylinder, twin SU carburettors
Valvegear	Twin overhead cam
Bore and stroke	78 × 90mm
Capacity	2580cc
Power	105bhp @ 5,000rpm
Transmission	Four-speed David Brown manual gearbox, rear-wheel drive
Chassis/body	Tubular steel frame, aluminium alloy body
Suspension	Trailing arms with coil springs and anti-roll bar front, coil-sprung live axle located by twin trailing arms and Panhard rod rear
Brakes	Four-wheel drum brakes, hydraulically operated
Performance	Top speed 110mph (177km/h), 0–60mph in 12.4sec

DB3

PROFESSOR ROBERT EBERAN von Eberhorst had been the chief engineer with the pre-war Auto Union Grand Prix team, and in 1950 he joined Aston Martin to work on a new racing car, the DB3. Although the DB2 had been competitive in the 3-litre racing class, it was too heavy to race for outright wins. Aston Martin hoped the purpose-built DB3 would be much lighter and much more competitive.

Eberan designed a new twin-tube chassis, with the main members made from sixteen-gauge tubes with a diameter of 4in (120mm). The bare chassis weighed just 151lb (68.5kg). Transverse torsion bar springs were used at both ends, with independent front suspension by trailing links, and a de Dion system at the rear. Alfin drum brakes were fitted all round, inboard at the rear. The DB2's 2.6-litre engine was used – at first driving through a five-speed David Brown gearbox, though later the DB3 would revert to the more reliable DB2 four-speed unit.

Development progressed only slowly through the first half of 1951, not least because Eberan was a perfectionist who liked to approach every problem from first principles. Sensing that the DB3 might not be ready for Le Mans, team manager John Wyer had a pair of lightweight DB2s built, and he was right to be concerned: the DB3 didn't turn a wheel until September 1951, when Lance Macklin had just one day of testing at the Motor Industry Research Association (MIRA) test track

near Nuneaton. The car was then shipped straight to Northern Ireland for the Tourist Trophy at Dundrod, where it ran its bearings after an oil leak from its new magnesium sump.

Testing at Montlhéry early in 1952 showed up some deficiencies in the de Dion suspension, which were rectified before the start of the racing season. DB2s were preferred for Aston Martin's early season appearance at the Mille Miglia, the full team of four DB3s making its debut at the Silverstone sports car race a week later. Motorcycle ace Geoff Duke, in his first major event for Aston Martin, retired when his DB3 developed steering problems, but the other three cars finished first, second and third in class. At the Bern sports car Grand Prix Duke's knowledge of the circuit helped him chase the Mercedes-Benzes home in fourth place.

That year's Monaco Grand Prix was for sports cars, and Aston Martin drove three DB3s to Monte Carlo for the race. All three suffered conrod failures in their new 2.9-litre engines, Parnell's sliding on its own oil into the straw bales on the outside of St Devote corner and being hit by several other cars. After the race, standard engines were flown out in David Brown's private plane and fitted to the two drivable DB3s so they could be driven to Le Mans. They were joined there by a new DB3 fitted with a fastback hardtop, which it was hoped would reduce drag and allow a higher top speed. It was planned that the fastback would replace the Parnell car, which had been

A new twin-tube chassis designed by Robert Eberan von Eberhorst underpinned the DB3 racing car, which made its debut late in 1951.

despatched by train to coachbuilder Henri Chapron in Paris for body repairs, but when another of the DB3s was badly damaged in an accident on the first day of Le Mans practice, the Parnell car was pressed into service. Henri Chapron had to finish repairs overnight, and saved time by giving the car a unique 'bob tail'. But all the effort came to nothing, as all three DB3s retired from the race with axle failures.

The bob-tailed DB3 was given a modified 2.9-litre engine for the Goodwood Nine Hours that August, and was going well until a final-drive oil seal broke up. Worse was to come: while the DB3 was being refuelled, one of the mechanics spilled fuel over the back of the car and it caught alight. Although the fire was soon under control, the car was badly damaged and three personnel (including Wyer) were badly burned. The second DB3 driven by George Abecassis and Dennis Poore retired with clutch failure – but the Peter Collins/Pat Griffith DB3 came through to win the race, salvaging some honour for the Feltham team.

Two DB3s with revised 2.9-litre engines were taken to Monza in December for testing, yielding useful results despite a circuit covered in snow! The 1953 season then kicked off early with a trip to Sebring, where Parnell was narrowly beaten by a Cunningham. Parnell was again the leading Aston Martin driver at the Mille Miglia, where he finished fifth despite broken rear suspension and a broken throttle cable – he brought the car home by wiring the throttle open and controlling the car with the ignition switch! It was the best Mille Miglia result a British car had ever achieved.

But it was almost the end for the DB3. Too big and too heavy – it was only slightly lighter than the 'lightweight' DB2s Wyer had built in 1951 – the DB3 was never likely to be fully competitive with the lightweight and larger-engined Jaguars. The solution to that problem came from Willie Watson, and it meant the construction of a new car.

■ 1952 DB3

Engine	In-line 6-cylinder, triple Weber 35DCO carburettors
Valvegear	Twin overhead cam
Bore and stroke	83 × 90mm
Capacity	2922cc
Power	163bhp @ 5,500rpm
Transmission	Four-speed David Brown manual gearbox, rear-wheel drive
Chassis/body	Tubular steel frame, aluminium alloy body
Suspension	Trailing arms with torsion bars front, de Dion with torsion bars rear
Brakes	Four-wheel drum brakes, inboard rear, hydraulically operated
Performance	Top speed 130mph (210km/h) (approx), 0–60mph in 7.5sec (approx)

**The DB3 was never as successful as Aston Martin hoped,
largely because it was heavier than it should have been.**

LAGONDA 3-LITRE

THE 2.9-LITRE ENGINE that had been developed for the DB3 race car went into production in 1953, and was first seen in a revised Lagonda. The extra capacity came from wider bores, which could only be accommodated by offsetting adjacent cylinders either side of the crankshaft centreline using asymmetric conrods. With a compression ratio of 8.16:1, the first 2922cc engines produced 140bhp, compared to the 125bhp of the Vantage-spec 2.6.

The new and more elegant Frank Feeley body was built by the Tickford coachbuilding company at Newport Pagnell in Buckinghamshire – an independent firm until David Brown took it over in 1955. The chassis and running gear were largely carried over from the Lagonda 2.6, which meant a hefty separate chassis and all-independent suspension.

A two-door, four-seat saloon was offered first, followed by a drophead coupé and then a four-door saloon. The two-door saloon was dropped in 1956. Later that year a MkII version of the Lagonda was introduced, with a floor-mounted gearshift instead of the earlier cars' column change. Production of the

In 1953 the race-proved 2.9-litre engine went into a revised Lagonda. Here the Queen and the Duke of Edinburgh watch as a drophead passes by during a parade at Windsor Castle. The Duke once owned a similar car.

drophead ended in 1957, and the final saloon was built early in 1958, by which time just 270 Lagonda 3-litre models of all types had been built. One high-profile customer was the Duke of Edinburgh, who ran a drophead Lagonda 3-litre, which even accompanied him on a visit to Australia in 1956.

The Lagonda's biggest problem was Jaguar, which was building fast, good-looking saloons such as the MkVII and selling them at very keen prices. After 1958 the Lagonda name would not reappear until 1961, and then on a very different car.

■ 1953 LAGONDA 3-LITRE

Engine	In-line 6-cylinder
Valvegear	Twin overhead cam
Bore and stroke	83 × 90mm
Capacity	2922cc
Power	140bhp @ 5,000rpm
Fuel system	Twin SU carburettors
Transmission	Four-speed David Brown manual gearbox, rear-wheel drive
Chassis/body	Cruciform platform chassis, aluminium alloy body
Suspension	Double wishbones and coil springs front, independent wishbones and torsion bars rear
Brakes	Four-wheel drum brakes, hydraulically operated
Performance	104mph (167km/h), 0–50mph in 9sec

DB2/4

THE DB2 HAD proved popular, but with only two seats and limited luggage space its appeal was limited. To make space for a rear seat the chassis cross-bracing over the rear axle was removed and the roofline raised at the rear. The rear window was enlarged and a lift-up rear door let into the bodywork to provide access to the luggage compartment, which was larger thanks to a repositioned spare wheel and smaller, lower fuel tank. The rear seat could be folded forwards for even more cargo space.

More substantial bumpers and a curved, single-piece windscreen completed the body modifications on what Aston Martin called the DB2/4, unveiled at the Motor Show in October 1953. It was a little heavier than the two-seater DB2, so to ensure that performance did not suffer, the 125bhp Vantage-spec engine was a standard fitment, and the 2.9-litre engine

already seen in the DB3 racer and Lagonda saloon was made available in the DB2/4 from the summer of 1954.

The DB2/4 was never intended to be a race car but it did have a competition career, which began early in 1955 when Aston Martin entered three cars in the Monte Carlo Rally. Reg Parnell was partnered by motor-racing photographer Louis Klemantaski in one car, Peter Collins and Graham Whitehead shared the second, while the third was crewed by two former Monte winners, Dutchman Maurice Gatsonides and Frenchman Marcel Becquart. Parnell and Collins put themselves out of contention by going flat out from the start and getting penalty points for arriving at controls early. Parnell was disqualified before the cars got back to Monte Carlo, but Collins was able to continue and won the traditional race around the Monaco GP circuit. The more experienced Gatsonides and Becquart

ABOVE: **Aston Martin added a rear seat and an opening luggage hatch to the DB2 in 1953 to produce the DB2/4 (background). Minor bodywork revisions produced the DB2/4 MkII (foreground) in 1955.**
LEFT: **Mid-1950s Aston Martins had simple but comfortable interiors with a full complement of instruments.**

This unique Bertone DB2/4 was one of several Italian-bodied DB2/4s commissioned by American industrialist Stanley H. 'Wacky' Arnolt.

led the rally until they passed a secret time-check early near Annecy and dropped to seventieth place. By the end they had recovered to seventh place, and without that one minor error they would have won easily. They were awarded the RAC Trophy for 'comfort and safety', and the preparation of the DB2/4 team was so neat that the organizers created a 'team prize' on the spot and awarded it to Aston Martin.

Two of the Monte Carlo DB2/4s reappeared in the Mille Miglia in place of the Lagonda V12s that Aston Martin had planned to enter, but which had engine trouble. Both retired with clutch problems.

At the Motor Show in October 1955 Aston Martin unveiled a Mark II version of the DB2/4 with a slightly higher roofline, a chrome strip above the windscreen, and tiny fins on the rear wings in accordance with mid-1950s fashion. At the front, the side panels of the engine bay were fixed to the body rather than the bonnet because the DB2's fold-forward front end had proved to be heavy and prone to shake on rough roads. As before there was also a drophead coupé, plus a notchback fixed-head coupé as an alternative to the standard fastback car. Two cars were sent to Carrozzeria Touring in Milan and fitted with open 'spyder' bodywork. One was given away as a competition prize by the *Daily Mail* newspaper.

Several standard DB2/4s appeared in films: the 1954 Motor Show car appeared in the Stanley Baker racing film *Checkpoint* in 1956, another DB2/4 starred in the Peter Sellers/Lionel Jeffries comedy *Two Way Stretch* in 1960, and most notably Tippi Hedren drove one in Alfred Hitchcock's *The Birds*.

■ 1953 DB2/4

Engine	In-line 6-cylinder
Valvegear	Twin overhead cam
Bore and stroke	78 × 90mm
Capacity	2580cc
Power	125bhp @ 5,000rpm
Fuel system	Twin SU carburettors
Transmission	Four-speed David Brown manual gearbox, rear-wheel drive
Chassis/body	Tubular steel frame, aluminium alloy body
Suspension	Trailing arms with coil springs and anti-roll bar front, coil-sprung live axle located by twin trailing arms and Panhard rod rear
Brakes	Four-wheel drum brakes, hydraulically operated
Performance	Top speed 114mph (183km/h), 0–60mph in 12.6sec

DB3S

THE DB3 HAD not been as successful as Aston Martin had hoped, the general feeling being that it was too big and too heavy to compete with the 3.4-litre, spaceframed C-type Jaguars. Early in 1953 Willie Watson came up with a plan for a smaller, lighter car, reshaping the main members of the DB3's twin-tube chassis so that they passed lower under the cockpit. Watson also reduced the wall thickness of the tubes, giving a useful reduction in weight. Frank Feeley designed a very pretty new body with cutaway front wheel arches, which were functional as well as ornamental: they provided an exit path for hot air from the engine. Mechanically it was much the same as the DB3 – but the DB3S, as the new car was known, tipped the scales 165lb (75kg) lighter than the DB3.

Aston Martin took the DB3S to Monza for testing with encouraging results, but the three DB3S cars that subsequently arrived at Le Mans were hurriedly prepared and suffered as a result. One retired with a failing clutch, one blew an engine, and

uncharacteristically Reg Parnell made a mistake and shunted one of the cars at Tertre Rouge.

Parnell hatched a plan to atone for his Le Mans error. With Wyer and Brown's approval he borrowed the DB3S prototype, which had been at Le Mans as a spares car, and entered it into the Empire Trophy in the Isle of Man, which was the following week. Parnell drove the car back to England, picked up mechanic Eric Hind from Feltham, then headed for Liverpool and the ferry to the Isle of Man. They arrived in time for the first practice session, where Parnell recorded the fastest time.

John Wyer flew in for the second practice session, where Parnell set a fast time but was then beaten by Moss in a Jaguar C-type and Reusch in a Ferrari. Parnell went out again and broke the lap record twice to win back pole position, only for the car to break a universal joint on the drive back to the hotel. They had no spares, and could not raise anyone at the factory. Late in the evening Wyer's wife Tottie phoned to see how he

Four DB3Ss line up at the BARC Aintree meeting in 1955. They took the top four places in the sports car race, led home by Roy Salvadori.

Many DB3S cars survive: this one won the Spa sports car race in Paul Frère's hands in 1955.

was, and was rapidly given instructions to get help. She located one of the Aston mechanics, who went to Feltham, removed a half-shaft from one of the Le Mans DB3Ss, drove to Liverpool, flew to the Isle of Man, helped fit it to Parnell's car, and then manned the pits during the race – which Parnell won.

It was the start of a run of success. Parnell won at Silverstone the following month, with DB3S drivers Salvadori and Collins second and third. The Parnell/DB3S combination won again at Charterhall in August, and then Parnell and Eric Thompson shared the winning DB3S in the Goodwood Nine Hours, with Peter Collins and Pat Griffith (who had won in a DB3 the year before) in second place. The situation was reversed at the Tourist Trophy, where Collins and Griffith won with the Parnell/Thompson DB3S – beating the Jaguars fair and square.

The DB3S had won everything it was entered for in the second half of 1953, and maybe that contributed to over-confidence in the Aston Martin camp the following season. Whatever the reason, Aston Martin spread their resources too thin

in 1954, with road-car work and the Lagonda V12 project on top of an ambitious race programme for the DB3S, which included the development of two new derivatives.

The season started early for the team, with a trip to the Buenos Aires 1,000km in January, which resulted in two retirements and a solitary third place for Collins/Griffith. The three cars then went to Sebring, where all three retired – and the story was little better at the Mille Miglia, where the Avon tyres the team used were unsuited to the wet conditions and both Parnell and Collins crashed out.

Two weeks later Aston Martin went to the Silverstone sports car race with three DB3Ss, treating the event as a shakedown for Le Mans. All three were fitted with new twin-plug cylinder heads, which liberated an extra 35bhp, pushing the total to 225bhp. Two were fitted with coupé bodies, which had been designed in conjunction with aircraft company Vickers and tested in their wind tunnel at Brooklands. But despite the low-drag body they finished behind the standard-bodied DB3S.

At Le Mans, Aston Martin ran a Lagonda V12, the two DB3S coupés, a regular DB3S, and DB3S/1, the original prototype, which was now fitted with a supercharged engine. The Lagonda crashed out early, and the two DB3S coupés (driven by Peter Collins/B. Bira and Graham Whitehead/Jimmy Stewart) followed soon after – the likely cause being instability due to rear-end lift, a common problem with low drag shapes but not one that was well understood at the time. The supercharged car proved fast, being timed at more than 150mph (240km/h) on the Mulsanne straight, but eventually the head gasket failed. The standard DB3S also dropped out with a stub-axle failure. Thus of the five cars entered by Aston Martin, not one finished.

David Brown was keen to raise morale by getting back into racing quickly, so Wyer combed through the Le Mans wreckage to put together a team for the Silverstone sports car race in July. The DB3S coupés were write-offs, but the two open DB3S cars were repaired, and the supercharged engine in DB3S/1 was replaced by an unblown unit. Wyer also co-opted David Brown's DB3S road car and installed a works twin-plug engine. It was a big boost to the team when Peter Collins won the race in DB3S/1, with Salvadori second and Texan Carroll Shelby third. Parnell was fourth in the repaired Lagonda. The Dundrod TT was another poor race, with two retirements and a distant thirteenth place for the DB3S of Poore and Whitehead – but the team salvaged some honour with second, third and fifth at Aintree in October.

The DB3S was back in action in the One-hour race at Silverstone in May 1955. The team entered two modified DB3S cars with bigger (Lagonda-spec) final drives, 11.5in Girling disc brakes and the latest twin-plug alloy cylinder heads, which Parnell and Salvadori used to beat Mike Hawthorn in the works Jaguar D-type OKV3. The following day Paul Frère won at Spa with a DB3S production car, and at Le Mans (where the DB3S lapped 15sec faster than the previous year) Frère and Peter Collins came home second behind the Hawthorn/Bueb D-type. More good news came at the British Grand Prix support race at Aintree a few weeks later, where the top four places were occupied by DB3Ss, and Crystal Palace, Goodwood and Oulton Park saw more wins for the DB3S. Aston Martin finished fourth and seventh at the TT, but the real highlight was a virtuoso drive from Collins, recovering from the back of the field after a starter motor failure, which sadly ended when the engine failed.

The 1956 season was the last for the DB3S as Aston Martin's frontline racing car. Stirling Moss joined the team, and in his first event at Sebring, where he shared DB3S/6 with Peter Collins, was running second until the oil pump drive broke. Parnell and Tony Brooks in DB3S/8 had the same problem, but Salvadori and Shelby in DB3S/7 managed to finish in fourth place. Moss finished second at Silverstone behind Salvadori (driving DB3S/5, which he had bought from the factory), but after the race there was a lot of ill feeling resulting from a first-lap accident which eliminated the Astons of Collins and Parnell and the Jaguars of Desmond Titterington and Ninian Sanderson. Salvadori entered DB3S/5 at Spa but then couldn't race through injury, so Parnell stepped in and brought it home in second place. At the Nürburgring 1,000km Salvadori's DB3S was borrowed back by the works Aston team for Collins and Brooks, who finished fifth.

For the Rouen sports car Grand Prix Collins asked for a drum-braked DB3S, feeling it might handle better. In practice Moss convinced Collins to swap with his disc-braked car, but it was Collins who led the Astons in the early part of the race until his engine blew. Moss finished second behind Castellotti's Ferrari, with Brooks fourth and Salvadori fifth. At Le Mans, Aston Martin entered a revised version of the DB3S with a smoother nose and faired-in headlamps. Moss and Collins in a rare partnership in DB3S/9 finished second, just a lap shy of the winning Flockhart/Sanderson D-type. At Oulton Park in August, Moss led an Aston Martin one-two-three-four finish; then Brooks and Salvadori finished first and second at Goodwood.

An experimental DB3S, with DB4 front suspension and fuel injection, ran in two races early in 1957, then one car was entered at the Nürburgring 1,000km in May 1957, driven by the Whitehead brothers. After that, Aston Martin concentrated on the DBR1.

■ 1956 DB3S

Engine	In-line 6-cylinder, triple Weber 35DCO carburettors
Valvegear	Twin overhead cam
Bore and stroke	83 × 90mm
Capacity	2922cc
Power	230bhp @ 6,000rpm
Transmission	Four-speed David Brown manual gearbox, rear-wheel drive
Chassis/body	Tubular steel frame, aluminium alloy body
Suspension	Trailing arms with torsion bars front, de Dion with torsion bars rear
Brakes	Four-wheel disc brakes, hydraulically operated
Performance	Top speed 145mph (233km/h) (approx), 0–60mph in 7sec (approx)

OPPOSITE PAGE:

TOP: **Stirling Moss kicks up the dust on his way to winning at the BARC Easter meeting at Goodwood in 1956.**

BOTTOM: **Later DB3Ss were given a revised nose, and this car tried coil and wishbone independent rear suspension.**

DB MARK III

THE DB2/4 WAS restyled in 1957, with a DB3S-style nose and neater tail. Inside there was a new facia panel, which echoed the shape of the radiator grille and grouped all the instruments in front of the driver for the first time.

Under the bonnet there was a heavily revised engine, called the DBA and designed by Polish engineer Tadek Marek. The block, crankshaft, inlet and exhaust manifolds, oil pump and timing chain were all new, and the engine produced 162bhp at 5,500rpm (compared to the standard DB2/4 MkII's 140bhp). By 1959 a 'competition' spec called the DBC was being offered for an extra £350, offering 214bhp. Girling front disc brakes were an option on early cars, and became standard fit after the first 100 cars were built. Overdrive and Borg Warner automatic transmission were also optional.

The new car, in theory a 'DB2/4 Mark III' to follow on from the MkII, was known to everyone as the DB Mark III (although Ian Fleming would later refer to it in *Goldfinger* as a 'DB III'). It was unveiled to the public at the Geneva motor show in March 1957, and was available for export only until the London Motor Show later that year. It was planned that it should have a short life as the DB4 was on the way, but in fact production continued until 1959, overlapping with the first DB4s, and 550 were built.

■ 1957 DB MARK III

Engine	In-line 6-cylinder, twin SU carburettors
Valvegear	Twin overhead cam
Bore and stroke	83 × 90mm
Capacity	2922cc
Power	162bhp @ 5,500rpm
Transmission	Four-speed David Brown manual gearbox, rear-wheel drive
Chassis/body	Tubular steel frame, aluminium alloy body
Suspension	Trailing arms with coil springs and anti-roll bar front, coil-sprung live axle located by twin trailing arms and Panhard rod rear
Brakes	Disc front, drum rear, servo assisted
Performance	Top speed 119mph (192km/h), 0–60mph in 9.3sec

The DB Mark III of 1957 adopted the stylish nose of the early-style DB3S and offered a heavily revised engine.

DBRI AND DBR3

WORK BEGAN ON a new racing Aston, the DBRI, in 1955. Ted Cutting, who had joined Aston Martin from Allard in 1949, masterminded the project and designed both the spaceframe chassis and the all-alloy engine. The 'barrel-type' crankcase, which had been a limitation for the LB6 and the downfall of the Lagonda V12, was gone and in its place Cutting used a conventional, light alloy block with bolted-in main bearing caps. The new engine, designated RB6, was planned to retain the dimensions of the DB3S unit, but at first it ran with a short stroke and 2493cc capacity in deference to new rules for 'prototypes' in the wake of the 1955 Le Mans accident. Initially the twin-plug alloy cylinder head was carried over from the old engine. Despite these limitations the early RB6 engines produced only 7bhp less than the existing 2.9-litre, with the promise of much more to come.

The RB6 went into a new 'perimeter' spaceframe chassis, largely made from steel tube with a diameter of 1in (25mm), which was perhaps too light to start with: after the prototype was built the design was reworked to add strength. The body-work was made from a mixture of eighteen- and twenty-gauge

alloys. The DBRI weighed 195lb (89kg) less than the DB3S, itself a featherweight compared to the DB2 and DB3.

Roy Salvadori recorded encouraging second place finishes with the 2.5-litre DBRI at Oulton Park and Goodwood early in 1957, before the car went to Spa for its first race in 2.9-litre form. Tony Brooks survived gearbox problems to win at Spa, with Salvadori second in another DBRI – beating a gaggle of Jaguar D-types. Brooks shared a DBRI with Noel Cunning-ham-Reid at the Nürburgring 1,000km, and the pair won by more than four minutes. But gearbox problems reappeared, the sister car of Salvadori and Les Leston finishing sixth after being stuck in fourth gear for the latter part of the race.

Aston Martin fielded the same cars and drivers at Le Mans (plus a DBR2 for Graham and Peter Whitehead), and ran into more transmission trouble. Brooks found it increasingly diffi-cult to select gears in his DBRI, and eventually crashed while battling the gearbox. The second DBRI was retired, stuck in fourth gear.

The Belgian GP at Spa was a sports car race that year, and the meeting started badly for Brooks in DBRI/2, the car he had

The DBRI had a new multi-tube chassis and 2.9-litre engine, which made it much more competitive than the DB3S.

driven at Le Mans. In practice the engine lost its oil pressure and the RB6 engine destroyed its crankshaft. A replacement had to be flown out in David's De Havilland Dove to get the DBR1 to the starting grid. But the race went well, Brooks emerging victorious despite constant concern over the health of the engine.

Stirling Moss rejoined Aston Martin for 1958. Regulation changes in sports car racing limited cars to 3-litre engines, ideal for the DBR1s with their 2.9-litre engines, and the team was optimistic that it would be their year – so much so that the DBR4 Grand Prix car was mothballed while Aston Martin concentrated on sports car racing. Moss and Brooks shared DBR1/2 at Sebring, but retired with yet more gearbox trouble – a growing embarrassment for the David Brown organization, which supplied the gearboxes. Salvadori and Shelby also retired when DBR1/1, the prototype, broke its early-type chassis.

At Silverstone in May, Moss drove the DBR3, which was a DBR1 fitted with a 2990cc version of the DB4 engine (and identifiable by a bonnet bulge to clear the cam covers on the taller engine). It was not a success: the car retired with a seized engine, and was subsequently converted to DBR1 spec. Moss suffered another transmission failure at the Targa Florio, but at the Nürburgring 1,000km the DBR1 he shared with Jack Brabham beat the Hawthorn/Collins Ferrari by nearly four minutes. The two sister cars fared less well, Brooks being hit by another car and Salvadori retiring with more gearbox trouble.

Yet another transmission failure put Brooks and Maurice Trintignant out at Le Mans, after Moss had his engine fail and Stuart Lewis-Evans slid off the road in rain. When the DBR1s finished first, second and third at the Tourist Trophy it was scant consolation, as pace-setters Ferrari had already wrapped up the championship and decided not to enter.

Aston Martin planned to concentrate on Le Mans (and F1) in 1959, but soon other races were added to the programme. The Sebring organizers pleaded with them to enter, so the 'spare' DBR1/1 was sent for Salvadori and Shelby – but the clutch failed. Moss wanted a car for the Nürburgring 1,000km, which he shared with Jack Fairman – though as in 1958, Moss did the lion's share of the driving. Fairman was forced off the road and into a ditch during his first stint, and had to heave the Aston bodily back on to the track, but despite that setback they went on to win – Aston's third successive victory at the Nürburgring.

Two weeks later, at Le Mans, the works DBR1s appeared with revised bodywork developed in a wind tunnel. The tail was higher and the rear wheels were shrouded, both in the pursuit

XSK497 makes regular appearances at historic motor-sport events such as the Goodwood Festival of Speed and Silverstone Classic in the hands of great drivers such as Stirling Moss (left).

The DBR1 dashboard is dominated by a huge rev counter. In this car a modern electronic instrument has replaced the original mechanical item, and there are additional controls for an ignition cutout and fire extinguisher.

Vents in the DBR1's front wings were designed to evacuate hot air from the engine compartment.

of lower drag and a higher top speed on the long Mulsanne straight. Moss again partnered Fairman, and was given the task of attacking hard in the early part of the race to force the Ferraris to chase. The pair were allocated DBR1/3, fitted with a more powerful but potentially less reliable four-bearing version of the RB6 engine. Salvadori paired up with Carroll Shelby, and they were given a comfortable target lap time of 4min 20sec to preserve the car. Maurice Trintignant, sharing with the young Belgian driver Paul Frère, would lap at 4min 22sec to act as a reserve. There was also a privately entered DBR1 shared by Whitehead and Naylor.

Moss led early on, lapping at an astonishing 4min 13sec – just two seconds shy of the best DBR1 practice laps. As afternoon became evening the Jean Behra/Dan Gurney Ferrari took over the lead, but the sister car of 'Nano' da Silva Ramos and Cliff Allison retired after just forty-one laps with gearbox trouble.

The Moss/Fairman DBR1 was next to crack, retiring with failing oil pressure. That left Shelby in the lead in DBR1/2, ahead of the third works Ferrari driven by 1958 winners Olivier Gendebien and Phil Hill. The Behra/Gurney Ferrari succumbed to gearbox problems after ten hours, but early on Sunday morning there was a scare for the Aston team when Salvadori brought the leading DBR1 into the pits complaining of a vibration: it was later found that one of the rear tyres had lost part of its tread.

The Ferrari challenge expired with five hours of the race still to run, when Gendebien retired with a failing head gasket. Reg Parnell, who had taken over from John Wyer as team manager, signalled to Salvadori that he could take it easy. Shelby took over two hours from the end and the DBR1 ran faultlessly to the finish – finally recording the Le Mans win that David Brown had wanted for so long. Trintignant and Frère finished second, just a lap adrift, despite the Frenchman suffering from a blistered foot thanks to heat from the DBR1's new under-floor exhaust.

Aston Martin now had a good chance to win the World Sports Car Championship: Ferrari led the championship with eighteen points, Aston Martin were second with sixteen, and Porsche third with fifteen points. Whichever team won the last round, the Tourist Trophy at Goodwood, would take the title.

Frequent tyre changes would be needed on the abrasive Goodwood surface, so to speed up pit stops the three Le Mans DBR1s were fitted with on-board jacks activated by com-pressed nitrogen, supplied from a bottle in the pit garage. Moss was teamed up with Salvadori and the pair led easily until the car caught light during refuelling – the second time Aston Martin had set its Goodwood pit on fire. Moss took over the second-placed Shelby/Fairman car for the rest of the race, and won by a lap from the Jo Bonnier/Wolfgang von Trips Porsche to give Aston Martin the World Sports Car Championship.

■ 1959 DBR1

Engine	In-line 6-cylinder, triple Weber 50DCO carburettors
Valvegear	Twin overhead cam
Bore and stroke	84 × 90mm
Capacity	2992cc
Power	254bhp @ 6,000rpm
Transmission	Five-speed David Brown manual gearbox, rear-wheel drive
Chassis/body	Tubular spaceframe chassis, aluminium alloy body
Suspension	Trailing links and transverse torsion bars front; trailing arms, Watt link and longitudinal torsion bars rear
Brakes	Four-wheel Girling disc brakes, hydraulically operated
Performance	165mph (265km/h), 0–60mph in 6sec (approx)

LEFT: **Texan Carroll Shelby hustles a DBR1 through the Goodwood chicane. Shelby shared the winning DBR1 with Roy Salvadori at Le Mans in 1959.**
BELOW: **Jack Fairman raced the DBR1 alongside the likes of Moss and Salvadori, and contributed to a famous win in the Nürburgring 1,000km in 1959.**

LAGONDA V12 AND DBR2

DAVID BROWN WAS keen to build a bigger, faster car that could beat Ferrari in international sports car racing. For 1954 Willie Watson designed a 4.5-litre V12 with a barrel-type crankcase like the LB6, but this time in aluminium alloy, with alloy 'cheeses' holding the main bearings. It went into a lengthened DB3S chassis, and the car looked similar – though it had different front end styling and Lagonda badges.

The engine's alloy block proved to be its downfall. In the LB6, the iron crankcase expanded less than the alloy bearing cheeses as the engine warmed up, so the block held everything together. In the V12, the block and the cheeses expanded at the same rate, and the result was that the engine would not hold its oil pressure. A great deal of effort went into the Lagonda in 1954, and again in 1955 when it was given a new spaceframe chassis,

but the engine problems continued. Ultimately the V12, which Brown had hoped would form the basis of future Aston Martin road cars, was abandoned.

But that wasn't the end of the story. In 1957 the spaceframe chassis was given an experimental 3.7-litre in-line six engine, ultimately destined for the DB4 road car. DBR1-style bodywork completed the package, which was known as the DBR2. Though not eligible for World Sports Car Championship classes, it was hoped the DBR2 could challenge for overall honours in races where larger-engined cars were permitted entry.

The highlight of the DBR2's career came at the end of 1957, when Roy Salvadori beat Archie Scott-Brown's Lister-Jaguar at Silverstone; the second DBR2 of Noel Cunningham-Reid was in third place, and Brooks was fourth in a DBR1.

■ 1957 DBR2

Engine	In-line 6-cylinder, triple Weber 50DCO carburettors
Valvegear	Twin overhead cam
Bore and stroke	92 × 92mm
Capacity	3670cc
Power	279bhp @ 5,750rpm
Transmission	Five-speed David Brown manual gearbox, rear-wheel drive
Chassis/body	Tubular spaceframe chassis, aluminium alloy body
Suspension	Trailing links and transverse torsion bars front; trailing arms, de Dion and transverse torsion bars rear
Brakes	Four-wheel Girling disc brakes, hydraulically operated
Performance	170mph (273km/h), 0–60mph in 6sec (approx)

ABOVE: **The V12 Lagonda was built to challenge Ferrari for outright wins in sports car racing, but the engine was fundamentally ill suited.**
TIM COTTINGHAM

RIGHT: **Lagonda chassis were re-used in the DBR2 cars, which looked almost identical to the DBR1 but were very different under the skin.**
TIM COTTINGHAM

DBR4 AND DBR5

ALTHOUGH ASTON MARTIN toyed with single-seater projects throughout the 1950s, serious work on a Grand Prix car did not begin until 1955. A narrower version of the DBR1's spaceframe chassis and a short-stroke 2.5-litre version of its RB6 engine created the DBR4, which was tested at MIRA in December 1957. But Aston Martin decided to concentrate on sports car racing in 1958, so the DBR4 did not race until 1959. It made a promising debut at Silverstone in May that year, Salvadori finishing second behind Jack Brabham in a Cooper.

But by the time it raced the DBR4 was already out of date, as Coopers were proving that the future of F1 was a rear-engined car. Bearing problems plagued the high-revving engines that year, leading to several retirements.

For 1960 Aston Martin built a new car, the DBR5, which was smaller and lighter than the DBR4 and had all-independent suspension and Lucas fuel injection. After problems with the CG537 transaxle (shared with the DBR1), the DBR4s and DBR5s were tried with a Maserati gearbox – which was ironic,

given that Aston Martin's parent company had long specialized in gears.

The DBR4 could have been competitive in 1958, but by the time it raced in 1959 it was outdated, and the DBR5 added more complication without any more performance. Thus Aston Martin's brief foray into Formula 1 was sadly unsuccessful.

Roy Salvadori tried his best with the DBR4 Grand Prix car and its successor the DBR5, but by the time Aston Martin entered Formula 1 its cars were already obsolete.

■ 1959 DBR4

Engine	In-line 6-cylinder, triple Weber 50DCO carburettors
Valvegear	Twin overhead cam
Bore and stroke	83 × 76.8mm
Capacity	2493cc
Power	250bhp @ 7,800rpm
Transmission	Five-speed David Brown manual gearbox, rear-wheel drive
Chassis/body	Tubular spaceframe chassis, aluminium alloy body
Suspension	Wishbones and coil springs front; trailing arms, de Dion and transverse torsion bars rear
Brakes	Four-wheel Girling disc brakes, hydraulically operated
Performance	180mph (290km/h) (approx), 0–60mph in 5sec (approx)

THE NEWPORT PAGNELL
DAVID BROWN YEARS

**The DB4/5/6 family is probably the most recognizable
series of cars that Aston Martin has ever built.**

1958–1972

DERIVATIVES OF THE DB2 were Aston Martin's bread and butter models for most of the 1950s, but in 1958 they would be replaced by a wholly new car, the DB4, which was to catapult Aston Martin into the very top league of performance car manufacturers. The DB4 would be the first of a family of cars that are probably the best remembered Astons of all.

Design work began in 1952 and a prototype, DP114, was built in 1954; however, its Frank Feeley-designed body was not thought sufficiently attractive. Instead an Italian styling house, Touring of Milan, was engaged to style the new Aston – and the adoption of Touring's Superleggera body construction system led to the design of a new platform chassis. Developments of that chassis would underpin almost all Aston Martins right through to the end of the V-car era in 2000. In addition to the new chassis, drawn up by Harold Beach, the DB4 featured a new 3.7-litre, twin-cam engine designed by Tadek Marek.

Despite early worries concerning engine reliability, the DB4 was an instant hit – fast and sure-footed, with handsome styling, it was a match for anything on offer from established performance car makers such as Ferrari, but at a much lower price. The road-going DB4 soon spawned a shorter, lighter and more powerful competition derivative, the DB4GT, and later there was the brutal DB4GT Zagato. But on the track these cars were campaigned by private teams, the Aston Martin works team having retired from sports car racing after its successful 1959 season. Instead, Aston Martin's own team concentrated on Formula 1 – but it had arrived too late, because F1 was quickly becoming the preserve of lightweight, rear-engined cars typified by the championship-winning Coopers of 1959 and 1960, and Aston Martin's front-engined cars were outclassed. So in

1962 the works racing team returned to sports cars with the DP212, and further 'Project cars' followed in 1963, with mixed success, before the team retired from racing altogether.

Newport Pagnell's road-car line-up was expanded in 1961 with the launch of a new Lagonda, the Rapide, with a DB4-derived chassis, de Dion rear suspension and a 4-litre version of the Marek straight-six engine. The Lagonda proved unpopular, largely due to its unhappy styling, and production was halted in 1964. But the larger engine survived in a revised DB4, the DB5 of 1963. When the DB5 appeared in a starring role in the James Bond film *Goldfinger* in 1964 it made Aston Martin a household name around the world. The DB6 of 1965 offered more interior space and more comprehensive equipment, but it also looked heavier and less athletic than the DB4 and DB5.

Touring produced two attractive DB6-based Aston-based concept cars, later known as the DBSC, but they were never developed into production cars. Instead David Brown planned to create a new line of William Towns-styled Aston Martins and Lagondas, beginning with the Aston Martin DBS in 1967. A 5-litre V8 engine was developed with the DBS in mind, but a disastrous appearance at the Le Mans 24-hours in 1967, where two Aston V8-engined Lolas both retired early with engine problems, led to a major redesign of the engine. The DBS launched in 1967 with the existing 4-litre 6-cylinder engine, and it was not until 1969 that the V8-powered car followed.

By then David Brown's long stewardship of the company was nearing its end. The sale of the company in 1972 would mark the end of one of the most stable and successful periods of Aston Martin's history – and it would be replaced by an era of crisis, doubt and change.

The DB5 was an evolution of the DB4, with the 4-litre engine that had been introduced in the Lagonda Rapide.

The DB4, identified by its uncowled headlamps, was the first of a successful family of cars for Aston Martin – though early cars were less than reliable.

Touring's **DBSC** was a fascinating project, but never became a production reality. Two were built.

DB4

ASTON MARTIN BEGAN work on a successor to the DB2 and its derivatives as far back as 1952, with the start of design work on a prototype, Development Project (DP) 114. Londoner Harold Beach, who had joined Aston Martin in 1950 after spells working on commercial and military vehicles and at the Barker coachbuilding concern, laid out a new perimeter frame chassis with rack-and-pinion steering, coil-and-wishbone front suspension and a de Dion rear end. DP114 was built in 1954, fitted with a 2.9-litre engine, and given a one-off body designed by Frank Feeley. The latter looked a lot like a DB2/4 hardtop coupé from the side, but more like an angular rework of the DB Mark III from the front. With a white body and blue roof it quickly acquired the nickname of 'Wall's ice cream van'. After many miles of testing, DP114 was adopted as a road car by David Brown and his wife.

Although DP114 had a promising start, its styling was considered rather frumpy so Aston Martin approached Touring of Milan, which had built a pair of DB2/4 'spyders' in 1956, to come up with designs for the new car. Harold Beach was despatched to Milan to liaise with the Touring team on the construction

of a new body, but he soon found that the Italians disliked his perimeter frame. Touring's Superleggera (superlight) construction method clothed a lightweight tubular steel body frame in alloy panels, and although the body frame contributed some stiffness to the car's structure it needed a strong, stiff chassis to take most of the loads. Touring suggested a platform chassis welded together from a multitude of small steel panels, on to which the Superleggera frame could be attached.

Once Beach understood the principles of Touring's construction system he set about designing a suitable platform chassis that could use the suspension systems already proven in DP114. The chassis was produced in something of a hurry, and turned out to be heavier than it would have been, had it been given the time for careful development – but that was to prove more of a benefit than a curse, as it meant the chassis had immense reserves of strength. Derivatives of this same chassis would go on to underpin several generations of Aston Martins, finally disappearing with the death of the V-cars in 2000.

While Beach was developing the chassis and body of the new car, Polish engineer Tadek Marek worked on a new engine

DP114/2 was the first prototype of what became the DB4. For a while it had a blue and white colour scheme and was nicknamed the 'Wall's ice cream van'.

Touring of Milan styled the DB4's body and provided the Superleggera construction system, which laid hand-made aluminium panels over a body frame built from small-diameter tubes.

to power it. Marek had been hired from Austin in 1954 to head Aston Martin's engine development team, and had already redesigned the LB6 engine to become the DBA, which would go into the DB Mark III in 1957. John Wyer, who had become Aston's technical director in 1955, wanted the new motor to be an all-alloy 3-litre six with enough 'meat' on the bores to allow expansion to 3.5 litres in due course. Marek was more cautious, and decided to opt for a less stressed engine of larger capacity, with a conventional iron block. Now that the British 'RAC horsepower' taxation system, which was based largely on the cylinder bore, had finally disappeared, manufacturers such as Aston Martin were able to design more modern engines with bigger bores and shorter strokes. While the 2.9-litre DBA engine in the DB Mark III was a long-stroke unit with a 78mm bore and 90mm stroke, Marek's new engine was 'square', with bore and stroke both set at 92mm, giving it a capacity of 3670cc.

The big iron block soon caused a headache, because apparently Aston Martin could not find a foundry to cast it. As it was easier to find an aluminium foundry, Marek switched back to the original plan, redesigning the engine with an alloy crankcase and wet iron cylinder liners. The engine, given the project code DP186, was running by 1956, and a prototype unit with triple Weber carburettors developing 287bhp went into the DBR2 racer – rather against Marek's wishes, as he had never intended the engine as a race unit. But the DBR2 was winning races in 1957, and in 1958 its engine was bored out to 95mm to displace 3910cc and generate 298bhp. The road-going 3.7-litre version

gave 240bhp using twin SU carburettors and an 8.25:1 compression ratio, and an engine in this tune was tested in a DB2/4 Mark II.

The complete DB4 package – the Beach chassis, bodywork by Touring's Carlo Felice Bianchi Anderloni and Federico Formenti, and the Marek engine – was brought together on DP184, the prototype of what became the DB4. It was on the road by the middle of 1957, and inevitably David Brown was one of the first to drive it, describing it as 'very promising'. DP184 was thrashed around Europe for a week, during which it covered more than 2,000 miles (3,220km), accelerating the development of the DB4 from prototype to production car.

One of the problems identified during testing was excessive engine-bay heat, which was dissipated by inserting vents into the wings behind the front wheel arches – known at Feltham as the 'letter boxes', and today an essential part of Aston Martin design 'DNA'. Another problem was that the de Dion rear end transmitted too much transmission noise to the interior, so it was dropped in favour of a coil-sprung live rear axle located by radius arms and a Watt link. In this form the DB4 was unveiled to the public at the London Motor Show in 1958, with a list price of £2,650 plus purchase tax.

Aston Martin licensed the Touring Superleggera system and built the bodies in house, Touring supplying construction jigs that were set up at the Newport Pagnell factory. The steel chassis were made at another David Brown outpost, a tractor factory at Farsley in Yorkshire.

ABOVE: **The elegant fastback shape of the DB4 emphasized its performance: at the time it was one of the fastest road cars available.**
RIGHT: **Early DB4s had a bigger air intake on the bonnet and a fine-mesh radiator grille.**

BELOW: **The wing vent allowed hot air to escape from the engine bay. It was set to become a key part of Aston Martin's styling DNA.**

Aston Martin claimed the DB4 could accelerate from rest to 100mph (160km) and then brake to a standstill in less than 30sec, so there was no doubting the DB4's performance. But reliability was less certain: early cars suffered from lubrication problems, caused by expansion of the alloy block when hot, which allowed the bearing clearances to grow and the oil pressure to disappear. The meagre 15-pint (9ltr) oil capacity served only to exacerbate the problem.

After the first fifty cars were built, the DB4 acquired chrome window surrounds, which helped to secure the glass more firmly, reducing wind noise, and bigger bumpers with overriders were fitted to give the car more showroom appeal in the important US market. An aluminium radiator cowl was added after the first 100 cars were built. In January 1960 a revised specification – later identified by the Aston Martin Owners Club as the 'Series 2' DB4 – was introduced, with a 17-pint (10ltr) sump, which helped alleviate the oil pressure problems, together with heavy duty front brake calipers and a radiator blind. At the same time the bonnet hinges were moved to the front, so that if the bonnet catch failed the bonnet would be unlikely to fly up and obscure the driver's view. An oil cooler was listed as an option, although this sensible extra was specified on only thirty-three of the 350 Series 2 DB4s built. Electric windows and overdrive were also available.

The Series 3 DB4 was introduced in April 1961, with detail differences including a second bonnet stay, electric rather than mechanical tachometer, extra demister ducts, and separate rear lights on a chrome plate in place of the original combination lamp units that had been carried over from the DB Mark III. Just 165 of these cars were built in the second half of 1961, three of them with DB4GT engines.

In September 1961 Aston Martin again upgraded the DB4 with another change of rear lamp style (this time the lights and their mounting plate were recessed slightly into the rear wing, for a neater appearance), and a neater nose with a smaller bonnet scoop and seven-bar grille. These 'Series 4' cars had an oil cooler as standard, though it seems some cars were supplied without. In addition to the GT engine option, which was fitted to five Series 4 cars, there was also a high-performance version of the standard engine known as the Special Series, with triple

SU HD8 carburettors, a big-valve cylinder head and a 9:1 compression ratio, which was claimed to deliver 266bhp at 5,750rpm. Usually DB4s with the Special Series engine were known as DB4 Vantages, and given a DB4GT-style nose with cowled headlamps (though they did not use the GT-style short wheelbase). At the 1961 London Motor Show Aston Martin also announced a DB4 convertible, with a list price of £3,050 before purchase tax, compared to a standard DB4 at £2,860. It was one of these cars that Michael Caine drove in the film *The Italian Job*, where it appears to be pushed off a cliff – fortunately for the Aston a Lancia 'double' made the plunge instead.

The Series 5 DB4 introduced in September 1962 had a host of detail changes. The most obvious was an increase of nearly 4in (100mm) in overall length, all of which went into the wheelbase to improve rear-seat legroom. At the same time the roofline was raised by 1in (25mm) to improve headroom, and the front wing and shoulder line of the body was reshaped to maintain the DB4's proportions – similar to the work that had been done to turn the prototype DB2 body into the more practical production car a decade earlier. The Series 5 also had 15in rather than 16in wheels to compensate for the higher roofline, and such refinements as a carburettor airbox, a vacuum advance system on the distributor and an electric fan

DB4 interior was simple rather than sumptuous. Note how the instrument binnacle mirrors the shape of the Aston Martin grille.

placed ahead of the radiator. All cars now received the DB4GT facia, the difference being that it had four separate instruments for water temperature, oil pressure, fuel level and amps instead of two combination dials.

Most of the Series 5 DB4s were DB4 Vantages, six of them Vantage GTs with the twin-plug GT engine. Three Series 5s were fitted with automatic transmission. As before there was a convertible option, although only seventy DB4 convertibles of all Series were sold, out of a total of 1,110 DB4s built between 1958 and the end of production in 1963.

Until the advent of the DB4, Aston Martin had built cars in tiny numbers for the well heeled few who could afford a high quality, hand-made car with fine handling and brisk performance. The DB4 built on those virtues, but pushed the performance to the next level: it was the fastest four-seater in the world, and it launched Aston Martin on the road to stardom.

■ 1958 DB4

Engine	In-line 6-cylinder, twin SU carburettors
Valvegear	Twin overhead cam
Bore and stroke	92 × 92mm
Capacity	3670cc
Power	240bhp @ 5,500rpm
Transmission	Four-speed David Brown manual gearbox, rear-wheel drive
Chassis/body	Steel platform chassis, tubular body frame with aluminium alloy body
Suspension	Double wishbones and coil springs front, live axle with trailing arms, Watt link rear
Brakes	Four-wheel Dunlop disc brakes, hydraulically operated
Performance	140mph (225km/h), 0–60mph in 9sec

LEFT: **Though the DB4's fastback shape looked as if it could incorporate a luggage hatch like that on the DB2/4 and DB Mark III, it reverted to a conventional boot lid.**
BELOW: **Early DB4s had Triumph rear light clusters, which were replaced by a group of separate lamps from April 1961.**

ABOVE: **The first-series DB4 had a conventional rear-hinged bonnet, but from the Series 2 cars of 1960 onwards, the bonnet was front-hinged.**

RIGHT: **Series 2 DB4s of 1960–1 added chrome window frames, but retained the rear-hinged bonnet and Triumph rear lights of earlier DB4s.**

DB4GT

BUILT PRIMARILY FOR GT-class racing, the DB4GT was a DB4 with the emphasis firmly on handling and speed: it was lighter and more manoeuvrable than the regular DB4, and was fitted with an engine that, though no bigger, was considerably more powerful.

The DB4GT was based on the same Harold Beach-designed steel platform chassis as the DB4, but with a 5in (127mm) slice taken out of the wheelbase, saving about 185lb (84kg) in weight. The space behind the front seats was much smaller than in the DB4, so most DB4GTs had no rear seats, the space instead being occupied by a carpeted luggage area – though tiny rear seats were shoehorned into a handful of GTs. A massive 30gal (136ltr) fuel tank with twin fillers dominated the boot space, and

a handful of DB4GTs was also fitted with twin 6gal (27ltr) wing tanks. Most of the remaining space under the boot lid was taken up by the spare wheel, a competition-specification 16in Borrani. The body, in eighteen-gauge magnesium aluminium alloy, followed the DB4 lines apart from at the front, where the headlamps were sunk into the wings and covered by plastic cowls.

Under the bonnet, the DB4's twin-cam 3670cc six was topped with a new twin-plug cylinder head. One set of spark plugs was controlled by a distributor driven from the intake camshaft, as on the six-plug engine, and the second set of plugs was controlled by a second distributor driven off the exhaust camshaft. With triple Weber 45DCOE twin-choke carburettors and a compression ratio of 9:1, it was claimed to deliver

The DB4GT was shorter, more powerful and faster than the DB4 on which it was based. The cowled headlamps were later adopted on the standard-length car, and retained for the DB5 and DB6.

302bhp at 6,000rpm, though in the fashion of the era that was probably optimistic. Power was delivered through a Borg and Beck 9in clutch and a close-ratio David Brown four-speed all-synchromesh gearbox to a 3.54:1 Salisbury final drive, fitted with a Powr-Lok limited slip differential as standard. As with the DB4, alternative axle ratios were available, and later there was the option of a wide-ratio gearbox. Suspension followed DB4 practice with double wishbones at the front, a well located live axle at the rear, and coil springs all round with telescopic dampers. The brakes – discs front and rear – were by Girling instead of Dunlop.

The combination of lighter weight and extra power made the DB4GT significantly swifter than the car it was based on. The DB4 has been claimed to dispatch 0–100mph (160km/h) in 30sec, and Aston Martin said the GT would complete the same test in 20sec. To confound the sceptics, Reg Parnell went out and proved it was possible!

The DB4GT was officially unveiled at the Earls Court Motor Show in October 1959, but by then it had already made its competition debut. That came at Silverstone in May, where Stirling Moss drove the prototype DB4GT, DP199/1, to a GT race win at the *Daily Express* meeting – setting a new lap record along the way. But the prototype DB4GT's next appearance, at Le Mans in June, was a less happy occasion. It was entered by a private team, Écurie Trois Chevrons, to be driven by Hubert Patthey (Aston Martin's Swiss distributor) and Renaud Calderari. As the DB4GT had yet to be officially announced, the car ran as a prototype, and had been modified to fit a short-stroke 2992cc version of Tadek Marek's 6-cylinder engine. In fact it was the same engine that had powered the DBR3 on its only outing, at Silverstone the previous year, when it had run its bearings. Because this engine had a dry-sump lubrication system, the DB4GT had to be fitted with an oil tank, located in the boot, and it was also given a five-speed gearbox. During practice the car's fuel consumption was higher than expected, so the fuel tank was enlarged to 38gal (173ltr). In this form the car lasted just three hours, Patthey bringing it into the pits on the twenty-first lap with a failed big-end bearing, later determined to be due to low oil pressure. While it was running the drivers complained of high temperatures and high noise levels in the cockpit, and brake wear had been severe enough that a pad change would have been required after twelve hours.

Between 1959 and 1963, ninety-four DB4GTs were built, at least five of them to a lightweight specification. One of these was the works experimental DB4GT, chassis 0167, which was road-tested by John Bolster in *Autosport* and also made an appearance in the Peter Sellers film *Wrong Arm of the Law*, after the GT they were using broke during filming. This car also had a tuned engine with a higher compression ratio, a specification intended for twenty-five Zagato-bodied cars (see p.57), which would have brought the total up to the 100 required for

GT-class homologation. In the end there were only nineteen Zagatos, making the DB4GT's racing appearances technically illegal!

The DB4GT's handsome styling, speed and rarity make it one of the most sought-after Astons of all. When these cars come up for sale, which inevitably is not very often, they command prices far in excess of the DB4 – though not in the league of the even rarer DB4GT Zagato.

DB4GTs are favourites in concours d'élégance events, and 54NMA has been winning concours trophies since the 1960s.

■ 1960 DB4GT

Engine	In-line 6-cylinder, triple Weber 45DCOE carburettors
Valvegear	Twin overhead cam
Bore and stroke	92 × 92mm
Capacity	3670cc
Power	302bhp @ 6,000rpm (claimed)
Transmission	Four-speed David Brown manual gearbox, rear-wheel drive, Powr-Lok limited slip differential
Chassis/body	Steel platform chassis, aluminium alloy body
Suspension	Double wishbones and coil springs front, live axle with trailing arms, Watt link rear
Brakes	Four-wheel Girling disc brakes, hydraulically operated
Performance	154mph (248km/h), 0–60mph in 6.2sec

DB4GT BERTONE JET

ASTON MARTIN HAD planned to make 100 DB4GTs, twenty-five of them Zagatos. But not all the chassis in the sequence were built (see the 1991 Zagato Sanction II/III, p. 120), and the body of the last car in the series, 0201, was made by a different Italian coachbuilder – Bertone.

The chassis was despatched to Turin late in 1960 to be clothed in a spectacular body designed by 22-year-old Giorgetto Giugiaro (who many years later designed the one-off DB7 Twenty Twenty). The bodywork had hints of the Alfa Romeo Giulietta SS in its form, and influenced a special Ferrari 250GT built by Bertone the following year. Curiously, the Bertone Aston's body was made of steel rather than aluminium, which meant that it was much heavier than a normal DB4GT, and probably heavier than the regular DB4.

The Jet, as it was known, made its public debut at the Geneva show in March 1961, and appeared at the Turin show later that year; it then spent many years in private ownership in the USA. In 1986 it was restored by the Aston Martin Works Service, and has since been seen at many Aston Martin events.

RIGHT: **Side vent on the Bertone Jet: the car had much more angular lines than the Touring-styled DB4GT, making it look considerably more modern.**
BELOW: **A young Giorgetto Giugiaro styled the Bertone Jet, a one-off based on a DB4GT chassis. The eye-catching body was built in steel rather than aluminium.**

■ 1961 DB4GT BERTONE JET

Engine	In-line 6-cylinder, triple Weber 45DCO carburettors
Valvegear	Twin overhead cam
Bore and stroke	92 × 92mm
Capacity	3670cc
Power	302bhp @ 6,000rpm (claimed)
Transmission	Four-speed David Brown manual gearbox, rear-wheel drive, Powr-Lok limited slip differential
Chassis/body	Steel platform chassis, aluminium alloy body
Suspension	Double wishbones and coil springs front, live axle with trailing arms, Watt link rear
Brakes	Four-wheel Girling disc brakes, hydraulically operated
Performance	150mph (241km/h), 0–60mph in 7sec (approx)

DB4GT ZAGATO

WHILE ASTON MARTIN pursued Formula 1 glory in 1959/60, with a notable lack of success, private teams were left to uphold the honour of the marque in sports car racing against the might of Ferrari. Teams such as John Ogier's Essex Racing Stable pitted DB4GTs against the Ferrari 250GTs, but the DB4GT was always at a weight disadvantage compared to the spaceframe Ferraris.

In 1960 Aston Martin revealed an even lighter DB4GT at the Earls Court Motor Show. The chassis and engine were largely that of the standard DB4GT, though the Marek straight six now had a higher compression ratio and a claimed 314bhp. The difference was in the bodywork, a lightweight creation hand made in the thinnest aluminium alloy by Milanese coachbuilder Zagato. The lines of the new car had been designed by Zagato stylist Ercole Spada, and gave the DB4GT a whole new mien:

gone was the genteel elegance of the Touring shape, and in its place came a mixture of muscle and aggression.

A run of twenty-five Zagatos was planned, starting with DB4GT chassis number 0200 and working backwards. Unlike the DB4 and DB4GT, which were built at Newport Pagnell, the Zagato was an Anglo-Italian affair: the chassis was built in England and shipped to Italy for Zagato to build the body, then the car was returned to Newport Pagnell for final trim and finishing. The result of this long and convoluted production line was that the DB4GT Zagato was considerably more expensive than the regular DB4GT. In 1961 a DB4 was £3,968 tax paid, a standard-bodied DB4GT was £4,668 and a Zagato was a colossal £5,470. The premium charged for the Zagato over the regular DB4GT would have bought a new Ford Consul. Even then, the Zagato was cheaper than a red car from Maranello…

RIGHT: **The DB4GT Zagato is one of the most famous of all Aston Martins, thanks to its rarity, its cost and its brutal shape.**
BELOW: **Each one of the nineteen original Zagatos was subtly different to the others. Most were bodied by Zagato, then trimmed and finished by Aston Martin, but this car is one of a handful to be completed in Italy.**

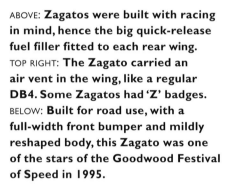

ABOVE: **Zagatos were built with racing in mind, hence the big quick-release fuel filler fitted to each rear wing.**
TOP RIGHT: **The Zagato carried an air vent in the wing, like a regular DB4. Some Zagatos had 'Z' badges.**
BELOW: **Built for road use, with a full-width front bumper and mildly reshaped body, this Zagato was one of the stars of the Goodwood Festival of Speed in 1995.**

Thanks to the lightweight bodywork, deleted bumpers, plexiglass windows and basic interior trim, the Zagato was around 100lb (45kg) lighter than a standard DB4GT, though it was still considerably heavier than a Ferrari 250GT – if, theoretically, more powerful. The Essex Racing Stable team, which had strong links to the factory, was supplied with a pair of Zagatos (registered 1VEV and 2VEV) that were even lighter. In this form seasoned Aston racer Roy Salvadori and up-and-coming star Jimmy Clark were sometimes able to compete with the Ferraris, but the Aston's weight always made it heavy and hard work to drive.

Just nineteen of the projected twenty-five Zagatos were built, each one different from the others. One had DB4-style headlamps instead of DB4GT-style cowls, another had thicker alloy bodywork to reduce the risk of dents, and a unique eggbox grille. A highly developed 'DP209' specification with a lower, curvier body was seen on two Zagatos and later adopted by one of the Essex cars, 2VEV, when it was rebuilt after a Goodwood crash. Following another accident in the 1990s, 2VEV was returned to its original specification.

The production of Zagatos ended prematurely because the factory could not find buyers for the cars, and the last two Zagatos were offloaded cheaply by the factory. It is ironic that now they are without doubt the most desirable Aston Martins of all, with values measured in millions of pounds.

◼ 1961 DB4 GT ZAGATO

Engine	In-line 6-cylinder, triple Weber 45DCO carburettors
Valvegear	Twin overhead cam
Bore and stroke	92 × 92mm
Capacity	3670cc
Power	314bhp @ 6,000rpm (claimed)
Transmission	Four-speed David Brown manual gearbox, rear-wheel drive, Powr-Lok limited slip differential
Chassis/body	Steel platform chassis, aluminium alloy body
Suspension	Double wishbones and coil springs front, live axle with trailing arms, Watt link rear
Brakes	Four-wheel Girling disc brakes, hydraulically operated
Performance	150mph (241km/h), 0–60mph in 7sec (approx)

'PROJECT' CARS: DP212, DP214 AND DP215

ASTON MARTIN RETIRED from sports car racing at the end of 1959 to concentrate on Formula 1, but the works team only survived until the end of 1960. Thereafter private teams upheld Aston Martin honour in motor sport, until pressure from the company's dealers for official competition involvement in sports car racing, and particularly the Le Mans 24-hour race, prompted a new effort in 1962.

The new car built to contest the Sarthe classic that year was Development Project 212, the first of the 'Project' cars. It was based on a production-type DB4GT platform chassis and powered by a DB4GT twin-plug engine with big-bore liners giving a capacity of 3995cc. The front suspension was similar to the DB4GT, but the DP212's relationship with its production brethren largely ended there. The rear suspension was a de Dion layout, and the whole lot was clothed in a lightweight, low-drag body with a very smooth nose featuring faired-in headlamps and a small oval air intake. Graham Hill and Richie Ginther were engaged to drive it, the 5ft 3in Ginther using a special seat that fitted inside six-footer Hill's. The race started well, Hill leading the pack at the end of the first lap by most of the length of the pits straight, but DP212 retired after six hours when a piston failed.

Wind-tunnel work at MIRA proved that DP212 generated massive rear-end lift, which explained why the drivers had complained of skittish handling in fast corners. For 1963 Aston Martin built three new Project cars incorporating rear spoilers,

RIGHT: **DP215 was the last of the 'Project cars' that upheld Aston Martin honour in sports car racing in the early 1960s. Though designed for the new V8 engine it was only ever run with a 6-cylinder unit.**
BELOW: **DP212 was the first of the 'Project' cars that returned Aston Martin to sports car racing in 1962.**
ASTON MARTIN HERITAGE TRUST

Two DP214s were built for 1963, with light box-section frames and aerodynamic improvements – note the upswept tail, which reduced rear-end lift. ASTON MARTIN HERITAGE TRUST

which Ginther had suggested based on his experiences with Ferrari. Two DP214s were built using chassis numbers from the DB4GT sequence, though the cars' chassis were light box-section frames instead of the production-type steel platform chassis. Both were fitted with 3750cc engines, mounted 8.5in (216mm) further back than standard to improve weight distribution. The other car was DP215, designed for the new V8 engine which was now being developed by Tadek Marek. As things turned out the V8 was never fitted to DP215, which instead made do with a 4-litre, dry-sump version of the DB4GT unit. DP215 also had a new double-wishbone rear suspension with a wide-based lower wishbone and a DBR1-style David Brown transaxle.

DP215 missed the Le Mans test, where the DP214s were the first cars ever to be officially timed at over 186mph (300km/h) on the Mulsanne straight. DP215 later recorded nearly 198mph (320km/h) in the same place. But while the Project cars had speed, they lacked reliability: both DP214s retired with holed pistons, and DP215's transmission failed. The cars appeared at several more sports car events in 1963, the last works win being recorded by Roy Salvadori in a DP214 at the Coppa Inter-Europa at Monza in September.

The Project cars then passed into private hands, one of the DP214s being scrapped after an accident at the Nürburgring, which killed Brian Hetreed. Happily the sister DP214 survives, as do DP212 and DP215, and there are at least two replicas.

	DP212	**DP214**	**DP215**
Engine	In-line 6-cylinder	In-line 6-cylinder	In-line 6-cylinder
Valvegear	Twin overhead cam	Twin overhead cam	Twin overhead cam
Bore and stroke	96 × 92mm	93 × 92mm	96 × 92mm
Capacity	3995cc	3750cc	3995cc
Power	327bhp @ 6,000rpm	317bhp @ 6,000rpm	323bhp @ 6,000rpm
Fuel system	Triple Weber 50DCO carburettors	Triple Weber 50DCO carburettors	Triple Weber 50DCO carburettors
Transmission	Four-speed David Brown manual gearbox, rear-wheel drive	Four-speed David Brown manual gearbox, rear-wheel drive	Four-speed David Brown manual gearbox, rear-wheel drive
Chassis/body	Steel platform chassis, aluminium alloy body	Steel box-section chassis, aluminium alloy body	Steel box-section chassis, aluminium alloy body
Suspension	Double wishbones and coil springs front, de Dion rear	Double wishbones and coil springs front, live axle with trailing arms, Watt link rear	Double wishbones and coil springs front and rear
Brakes	Four-wheel Girling disc brakes, hydraulically operated	Four-wheel Girling disc brakes, hydraulically operated	Four-wheel Girling disc brakes, hydraulically operated
Performance	170mph (273km/h), 0–60mph in 6sec (approx)	186mph (300km/h), 0–60mph in 6sec (approx)	199mph (320km/h), 0–60mph in 6sec (approx)

LAGONDA RAPIDE

WHEN DAVID BROWN brought Aston Martin and Lagonda together in 1947, his aim was not simply to adopt the Watson/Bentley 2.6-litre engine to power a new generation of Aston Martins. Brown was keen to make Lagonda a successful marque in its own right, and to that end the Bentley-designed 2.6 saloon was readied for production in 1949 and a 3-litre successor followed in 1953.

But luxurious and beautifully made as they were, the Lagondas struggled to make their mark in the marketplace against competition from Jaguar, which was building the big MkVII and a family of compact sports saloons. The Jaguars offered extremely good performance, thanks to the excellent XK twin-cam engine, together with fine handling and – crucially – very affordable prices. Lagonda simply could not compete (a problem it shared with other aristocratic marques such as Armstrong-Siddeley), and the last of the 3-litre cars was built early in 1958.

Aston Martin then concentrated on the new DB4, but Lagonda was not entirely forgotten. In 1961 a new Lagonda appeared, sharing practically nothing with the Bentley-era cars of the 1950s. Instead the new car was based on a lengthened DB4 platform chassis, and powered by a big-bore 4-litre version of the DB4's twin-cam engine with twin Solex carburettors.

A Borg-Warner three-speed automatic transmission was standard, though a David Brown manual gearbox was available as an option. Dunlop disc brakes were fitted on all four wheels. The front suspension was a wishbone set-up similar to the DB4, but the rear end used a de Dion system, just as Harold Beach had originally proposed for the Aston, with fabricated trailing arms, a Watt linkage and torsion bar springs.

The original styling proposal had been for the Lagonda to follow closely the DB4's looks, but using a longer wheelbase to provide greater interior space and four doors. The shape that emerged carried a clear family resemblance to the DB4 at the back and to some extent from the side, but the nose was reshaped as it was felt that the Lagonda needed to have its own identity. The new four-headlamp front end carried forwards a styling theme from the abortive Lagonda V12 racer of the 1950s, with a horseshoe-shaped main grille and horizontal side grilles. It was widely disliked.

Largely as a result of the uninspiring styling (plus some problems with spline wear on the driveshafts) 'the finest of fast cars' was unsuccessful. Just fifty-five were made between 1961 and 1964, when production was ended so that the company could concentrate on building Aston Martins. A shooting-brake

There are hints of DB4 in the Lagonda Rapide's styling, which indicate the origins of the project. Few were convinced by the front-end design.

version of the Lagonda had been planned, but the Rapide's slow sales put paid to that idea, and the shooting brake was never built by the factory – though one car was converted to this specification by the Carrosserie Company many years later.

After the demise of the Rapide, the Lagonda name would lie dormant until the mid-1970s, while the Rapide model name would not return until the new millennium. Nearly all the 1960s Rapides built still survive, but despite their rarity their values are low in comparison to DB4-6 Astons.

BELOW: **The Rapide offered comfort, quality and space for four but never found a place in the market. Just fifty-five were built in three years.**
BOTTOM LEFT: **After the demise of the Rapide in 1964, the Lagonda name remained dormant until 1969.**

■ 1961 LAGONDA RAPIDE

Engine	In-line 6-cylinder, twin Solex carburettors
Valvegear	Twin overhead cam
Bore and stroke	96 × 92mm
Capacity	3995cc
Power	236bhp @ 5,500rpm
Transmission	Borg-Warner automatic transmission, four-speed David Brown manual gearbox optional, rear-wheel drive
Chassis/body	Steel platform chassis, tubular body frame with aluminium alloy body
Suspension	Double wishbones and coil springs front, de Dion rear
Brakes	Four-wheel Dunlop disc brakes, hydraulically operated
Performance	125mph (201km/h), 0–60mph in 9sec (approx)

RIGHT: **A shooting brake was planned by the factory, but slow sales of the saloon meant it was never built. This car was built by the Carrosserie Company for a private owner many years later.**

DB5

DESPITE A SHAKY start caused by reliability concerns, the DB4 became a huge success for Aston Martin, with more than 1,100 sold during a four-and-a-half year production run. Its replacement, the DB5 of 1963, would sell even faster.

Externally there was little difference between a Series 5 DB4 Vantage and a DB5. Both were slightly longer than the earlier DB4s, with a higher roof and reprofiled wings. Even the dual fuel fillers often used as a recognition point for the DB5 were fitted on some Series 5 DB4s, and like all previous Astons, early DB5s carried no model identification badges. It was only part-way through the production run that the DB5 acquired model badges, fitted on its boot lid and near the bottom of both front wings.

Despite the external similarity between the DB5 and the car it replaced, there were significant changes under the skin. The biggest difference was the adoption of a larger engine, a 3995cc version of the Marek 6-cylinder using the 96mm bore which had already been seen in the DP215 race car and the Lagonda Rapide production machine. While the Lagonda's 4-litre engine was fitted with two Solex twin-choke carburettors, the DB5 was given triple SUs, boosting the claimed power output to 282bhp. Early DB5s used the four-speed David Brown gearbox, which had been standard on the DB4, with overdrive and a five-speed ZF gearbox as options. Numerous detail improvements over the DB4 included an alternator instead of a dynamo, Triplex Sundym tinted glass and electric windows, four exhaust silencers rather than two, and an oil cooler. Girling disc brakes with twin master cylinders replaced the Dunlop brakes on the DB4. There was even a change in the toolkit, a hydraulic jack replacing the previous mechanical item.

For many people the DB5, with its classic styling and James Bond connection, is the ultimate classic Aston.

The DB5 was very similar to the last of the DB4s, but was powered by a 4-litre engine similar to that of the Lagonda Rapide.

David Brown was always keen on estate cars – or 'shooting brakes' as they were known at Newport Pagnell. A dozen DB5 shooting brakes were built, but to avoid disruption to the Aston factory they were made by coachbuilder Harold Radford.
ASTON MARTIN HERITAGE TRUST

The DB5 interior was broadly similar to the DB4, but with detail improvements.

A convertible version of the DB5 was available from the start, at a price of £4,490 including UK purchase tax, a £305 premium over the DB5 saloon. There was also a DB5 shooting brake: David Brown had one made as a one-off, then a handful of replicas was built up by London coachbuilder Harold Radford using complete DB5 saloons as the basis.

In 1964 the five-speed ZF gearbox was standardized, and at the same time a three-speed Borg-Warner automatic transmission was offered as a £72 option. A Vantage engine option was also made available, with triple Weber carburettors and a claimed (though optimistic) output of 314bhp at 5,750rpm.

In just two years Aston Martin built 1,023 DB5s, 898 of them standard saloons, with 123 convertibles and just twelve Radford shooting brakes.

Today the DB5 is one of the best known Aston Martins of all, thanks to its appearance in the 1960s James Bond films *Goldfinger* and *Thunderball* (though one of the two cars used was actually a late DB4 Vantage!) and much later in *GoldenEye* and *Tomorrow Never Dies*. It is also an attractive package, with a host of worthwhile detail improvements over the DB4 but without the arguably less stylish body of the DB6. As a result, good

examples are worth considerably more than either the DB4 or DB6.

■ 1963 DB5

Engine	In-line 6-cylinder, triple SU carburettors
Valvegear	Twin overhead cam
Bore and stroke	96 × 92mm
Capacity	3995cc
Power	282bhp @ 5,500rpm
Transmission	Four-speed David Brown manual gearbox, overdrive optional, five-speed ZF gearbox optional, Borg-Warner automatic transmission optional, rear-wheel drive
Chassis/body	Steel platform chassis, tubular body frame with aluminium alloy body
Suspension	Double wishbones and coil springs front, live axle with trailing arms, Watt link rear
Brakes	Four-wheel Dunlop disc brakes, hydraulically operated
Performance	145mph (232km/h), 0–60mph in 8sec

JAMES BOND'S DB5

Sean Connery as James Bond with 007's Aston Martin DB5. Two cars were used for filming *Goldfinger* – one of them not a DB5 at all!

IT WAS IAN Fleming himself who started the relationship between his famous secret agent, James Bond, and Aston Martin. In the *Goldfinger* book Bond selects a pool car, opting for a DB Mark III rather than a Jaguar 3.4.

For the *Goldfinger* film, special effects supervisor John Stears and production designer Ken Adam wanted a more modern Aston, originally considering a DB4GT Zagato. When Stears approached Aston Martin they were sceptical about the whole project, and particularly the gadgets Stears proposed to fit, but eventually agreed to lend the film company Eon Productions two cars – not Zagatos, but instead a production DB5 and a pre-production prototype, DP216/1, which had started life as a DB4 Vantage. The production car, originally registered FMP7B, would be used for close-ups while the well used DP216/1 could be modified to incorporate the gadgetry that Bond would use in the film (and more that was never used). Both cars used DP216/1's registration, BMT216A, during filming.

The gadgets included an arsenal of offensive and defensive weapons, and other useful items for a secret agent in the field: thus the bumper over-riders extended into battering rams, machine guns were concealed behind lamps, and the rear window could be protected by a bullet shield. There was a tracking device with a screen hidden behind a speaker grille in the centre console, and a car phone was concealed in the driver's arm rest. Pursuers could be deterred by tyre slashers extending from the rear wheel hubs (apparently inspired by the chariot-racing scene in *Ben Hur*), while oil slicks, smoke and nails could be spread from the rear of the car. *Goldfinger* director Guy Hamilton kept getting parking tickets in London and wished his car had revolving number plates so he could quickly change its identity, so they were fitted to Bond's DB5 – giving a choice of British, French and Swiss plates. Most of the equipment was controlled from a switch panel hidden under the centre arm rest, though famously the car was also fitted with a passenger ejector seat, operated by a button hidden under a flip-top gear knob. Flame throwers and an automatic cocktail shaker were proposed, too, but never made it on to the car.

The gadget-laden DB5 proved to be a huge hit with cinema audiences, and two replicas were built for promotional duties. *Goldfinger* earned back its $3 million production cost in just two weeks, making it the fastest grossing film ever made. Corgi made a scale model of the DB5, and US company Gilbert made a '007

Road Race Set' with a DB5 and Ford Mustang. Bond's DB5 reappeared in the pre-title sequence for the next film, *Thunderball*, in which it uses a new gadget – a rear-facing water cannon.

DP216/1 was later returned to standard and sold, but its identity was soon discovered and replica gadgets installed. Sotheby's sold the car at auction in 1986 for $250,000 to Florida property developer Anthony Pugliese, whose collection of 1960s memorabilia also included the gun Jack Ruby used to shoot Lee Harvey Oswald. The Aston toured the world, appearing at museums and events until June 1997, when it was stolen from the hangar at Boca Raton where it was being stored. It has never been seen since.

The close-ups car, FMP7B, was fitted with replicas of some of the Bond gadgets and was also sold to the USA. In 2010 it was sold at auction for a (surprisingly modest) £2.6 million.

James Bond moved on to a DBS in *On Her Majesty's Secret Service*, and then toyed with other marques before briefly returning to the DB5 in 1995. Four more DB5s were used for sequences in *GoldenEye* and *Tomorrow Never Dies*, before Bond was allocated an Aston Martin Vanquish in *Die Another Day*.

LEFT: **The famous film gadgets fitted to FMP7B include a removable roof panel – supposedly for a passenger ejector seat.**
BELOW: **FMP7B, one of the two *Goldfinger* cars, was sold by RMA Auctions in November 2010, making £2.6m.**

DB6 AND DB6 MARK 2

THE SUCCESS OF the *Goldfinger* film garnered worldwide acclaim for Aston Martin, and the company took advantage of its new-found fame by launching two new models at the London Motor Show in 1965.

Aston Martin moved its engineering operations from Feltham to Newport Pagnell early in 1964, but of the design and technical staff only Harold Beach and Tadek Marek made the move, so plenty of new recruits were involved in the development of the DB5's successor, the DB6. From the front the new car was clearly a development of the old, retaining the familiar Aston Martin nose with faired-in headlamps which dated back to the DB4GT of 1959. For the DB6 the bumper was split, and there was a prominent oil cooler intake grille between the two halves. At the back there was evidence of new thinking: the DB5's vestigial fins were gone, and in their place was a vertical tail topped by a built-in spoiler. It was clearly derived from the aerodynamic work that had gone into the DP214 and DP215 Le

Mans cars, and it meant the DB6 not only generated less aerodynamic drag than the DB5, it was also more stable at speed.

The wheelbase was 4in (100mm) longer to improve rear passenger accommodation, but the overall length of the new car was only 2in (50mm) more than the old. Kerb weight hardly changed, the DB6 weighing in just 17lb (8kg) heavier. Although in practice the differences in weight and length between DB5 and DB6 were relatively minor, the DB6 looked considerably longer and heavier, partly because the roof had been raised slightly and remained higher over the rear of the cabin to improve rear headroom. The DB5's triangular rear side windows were replaced by squarish windows similar to those on the DB4GT Zagato, with thick C-pillars on either side of the rear window. The raised, reprofiled roof and longer wheelbase made the rear seats of the DB6 much more usable, and slimmer seat cushions liberated even more space, making the new car a genuine four-seater.

ABOVE: **The DB6 looked bigger and heavier than the DB5, but in practice the differences in size and weight were marginal.**
RIGHT: **The reshaped tail of the DB6 incorporated a spoiler, developed from Aston Martin's experience in racing with the Project cars.**

LEFT: **The DB6 Mark 2, introduced in 1969, shared components with the DBS as a cost-cutting measure.**
BELOW: **Wider wheels and flared arches give the DB6 Mark 2 a more muscular stance than the earlier car, but both have their fans.**
BOTTOM: **The DB6 Mark 2 was the last of the DB4/5/6 family, continuing in production until 1970.**

Comparison of the DB6 and DB6 Mark 2: the flared arches and wider wheels of the Mark 2 (*right*) are easy to see.

Although the platform chassis was much the same as before, just lengthened in the wheelbase, the body was constructed in a slightly different way. The framework of small-bore tubes that made up the body frame on the DB4 and DB5 – Touring's Superleggera construction system – made way for a new framework consisting of folded box sections. Unlike the Touring system, which used the same size tubing throughout, the box sections were sized according to their function throughout the structure, which meant the new body frame was both stiffer and lighter than before. Aston Martin would continue to use the same construction method for many years.

Mechanically the DB6 was much the same as before, with the DB5's 4-litre, triple-SU version of the twin-cam straight six engine, developing the same 282bhp. In theory, at least – but Aston Martin were having to compete with American manufacturers who routinely overestimated their engines' outputs, often by as much as 30 per cent. John Wyer had only ever allowed Aston Martin's figures to be 15 per cent optimistic, a practice that continued until DIN standard power measurements restored some order in the 1970s. So the true output of the standard 4-litre six was closer to 245bhp, while the Vantage specification (which now included a 9.4:1 compression ratio), which had a claimed output of 325bhp at 5,750rpm, in fact had a real output of around 275bhp.

The ZF five-speed gearbox was carried over from the DB5, and a Borg-Warner three-speed automatic transmission was a no-cost option, though it was criticized for its low gearing. Armstrong Selectaride adjustable dampers, optional on the DB5, were standard fit on the DB6. There were only two optional extras: power steering and Normalair air conditioning.

The DB6 was produced alongside two different Volante models (*see* p.71) until 1969, when it was replaced by a Mark 2 model. Under the bonnet the only change was the availability as an optional extra of AE Brico electronic fuel injection,

introduced the previous year as an option on the DBS. As the injection option cost £299 (on top of the list price of the DB6 Mark 2 of £4,798) there were few takers, just forty-six injected cars being sold.

Other changes were largely aimed at reducing manufacturing cost and complexity by sharing parts wherever possible with the DBS. The DB6 Mark 2 was given the same seats and the wider 6 × 15in wire wheels that were used on the DBS. Wheel-arch flares were added to the front and rear, largely to make the car look wider and more modern. There was also a larger clutch and a lower first-gear ratio, and power steering was standardized. There was also a Volante version of the Mark 2 (*see* p.71).

The DB6 Mark 2 lasted for only a year, during which 240 were made. It was phased out in 1970 so that Newport Pagnell could concentrate on the DBS and the newly launched DBS V8.

■ 1965 DB6

Engine	In-line 6-cylinder, triple SU carburettors, AE Brico fuel injection optional on Mark 2
Valvegear	Twin overhead cam
Bore and stroke	96 × 92mm
Capacity	3995cc
Power	282bhp @ 5,500rpm
Transmission	Five-speed ZF manual gearbox, Borg-Warner automatic transmission optional, rear-wheel drive
Chassis/body	Steel platform chassis, tubular body frame with aluminium alloy body
Suspension	Double wishbones and coil springs front, live axle with trailing arms, Watt link rear
Brakes	Four-wheel Dunlop disc brakes, hydraulically operated
Performance	145mph (232km/h), 0–60mph in 8sec

DB GT SPECIAL

DB4GT CHASSIS NUMBER 0148 was originally owned by Max Aitken (later chairman of Express Newspapers). It was then acquired by Bobby Buchanan-Michaelson, who returned it to Newport Pagnell to be rebuilt to his own, unique specification. During 1967/68 it was given a DB5-style front end and a cut-off DB6-style tail, and the ZF five-speed gearbox used on the later models. In total the modifications cost almost £5,000, which would have comfortably bought a brand new DB6. The result, named the DB GT Special, was less than the sum of its parts: aesthetically it was dubious, and it was very heavy. But that wasn't the end of its curious history.

After passing through the hands of several owners, one of which was Aston Martin chairman Victor Gauntlett, 0148 was given a mechanical restoration by respected Aston Martin specialist R. S. Williams, and sent to Zagato in Turin to be clothed in a DB4 GT Zagato body. On its completion in 2003 it was effectively a brand new 1961 DB4GT Zagato – not quite one of the original cars, and not quite a Sanction II/III Zagato either. Instead it is a unique addition to the Aston Martin/Zagato family, which has since been campaigned on track by Chris Scragg.

■ 1961 DB GT SPECIAL

Engine	In-line 6-cylinder, triple Weber carburettors
Valvegear	Twin overhead cam
Bore and stroke	92 × 92mm
Capacity	3670cc
Power	345bhp @ 6,000rpm
Transmission	Five-speed ZF manual gearbox, rear-wheel drive, Powr-Lok limited slip differential
Chassis/body	Steel platform chassis, aluminium alloy body
Suspension	Double wishbones and coil springs front, live axle with trailing arms, Watt link rear
Brakes	Four-wheel Girling disc brakes, hydraulically operated
Performance	150mph (242km/h), 0–60mph in 6sec

Not quite what it seems: 616JGY, the DB GT Special, originally had a short-wheelbased DB5/6 body but was rebodied by Zagato in 2003.

VOLANTE

THREE DIFFERENT CONVERTIBLES were built alongside the DB6 and DB6 Mark 2 saloons between 1965 and 1970, all of them under the same model name – Volante, the Italian word for 'flying'.

The first Volante was unveiled alongside the DB6 at the London Motor Show in October 1965. It shared the DB6's revised front-end styling with a split front bumper and central oil-cooler intake, but it was built on the shorter DB5 platform (in fact using up a stock of unsold DB5 chassis) and had a DB5-style tail carrying a Volante badge on the boot lid. Just thirty-seven of these cars were built, two of them with Vantage engines. This model later came to be known as the 'short chassis' Volante.

It was replaced in 1966 by a DB6-based Volante with the same 4in (100mm) wheelbase stretch and vertical bespoilered tail as the saloon. A power-operated hood was standard, though a tonneau cover was a £59 option. Of the 140 made, twenty-nine were fitted with Vantage engines and almost half (sixty-eight) had automatic transmission.

The Mark 2 Volante was launched alongside the DB6 Mark 2 in 1969. It was fitted with the same DBS-type wider wheels and flared arches and, like the saloon, had power steering as standard and AE Brico injection as an option (though possibly only one Mark 2 Volante had an injected engine).

The short-chassis Volante was built alongside the DB6 and shared its front-end styling, but used a shorter wheelbase DB5 chassis.

1970 VOLANTE MARK 2

Engine	In-line 6-cylinder, triple Weber carburettors
Valvegear	Twin overhead cam
Bore and stroke	96 × 92mm
Capacity	3995cc
Power	325bhp @ 6,000rpm
Transmission	Five-speed ZF manual gearbox, Borg-Warner automatic optional, rear-wheel drive, Powr-Lok limited slip differential optional
Chassis/body	Steel platform chassis, aluminium alloy body
Suspension	Double wishbones and coil springs front, live axle with trailing arms, Watt link rear
Brakes	Four-wheel disc brakes, hydraulically operated
Performance	150mph (242km/h), 0–60mph in 6sec

The Mark 2 Volante was available for just one year, during which thirty-eight were made.

Comparison of Volante tails: the short-chassis Volante (*top*) and the later DB6-based Volante (*above*).

TOURING DBSC

AS SOON AS the DB4 had gone into production and the earliest teething troubles had been sorted out, Aston Martin started thinking about how to replace it. David Brown had always been keen to take the marque further upmarket so that it could compete on level terms with the fastest Ferraris. That meant increasing the engine size, and the existing 6-cylinder engine had been run experimentally at 4.2 litres – but that was barely enough. What was needed was a considerably bigger engine, and development of that unit – the V8 – began in 1962. The car it was originally intended to power was known internally as MP220, a wider four-seat grand touring car.

Meanwhile the DB4 was progressively developed into the DB5 and then the DB6, each car longer than its predecessor with better interior accommodation and greater practicality. But to some eyes the DB6 lacked the grace of the older cars, and represented a shift in emphasis from refined road-burner to family man's sports car – a shift that would be firmly under-lined by the production version of MP220. That left a gap in the market for a smaller, two-seater car with the emphasis more on performance and driving enjoyment than on refinement and practicality.

In January 1966 work began on a chassis for this two-seater car, retaining the longer wheelbase of the DB6 but with short-er overhangs. At the front there was space for the V8 engine, and at the rear there was a de Dion suspension system – this time carefully designed to avoid running the driveshafts at a compound angle, which in the Lagonda Rapide caused them to wear.

Within Aston Martin the two-seater was often referred to as 'the 170mph car', that being the top speed expected with the V8 engine, and the soubriquet stuck even when delays to the V8 project (see p.78) led to the adoption of a Vantage-spec 6-cylinder engine. Carrozzerria Touring, the Italian design house that had shaped the DB4, was invited to draw up the design

ABOVE: **Touring's DBSC was powered by the 4-litre 6-cylinder engine, but offered a more modern body style. Only two were built.**
RIGHT: **The interior of the DBSC also brought Aston Martin up to date, with more luxurious appointments than the existing production cars.**

and submitted its ideas in April, with the initial schedule aiming to complete the two MP226 cars by October 1967. But in mid-1966 the Labour government increased taxes and reduced tax relief on hire purchase payments, which made Aston Martins rather more expensive – and sales collapsed almost overnight.

To drum up some interest Aston Martin now planned to show MP226 at the most important motor shows in the latter part of 1966, at Paris and London, and that meant the cars needed to be ready in September 1966 – more than a year ahead of schedule. Touring reluctantly agreed to a crash build programme and the cars were externally complete for their show debuts, though still far from finished under the skin. At first referred to publically as 'the Touring', they had acquired the name DBS by the time of the Earls Court show in October.

But these were very much hand-built prototypes rather than production-ready machines. The long 6-cylinder engine was mounted much further back in the chassis than it was in the

DB6, leaving no room for a heater. The cylinder head could not be removed with the engine in the car. There were few production drawings, and Aston Martin's engineering director Dudley Gershon estimated at least six months' further work would be needed to ready the cars even for a limited production run.

These problems, together with the worsening financial situation at Touring (the company ceased trading shortly after) and David Brown's preference for the bigger four-seater car, led to the MP226 project being shelved. The two Touring-built cars were completed over the next few months and sold on to wealthy enthusiasts, while the factory concentrated on the development of the four-seater car. When that was launched in October 1967 – with a stop-gap 6-cylinder engine – it also used the name DBS, which was by now well known thanks to the impact of the Touring cars. To save any future confusion, the MP226 cars were redesignated DBSC. Despite their drawbacks they remain a fleeting glimpse of a new age of Aston Martins, which never quite happened.

DBSC had packaging compromises that made it impractical: there were only two seats, and the engine installation was problematic.

The rear pillars of the DBSC carried air-exit louvres for the ventilation system.

Although the DBSC was attractive from some angles, some of its details were odd – such as the curious cut-outs for the circular rear lamp units.

Probably the DBSC's best feature is its striking nose with the cowled lamps. The grille retains a hint of the now-classic Aston Martin shape.

■ 1966 DBSC

Engine	In-line 6-cylinder, triple Weber 45DCO carburettors
Valvegear	Twin overhead cam
Bore and stroke	96 × 92mm
Capacity	3995cc
Power	325bhp @ 6,000rpm
Transmission	Five-speed ZF manual gearbox, Borg-Warner automatic optional, rear-wheel drive, Powr-Lok limited slip differential optional
Chassis/body	Steel platform chassis, aluminium alloy body
Suspension	Double wishbones and coil springs front, live axle with trailing arms, Watt link rear
Brakes	Four-wheel disc brakes, hydraulically operated
Performance	165mph (266km/h), 0–60mph in 5.5sec (approx)

LOLA-ASTON MARTIN

IT WAS TRADITIONAL for Aston Martin to prove its products in motor sport. The new V8 engine under development since 1963 had been intended to power DP215, but by the time the V8 was ready, the front-engined 'Project' GT cars were obsolete, and in any case Aston Martin had withdrawn from works competition. So in September 1966 Aston Martin announced a partnership with the racing car constructor Lola, and at the Racing Car Show in January 1967 the Surtees Racing stand displayed the new four-cam, all-alloy Aston Martin V8, said to be producing more than 450bhp in its racing specification, which included dry-sump lubrication and Lucas fuel injection. At the same show Lola revealed a new 'Mark III' version of its successful mid-engined sports racing car, the T70, and it was announced that an Aston-powered version would soon be under construction.

Two Lola-Astons were built, with Le Mans in mind. John Surtees took one car to the Nürburgring for the 1,000km race two weeks before Le Mans, where the car proved to be fast in practice but retired early with suspension failure. At Le Mans, Surtees managed only three laps before a piston failed, and the sister car of Chris Irwin and Piet de Klerk did little better, retiring with fuel system problems after twenty-five laps. When the engines were stripped after the race they were found to be badly distorted – the block design clearly was not up to the job and needed a major redesign.

Both cars survive, though one suffered the indignity of being disguised as a Ferrari and deliberately crashed during the making of Steve McQueen's *Le Mans* film.

Aston Martin's V8 engine first appeared in a pair of Lola T70 racing cars built by John Surtees. Early engines were woefully unreliable.

■ 1967 LOLA-ASTON MARTIN

Engine	V8, fuel injection
Valvegear	Twin overhead cam per bank
Capacity	5064cc
Power	460bhp
Transmission	Five-speed manual gearbox, rear-wheel drive
Chassis/body	Tubular spaceframe chassis, aluminium alloy body
Suspension	Double wishbones and coil springs front and rear
Brakes	Four-wheel disc brakes, hydraulically operated
Performance	206mph (332km/h), 0–60mph in 4sec (approx)

DBS

ALTHOUGH THE EVOLUTIONARY change from DB4 to DB5 to DB6 looked logical and orderly, the mid-1960s was a chaotic period behind the scenes at Newport Pagnell. A new V8 engine was being developed, but testing quickly showed that the block was not stiff enough, and its competition career in the Lola-Astons in 1966 was both brief and disastrous. A major redesign followed, which delayed the introduction of the production engine until 1969.

Aston Martin's new models were planned around the new V8 engine. The two-seater Touring DBSC (see p.73) had its

ABOVE: **The DBS of 1967 was built for the V8 engine, but when the new unit was delayed the car was launched with the old 4-litre six.**

BELOW: **Wider and heavier than the DB6, the DBS offered greater comfort and refinement but lost some outright performance.**

Aston Martin debated whether or not to use the 'DB7' name, but 'DBS' had already won some positive publicity thanks to the Touring DBS show cars.

own problems and never made it to production, but plans went ahead for a larger, four-seat car based on a widened version of the existing platform chassis. Styling proposals from Touring were rejected in favour of an in-house scheme from William Towns, who had joined Aston Martin as a seat designer. It was designed from the outset to work on several wheelbase lengths, from four-door Lagonda down to short-wheelbase GT.

The new car was shown to the press at Blenheim Palace in September 1967 and then formally announced at the Motor Show the following month. Logically it should have been called DB7 and it very nearly was – DB7 badges were made – but the Touring two-seater had generated a lot of useful publicity in 1966 under the name DBS, so that name was used instead. Towns' design was much more modern than the decade-old DB4/5/6 shape, with an imposing four-headlamp front end incorporating a wider version of the traditional Aston Martin grille and peaked front wings, supposedly inspired by the Ford Mustang. Considerably wider than the DB6, though lower and shorter, it offered much more passenger space and an even more luxurious interior.

While the chassis was closely related to the previous cars, the DBS had new rear suspension – a de Dion layout similar to that on the ill-fated Lagonda Rapide. The new car was powered by the existing 4-litre straight six engine, with triple SU carburettors and a claimed 282bhp – though a triple Weber Vantage engine with a theoretical 325bhp was available as a no-cost option, and AE Brico fuel injection was also available. But the DBS had no more power than the DB6, and with its increased width it had more weight and a greater frontal area leading to more drag, which meant that its straight line performance suffered – though the more effective rear suspension meant that it was more than a match for the earlier cars on a twisty road.

As a result, reaction to the new car was mixed. It was common knowledge that the V8 engine was on the way, and that it had failed at Le Mans earlier that year. The DBS was criticized for being too heavy and too slow, even though in Vantage form it was still capable of 140mph (225km/h) and 0–60mph sprint times under eight seconds.

Unusually for Aston Martin no official convertible version of the DBS (or its later DBS V8 cousin) was ever made, though there have been private conversions. FLM Panelcraft also built a DBS shooting brake.

The DBS was in production for four and half years, initially running alongside the DB6 and later the DBS V8. In that time 790 were built. It was replaced in 1972 by the Aston Martin Vantage.

■ 1967 DBS

Engine	In-line 6-cylinder, triple SU carburettors, triple Weber carburettors or AE Brico fuel injection optional
Valvegear	Twin overhead cam
Bore and stroke	96 × 92mm
Capacity	3995cc
Power	282bhp @ 5,500rpm
Transmission	Five-speed ZF manual gearbox, Borg-Warner automatic transmission optional, rear-wheel drive
Chassis/body	Steel platform chassis, box-section body frame with aluminium alloy body
Suspension	Double wishbones and coil springs front, de Dion with trailing arms and Watt link rear
Brakes	Four-wheel Girling disc brakes, hydraulically operated
Performance	140mph (225km/h), 0–60mph in 7.5sec

DBS V8

AFTER FAILURES DURING testing and in the Lola-Aston racing programme, Aston Martin's new V8 engine had to be substantially reworked before it would be ready for production. Stiffening ribs were added and the main bearing housings strengthened, and longer cylinder-head bolts were used so that the stresses were fed into the bottom of the block rather than the top. Much of the detail redesign was done by Alan Crouch, who later moved on to the renowned engine development company Ricardo.

At the same time the bore and stroke were increased to expand the engine's capacity to 5340cc, and Bosch fuel injection was added; the revised engine was then put through an extensive test programme using modified DBSs. The result was a very

reliable and tractable engine, which produced around 345bhp – and it was just 30lb (13.6kg) heavier than the old 6-cylinder unit with its true output of around 275bhp. After years of fibbing in an attempt to keep up with rivals who had no scruples about publishing 'optimistic' power figures, Aston Martin declined to state officially the power output of the new engine, though they did point out how flat the torque curve was by revealing that the engine produced more than 300lb ft from 2,000rpm all the way to 6,000rpm, and the more technically aware journos realized this data could be used to calculate the power output.

The car it went into, the DBS V8, was visually very similar to the 6-cylinder DBS. The most noticeable change was the addition of a small air dam under the front bumper, which

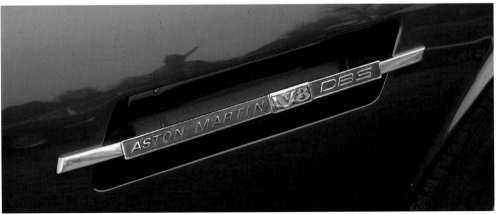

ABOVE: **The DBS V8 of 1969 was altogether swifter than the 6-cylinder car, and Aston Martin added a front air dam to ensure stability at high speed.**
LEFT: **DBS V8 was denoted by different wheels, a front air dam, and these badges across the front wing air vents.**

reduced aerodynamic lift at the very high speeds of which the new car was capable. Indeed, the DBS V8 was expected to be stable well beyond the 171mph (275km/h) maximum recorded in testing, it being Aston Martin practice to ensure its cars handled well even beyond production cars' theoretical top speed.

The wheels were another difference between the DBS and the V8. The new car swapped the 6-cylinder's traditional wire-spoked wheels for modern GKN light-alloy wheels shaped to draw hot air away from the larger Girling brakes, which now had internally ventilated front discs. The wheels were fitted with Pirelli tyres, which were chosen for their high top-speed rating, though they lacked the wet grip capability of Aston's usual Avons. The spring rates were increased and power steering – still only an option on the DBS – was now a standard fitment. The DBS V8 was offered with either the familiar ZF five-speed manual gearbox or a three-speed Chrysler Torqueflite automatic (which was altogether better than the old Borg-Warner transmission available on previous Astons). The only other option was air conditioning.

The DBS V8 was unveiled in September 1969 and sold alongside the 6-cylinder DBS (and, for a while, the DB6 and Volante Mark 2 models). By April 1972, when the DBS V8 was replaced

by a revised V8 saloon model, 405 had been built. A 375bhp Vantage model, proposed in 1968, was never developed for production – though much more powerful V8 Astons would follow in due course.

■ 1969 DBS V8

Engine	V8, Bosch fuel injection
Valvegear	Twin overhead cam per cylinder bank
Bore and stroke	100 × 85mm
Capacity	5340cc
Power	345bhp @ 6,000rpm
Transmission	Five-speed ZF manual gearbox, Chrysler Torqueflite automatic transmission optional, rear-wheel drive
Chassis/body	Steel platform chassis, box-section body frame with aluminium alloy body
Suspension	Double wishbones and coil springs front, de Dion with trailing arms and Watt link rear
Brakes	Four-wheel Girling disc brakes, hydraulically operated
Performance	170mph (275km/h), 0–60mph in 6sec

Aston Martin never made a convertible DBS, though some cars were converted by coachbuilders. This is a V8.

LAGONDA MP230/1

FROM THE START, William Towns had planned his DBS design so that it could be lengthened into a four-door car, or shortened to make a close-coupled GT. The shorter version was never built, but a prototype of the longer car, MP230/1, was slowly put together in 1968/69.

It was 11in (279mm) longer than the DBS, the extra length providing more rear legroom and greater boot space in addition to the extra pair of doors. Mechanically it was much the same as the DBS V8, though the longer propshaft had an extra centre bearing and initially the car was fitted with a prototype 5-litre engine with AE Brico electronic injection, though it soon reverted to a standard Bosch-injected V8. It was also fitted with wire wheels at first, later replaced by production-type alloys.

After some high-level arguments about what the identity of the new car should be, it was announced to the press, and registered for the road, as a Lagonda. Sir David Brown used it extensively and it was all set for production in 1970. But Aston Martin was already struggling to build V8 engines in sufficient quantity to keep up with orders for the DBS V8, so another new car creating further demand for the engine was a headache

1969 LAGONDA MP230/1

Engine	V8, Bosch fuel injection
Valvegear	Twin overhead cam per cylinder bank
Bore and stroke	100 × 85mm
Capacity	5340cc
Power	345bhp @ 6,000rpm
Transmission	Chrysler Torqueflite automatic transmission, rear-wheel drive
Chassis/body	Steel platform chassis, box-section body frame with aluminium alloy body
Suspension	Double wishbones and coil springs front, de Dion with trailing arms and Watt link rear
Brakes	Four-wheel Girling disc brakes, hydraulically operated
Performance	170mph (274km/h), 0–60mph in 6sec

the company did not need. So the Lagonda was mothballed – though it would return, in a mildly modified form, a few years later.

Lagonda returned – briefly – in 1969 when this four-door version of the DBS V8 was built for David Brown. A production car would not follow until 1974.

SIVA S530

IT'S NOT AN Aston Martin, but the Siva S530 is a fascinating 'might have been' and a turning point in Aston Martin history. Conceived by British designer Neville Trickett and displayed at the Earls Court Motor Show in 1971, the S530 was originally intended to use a mid-mounted Aston Martin V8 engine, which was mated to a ZF transaxle similar to that used by Ford's GT40. The plush interior featured bucket seats and a rectangular steering wheel.

Aston Martin did seriously consider putting the car into production. That it never became a production reality was less about the merits of the car itself and more about a struggle for control within the company, which, temporarily, was resolved in favour of the Brown family. Management changes were made within Aston Martin – and suddenly the Siva project was cancelled.

Had the S530 gone into production as an Aston Martin it would have been a major break with the past – not just in its ultra-modern styling, but also because of the mid-engined layout and glassfibre body. It's easy to see why David Brown – and perhaps many staunch Aston Martin customers – would have been against it. But it would have put Aston Martin ahead of Ferrari, Lamborghini and Maserati, all of which launched wild, wedge-shaped supercars in the early 1970s.

The car itself was re-engined with a Chevrolet V8, but only the prototype was ever built. It still exists today.

SIVA S530

Engine	V8, Bosch fuel injection
Valvegear	Twin overhead cam per cylinder bank
Bore and stroke	100 × 85mm
Capacity	5340cc
Power	345bhp @ 6,000rpm
Transmission	Five-speed ZF manual transaxle, rear-wheel drive
Chassis/body	Tubular spaceframe chassis, glassfibre body with gullwing doors
Suspension	Double wishbones and coil springs front and rear
Brakes	Four-wheel disc brakes, hydraulically operated
Performance	170mph (275km/h), 0–60mph in 5sec (approx)

The Siva S530 was a radical departure from the existing Aston Martin range. Some factions at Newport Pagnell wanted to put the car into production, but only a single prototype was ever built.

SOTHEBY SPECIAL/OGLE ASTON MARTIN V8

THE DBS V8 contributed its engine and chassis to a concept car by British design studio Ogle in 1971. The car was used in the promotion of the new Sotheby cigarette brand, and became known as the Sotheby Special. Its public debut came at the Montreal Motor Show in January 1972.

The Sotheby Special was unlike any previous Aston. The lower part of the wedge-shaped bodywork was in glassfibre, while above the waistline was predominantly glass. The low nose managed to retain the classic Aston Martin grille shape, while the tail incorporated twenty-two separate lamp units in two rows. The top row were direction indicators, which flashed in sequence from the centre of the car to the side. The bottom row were brake lights, more lights illuminating the harder the car braked. The car was a three-seater, with a 'chaise longue' seat for one at the back.

Sotheby cigarettes did not last long. Originally dark blue with gold coachlines and a brown interior, the Sotheby Special was repainted in Embassy white with red coachlines and used by Graham Hill, who had Embassy sponsorship for his F1 team.

Ogle built a replica later in 1972 for Mrs Mary Agate, based on the then-current Series 2 V8 but costing around three times as much. This second car, which survives, was originally burgundy with a dark green roof. It is now a brighter red and has a carburettored engine in place of the original injected unit.

LEFT: **Ogle's Sotheby Special was based on a DBS V8. This is the second car, built at great expense for a private customer in 1972.**

RIGHT: **The Ogle Aston has a very modern wedge-shaped body with a myriad of lights in the tail.**

■ 1972 SOTHEBY SPECIAL/OGLE ASTON MARTIN V8

Engine	V8, Bosch fuel injection (Agate car later used Weber carburettors)
Valvegear	Twin overhead cam per cylinder bank
Bore and stroke	100 × 85mm
Capacity	5340cc
Power	345bhp @ 6,000rpm
Transmission	Five-speed ZF manual gearbox (Sotheby Special), Chrysler Torqueflite automatic transmission (Agate car), rear-wheel drive
Chassis/body	Steel platform chassis, glassfibre body
Suspension	Double wishbones and coil springs front, de Dion with trailing arms and Watt link rear
Brakes	Four-wheel Girling disc brakes, hydraulically operated
Performance	175mph (281km/h), 0–60mph in 5.5sec (approx)

MOSTLY V8s –
NEWPORT PAGNELL

William Towns' 1975 Lagonda was one of the most striking
shapes ever put into production by a British manufacturer.

1972–1989

D AVID BROWN RAN Aston Martin as little more than a hobby for twenty-five years. During that time he saw the company develop three distinct generations of car, from the Atom-based machines of the immediate postwar years, through the DB4 family in the 1960s, to the big DBS series. Brown had achieved his aim of winning at Le Mans, had seen Aston Martin clinch the World Sports Car Championship in 1959, and had even dabbled with Grand Prix racing.

What Brown had not done was turn Aston Martin into a profitable company. While Astons were winning races and the David Brown group was benefiting from the reflected glory, that did not matter. But Aston Martin withdrew from motor sport in the 1960s, and by the end of the decade the British motor industry was in a turmoil of mergers and takeovers. The David Brown group was losing money, and the red ink on the Aston Martin balance sheet made it an easy target. Early in 1972 Brown concluded a deal with property developer Company

ABOVE: **Aston Martin relied on the Tadek Marek V8 engine exclusively from 1973 until 1994. Each one was hand built by a single technician.**
LEFT: **After David Brown sold Aston Martin, the DBS nomenclature was dropped to create this car – simply known as the V8. The new nose had been under development for some time.**

Developments to take over Aston Martin and Lagonda – and their debts – for just £100.

Aston Martin's new chairman, William Willson, sold off the Newport Pagnell sportsground to pay off some of the debts and announced revisions to the model range, including new front-end styling and a return to carburettors for the V8 engine. A new Lagonda was launched to a surprised media at the Motor Show in 1974, and from the outside it looked as if Aston Martin was forging ahead under its new owners – but in reality Willson was reaping the benefits of development work carried out under David Brown's ownership. The new two-headlamp front end had been designed by William Towns in 1971, work had started on a Weber carburettor installation

to replace the troublesome fuel injection, and the Lagonda had been planned right at the start of the DBS project – a prototype had been running since 1969 and was used by David Brown as his personal car (*see p.80*).

The reality was that Aston Martin was living on borrowed time. It was already struggling to survive as an independent car maker, rather than relying on the financial support and also the production facilities of the David Brown group, and it was battling to get the V8 and Lagonda through the emissions certification that would allow them to be sold in the United States. Then it was dealt another blow when the Yom Kippur war led to an oil crisis, and suddenly powerful, thirsty cars were out of fashion.

LEFT: **The Lagonda announced Aston Martin was back in business following bankruptcy in 1974.**
BELOW: **Aston Martins were built slowly, by craftsmen. Here a V8 Vantage takes shape at Newport Pagnell.**

With Aston Martin in crisis, Willson approached the government for a loan to help them complete the US certification work, but the Labour government of the time had no interest in subsidising performance cars for plutocrats – and in any case had its hands full with the much larger mess that was British Leyland. Aston Martin ran out of money at the end of 1974, the company went into voluntary receivership, the doors closed at Newport Pagnell, and the 500-strong workforce was made redundant. Some of them headed north to go to work for Rolls-Royce in Crewe.

It seemed like the end, but the Aston Martin Owners Club had different ideas. A 'Save Aston Martin' campaign was established to drum up support and raise money. Rex Woodgate of Aston Martin Incorporated, the US sales company, looked around for a possible buyer. The result, late in 1975, was the formation of a consortium of interested parties: Peter Sprague from the USA, George Minden from Canada, and Britons Alan Curtis and Denis Flather, all of them long-time Aston Martin drivers. Between them they bought Aston Martin from the receiver and got production going again.

The revitalized company marked its return with an extraordinary new Lagonda, a futuristic wedge-shaped saloon designed by William Towns, which was unveiled in 1976. It was fitted with advanced electronic instrumentation, which must have seemed dazzlingly modern at a time when digital watches were the latest must-have gadget. Under the skin the Lagonda used a revised version of the existing V8 engine and shared much of its chassis and suspension design with the Aston Martins, but the instrumentation was all new and took far longer to develop than the company had planned. Production of the Lagonda was delayed until 1978 as a result.

LEFT: **The twin-turbo Bulldog was for some time the fastest Aston Martin ever made. Just one example was built.**
BELOW: **Victor Gauntlett steered Aston Martin through troubled economic times and brokered a deal with Ford that gave the company unprecedented stability.**

A healthy order book for the Lagonda had led to speculation that the DBS-derived V8 saloon would be phased out, but with Lagonda production delayed, the V8 retained its place in the range and it continued even after Lagonda production finally began. In the mid-1970s two new V8 derivatives were introduced: a drophead Volante aimed largely at the American market, and a high-performance V8 Vantage, which benefited from engine development work carried out for the Lagonda. Aston Martin began the 1980s by unveiling the ultimate V8-engined car: the mid-engined, twin-turbocharged Bulldog. Although it was the fastest car Aston Martin had created up to that time, it was never turned into a production reality: just one example was built.

But another oil crisis threatened Aston Martin's survival. CH Industrials and Victor Gauntlett's Pace Petroleum business took control of the company in the early 1980s and concentrated on improving production efficiency. Gauntlett also took the opportunity to return the Aston Martin name to the top levels of sports car racing with the Nimrod project, born out of Robin Hamilton's efforts with a much modified V8 saloon. The racing engines developed by the Aston Martin Tickford subsidiary for the Nimrod – which were based on the long-running road car V8 – also powered the EMKA and Cheetah race cars. The high point of Aston Martin's return to sports car racing came in 1982 when Viscount Downe's Nimrod finished seventh overall at Le Mans and fourth in the Group C class.

A return to the big screen alongside James Bond in the 1983 film *The Living Daylights* – after a long period where the famous secret agent had dabbled with other cars – provided welcome publicity for Aston Martin. In 1984 the company's ownership changed again as CH Industrials moved on, being replaced by Automotive Investments, a company owned by the Greek Papanicolau and Livanos families. By then the economic conditions were improving and Aston Martin could think of developing new cars, including a renewal of the tie-up with Zagato that led to the exclusive Aston Martin Vantage Zagato and Zagato Volante cars. Further revisions to the long-running V8

would keep it going until a replacement, the Virage, could be readied. The standard V8 was given electronic fuel injection with a sophisticated Weber-Marelli engine management system. The tuned engine of the Vantage was offered in a wide-arch version of the convertible Volante body to produce the Vantage Volante, and there was a 'Prince of Wales' Volante with the same engine in a subtler standard body. Even after the Virage was launched the V8 Volante remained in production to satisfy demand for drophead Astons until a Virage Volante could be developed.

To put the Virage into production Aston Martin needed the support of a big industry partner, which would arrive in 1987 – and it would be the start of a whole new era for the company.

V8

AVID BROWN SOLD Aston Martin in February 1972 and a new model was released in April of that same year. From the outside it might have looked as if the new proprietors were really on the ball, but in reality the new car had been under development for some time under the old regime.

The new model was simply called the Aston Martin V8 (though more recently the Aston Martin Owners Club has termed it the Series 2, Series 1 being the DBS V8). The major change was the adoption of a new two-headlamp front end, which improved the lighting and freshened up the four-year-old shape at the same time. William Towns, now a freelance stylist, designed the new front end and also proposed changes at the rear to improve boot space, but these did not make production. But there were many other useful detail improvements: a reshaped fuel tank and horizontal spare wheel improved the shape and size of the boot, there was better insulation to isolate the cabin from heat and noise from the engine bay, and Lucas Opus electronic ignition was now a standard feature.

Bosch mechanical fuel injection continued to be used until August 1973 when Aston Martin reverted to carburettors for what is now known as the Series 3 V8. A taller bonnet bulge was required to clear the intakes of the four downdraught Webers, which were cheaper and more reliable than the injection system and improved both drivability and fuel consumption, though at the expense of some top-end power.

Throughout the early 1970s Aston Martin struggled with the oil crisis, lengthy development of US-certified engines, and then receivership, rescue and the development of the new Lagonda, Vantage and Volante (*see* pp.91, 94, and 96). It was not until 1978 that the V8 was significantly revised, the new version (Series 4) being known inside Newport Pagnell as 'Oscar India' – 'pilot speak' for the letters 'O' and 'I', which stood for

RIGHT: **Officially this car was called the Aston Martin V8 – though it still has DBS badges on the sides!**
BELOW: **Newport Pagnell made cars the old-fashioned way, with hand-shaped aluminium panels. This picture could have been from almost any time in the twentieth century, but was taken in 1984.**

■ 1972 V8 (SERIES 2)

Engine	V8, Bosch fuel injection
Valvegear	Twin overhead cam per cylinder bank
Bore and stroke	100 × 85mm
Capacity	5340cc
Power	345bhp @ 6,000rpm
Transmission	Five-speed ZF manual gearbox, Chrysler Torqueflite automatic transmission optional, rear-wheel drive
Chassis/body	Steel platform chassis, box-section body frame with aluminium alloy body
Suspension	Double wishbones and coil springs front, de Dion with trailing arms and Watt link rear
Brakes	Four-wheel Girling disc brakes, hydraulically operated
Performance	160mph (257km/h), 0–60mph in 6sec

ABOVE: **Apart from the new nose, the Aston Martin V8 also had detail improvements over the DBS – but it looked much the same.**
LEFT: **The V8 gradually evolved throughout its twenty-year production run. This is a Series 5 car from the late 1980s, recognizable by its BBS cross-spoke alloy wheels.**

'October introduction'. Oscar India shared some revisions developed for the Vantage and Volante, such as a neat tail spoiler, tidier bonnet and upgraded interior.

There were continual minor updates, including retuned engines in 1980 (which improved fuel economy without harming performance) and the adoption of BBS wheels in 1983. The final major version of the V8 saloon was the Series 5, introduced at the New York show early in 1986. Fuel injection made a comeback, this time a Weber-Marelli system with full electronic engine management. For the first time in a long while Aston Martin quoted an official power figure – 305bhp, considerably less than the first DBS V8. Significantly, emissions performance was much improved, which was essential to pass ever-more stringent regulations. The injection system reduced the height of the engine, so the bonnet bulge was no longer needed.

The V8 saloon finally died in 1989 after more than 2,000 had been built, making way for the Virage.

■ 1986 V8 (SERIES 5)

Engine	V8, Weber-Marelli fuel injection
Valvegear	Twin overhead cam per cylinder bank
Bore and stroke	100 × 85mm
Capacity	5340cc
Power	305bhp @ 6,000rpm
Transmission	Five-speed ZF manual gearbox, Chrysler Torqueflite automatic transmission optional, rear-wheel drive
Chassis/body	Steel platform chassis, box-section body frame with aluminium alloy body
Suspension	Double wishbones and coil springs front, de Dion with trailing arms and Watt link rear
Brakes	Four-wheel Girling disc brakes, hydraulically operated
Performance	150mph (241km/h), 0–60mph in 7sec

VANTAGE

**The Vantage was simply a post-David Brown version of the 6-cylinder
DBS. It shared its two-headlamp nose with the 1972 V8.**

COMPANY DEVELOPMENTS INHERITED a two-car model range when they took over at Aston Martin in 1972, with the 6-cylinder DBS Vantage still being sold alongside the flagship DBS V8. Work was already well advanced on William Towns' new two-headlamp front end and the reorganized boot, revealed in April 1972. At the same time the 'DB' names of both models were now clearly inappropriate, so 'DBS' was dropped from both cars' names: the DBS V8 was simply known as the Aston Martin V8, and the 6-cylinder car became the Aston Martin Vantage. However, the first few cars were fitted with 'David Brown Aston Martin' badges – no doubt a result of the time-honoured process dating back to the 1920s of using up a stock of parts before ordering new.

Mechanically the Vantage was largely the same as the DBS it replaced, with the triple Weber 6-cylinder engine and a choice between manual or automatic transmissions. It still rolled on wire-spoked wheels, which were by now a throwback to an earlier era and rapidly becoming obsolete. Vantages were made in small batches, just seventy examples being built before production ended in July 1973.

■ 1972 VANTAGE

Engine	In-line 6-cylinder, triple SU carburettors, triple Weber carburettors or AE Brico fuel injection optional
Valvegear	Twin overhead cam
Bore and stroke	96 × 92mm
Capacity	3995cc
Power	282bhp @ 5,500rpm
Transmission	Five-speed ZF manual gearbox, Borg-Warner automatic transmission optional, rear-wheel drive
Chassis/body	Steel platform chassis, box-section body frame with aluminium alloy body
Suspension	Double wishbones and coil springs front, de Dion with trailing arms and Watt link rear
Brakes	Four-wheel Girling disc brakes, hydraulically operated
Performance	140mph (225km/h), 0–60mph in 7.5sec

LAGONDA (SERIES 1)

ASTON MARTIN SPRANG a surprise on press and public alike at the Earls Court Motor Show in October 1974, introducing a new model and reintroducing an old name: Lagonda.

The new car was a production version of MP230/1, the long-wheelbase, four-door car, which had been built in 1968/9 and used extensively by Sir David Brown. Since then Aston Martin had adopted a new two-headlamp front end (on the V8 and Vantage), and the new Aston Martin Lagonda combined the four-door body style of the prototype with the two-headlamp nose of the latest Aston Martins. The grille was subtly reworked to differentiate the Lagonda from the Astons, and to give hints of previous Lagonda models. The attractive result won a gold medal for coachwork from the Society of Motor Manufacturers and Traders.

But the timing was hardly right for a new model. Aston Martin was suffering because war in the Middle East had created an energy crisis in the West, and fuel prices were soaring. At the same time the company was spending large sums to get the V8 engine certified for sale in the USA. Just a few weeks after the Lagonda's debut, the company was in receivership.

Just seven of these 'Series 1' Lagondas were built between 1974 and 1976. An eighth was built up from the only remaining unfinished chassis by Roger Bennington of Aston Martin dealer Stratton Motor Company, a nine-year project that was completed in 2007.

▮ 1974 LAGONDA

Lagonda reappeared in 1974, with a long-wheelbase four-door version of the V8 saloon. The wedge-shaped car, in the background here, was still in the future. Both cars were styled by William Towns.

Engine	V8, Weber carburettors
Valvegear	Twin overhead cam per cylinder bank
Bore and stroke	100 × 85mm
Capacity	5340cc
Power	325bhp @ 6,000rpm (approx)
Transmission	Five-speed ZF manual gearbox, Chrysler Torqueflite automatic transmission optional, rear-wheel drive
Chassis/body	Steel platform chassis, box-section body frame with aluminium alloy body
Suspension	Double wishbones and coil springs front, de Dion with trailing arms and Watt link rear
Brakes	Four-wheel Girling disc brakes, hydraulically operated
Performance	160mph (257km/h), 0–60mph in 7sec (approx)

LAGONDA (SERIES 2/3/4)

BY THE END of 1974 Aston Martin was in receivership, and it looked as if the fine old marque was finally finished. But over the next year and a half the company was rescued and rebuilt. Early in 1976, with production once again under way in earnest, the new owners began to plan a spectacular new car that would show that Aston Martin Lagonda was back to stay.

William Towns once again styled the car and, as with the genesis of the DBS in the 1960s, he proposed the concurrent development of two cars: a short-wheelbase Aston and a long-wheelbase Lagonda. But the new cars he proposed were very different to anything Aston Martin had attempted before, with a brave modern shape and plenty of innovation under the skin.

The new management decided to concentrate on the Lagonda, a car that the Aston Martin Owners Club were later to refer to as the 'Series 2' to differentiate it from the rare 1974–76 Series 1. Towns worked twelve-hour days to turn his initial sketch and scale model into a full-size mock-up from which measurements could be taken to begin the body tooling process. The body itself was made in the now traditional Aston way, with hand-rolled aluminium alloy panels laid over a box-section body frame – but the shape was something else: a futuristic, sharp-nosed wedge. At the front, pop-up headlamps were inset into the bonnet, with two pairs of auxiliary lights flanking a vestigial 'radiator' grille, which actually provided an intake for the gearbox oil cooler. Straight lines and sharp creases defined the shape of the cabin and tail. A glass panel was let into the rear half of the roof, so the Lagonda's cabin felt surprisingly bright and airy.

RIGHT: **The 'Series 2' Lagonda had an eye-catching shape and advanced electronic instruments, but it proved difficult to get into production.** BELOW: **Despite the modern shape, the Lagonda used a similar chassis and drivetrain to the V8 cars and was built in much the same way.**

Underneath, the Lagonda was based on the usual Aston Martin platform chassis, but considerably lengthened: the new car was 14in (356mm) longer than the old Lagonda, itself 12in (305mm) longer than the Aston Martin V8. Suspension was carried over from the Aston, so the Lagonda retained the wishbone front suspension and the de Dion rear with inboard rear brakes.

Mike Loasby was now leading Aston Martin's engineering team, and in addition to the chassis work, his men were given the apparently impossible task of making the Aston Martin V8 engine fit under the incredibly low bonnet of the new Lagonda. It was mounted as far back as possible, but still needed a new low-line intake system to squeeze under the bonnet – and the unwelcome side effect of that was a drop in mid-range torque. To restore the V8's output, big-valve cylinder heads were developed, together with lower-lift cam profiles to maintain piston/valve clearances. The result was the same power and torque as the Aston-spec V8, delivered at lower engine speeds.

The main focus of attention, however, was inside the Lagonda. The interior was the most luxurious that Aston Martin had ever created, and there was adequate, if not generous, space for four people. But it was the Lagonda's instruments and controls that really got people excited: they were to be at once the Lagonda's biggest attraction and its greatest headache.

There were no conventional instruments at all, instead just a flat black plastic panel ahead of the driver, which lit up with LED readouts and graphic displays when the ignition key was turned. In addition to replacing the usual instruments, the Lagonda system provided a wealth of new information, such as elapsed journey time and average speed – in fact there was so much data that an 'Essential Services Only' switch was provided to turn off everything except speed, time and fuel level for driving at night. The controls were equally innovative, with conventional column stalks replaced by pods behind the wheel carrying touch-sensitive switches. In an era when computers were room-sized and digital watches a novelty, the advanced electronics in the Lagonda were headline news.

But when the Lagonda was unveiled to the press at The Bell Inn, Aston Clinton, in October 1976 it was far from finished, and needed a major redesign before it was ready for production. Aston Martin had promised the first customer cars for the summer of 1977, but it was April 1978 before the first car was delivered, and production did not get under way until months later.

Despite the development problems, the Lagonda was a hit, and became particularly popular in the Middle East. Gradual improvements in the specification included the adoption of BBS wheels (of a different type to those used on the Aston V8) in 1983, and later that year Aston Martin Tickford launched an £85,000 super-luxury conversion (the standard car was £66,000). That was followed in 1984 by a £110,000 long-wheelbase limousine, of which three were built. Also that year came new instruments using cathode-ray tubes, which could display messages in four different languages (English, French, German and, inevitably, Arabic).

In January 1986 the Lagonda adopted Weber-Marelli injection, as did the Aston V8, on what the Aston Martin Owners Club calls the 'Series 3'. A year later the instruments changed again, this time adopting more modern, vacuum fluorescent displays.

ABOVE: **The Lagonda shape has not aged well, but the car has its devotees. Here two early models line up at an Aston Martin Owners Club event.**
LEFT: **The low nose of the Lagonda incorporated indicators and auxiliary lights. The main headlamps were pop-up units sunk into the bonnet.**

Shortly after, a restyled Series 4 Lagonda made its debut at the Geneva Motor Show. The sharp edges were rounded off to suit modern styling preferences, the pop-up headlamps were replaced by six forward-facing lamps inserted into a restyled nose and the indicators dropped down into the front bumper.

The final Lagondas were built in 1989, but the car was not directly replaced, although the Lagonda name was to reappear a couple of years later when Works Service started applying the name to the Virage-based four-door saloons and shooting brakes it built.

Two 'one-off' Lagondas deserve a mention. The first is chassis number 4, one of the first development prototypes, which was later used to explore a high-performance engine specification. The Vantage engine was too tall to fit under the Lagonda's low bonnet, so instead Aston Martin turned to turbocharging. Two Garrett T03 turbos were fitted, blowing through the standard Weber carburettors. Though effective (the turbo Lagonda could hit 60mph from rest in as little as 6sec), the installation never progressed beyond the prototype stage, and the car was later dismantled.

The other Lagonda one-off was DP2034, a two-door Lagonda, which was the development 'mule' for the chassis and suspension to be used on the Aston Martin Virage. Though Victor Gauntlett, Aston Martin's chairman at the time, said he wondered if there would be a market for the short-wheelbase Lagonda, no production versions were ever made.

RIGHT: **The Lagonda's original LED instruments were replaced by LCDs, then by cathode ray tubes. The final change came in 1987 when these vacuum fluorescent displays were adopted.**
BELOW: **The rounded-off styling of the Series 4 Lagonda made its debut at the Geneva show in 1986.**

■ 1976 LAGONDA

Engine	V8, four Weber 42DCNF carburettors
Valvegear	Twin overhead cam per cylinder bank
Bore and stroke	100 × 85mm
Capacity	5340cc
Power	325bhp @ 6,000rpm (approx)
Transmission	Five-speed ZF manual gearbox, Chrysler Torqueflite automatic transmission optional, rear-wheel drive
Chassis/body	Steel platform chassis, box-section body frame with aluminium alloy body
Suspension	Double wishbones and coil springs front, de Dion with trailing arms and Watt link rear
Brakes	Four-wheel Girling disc brakes, hydraulically operated
Performance	(Series 2) 148mph (238km/h), 0–60mph in 7.9sec (approx)

V8 VANTAGE

A HIGH-PERFORMANCE VANTAGE model had been considered when the DBS V8 went into production in 1969, but at the time Aston Martin had enough trouble keeping up with demand for the standard car, so neither the more powerful V8 nor the DBS-based Lagonda ever reached production. But engine modifications that were a spin-off from the 1976 Lagonda project would prove to be the beginning of a V8 Vantage in the mid-1970s. The low bonnet line on the Lagonda required a revised intake system but this strangled the engine, so Mike Loasby's engineering team developed big-valve heads to restore the power. Loasby then decided to use the big-valve heads to build a high-performance V8.

For the Lagonda the emphasis had been on mid-range torque, but for the Vantage-spec engine Loasby was after more power. The heads were skimmed to raise the compression ratio, and higher-lift camshafts (actually the same profile as the old fuel-injected V8) were fitted. Valve cutouts were machined in the piston crowns to avoid contact with the huge 53mm valves. The intake system was heavily revised to handle greater airflow, with larger diameter trunking from the airbox to the bigger Weber 48IDA carburettors, which sat on a new manifold with wider ports. Hotter spark plugs and a larger bore exhaust system were fitted, all of which helped the new engine deliver around 380bhp.

The revised engine was fitted in a V8 development car, which Loasby took to the Aston Martin Owners Club's annual St John Horsfall race meeting at Silverstone in the summer of 1976, raising a few eyebrows with the car's prodigious speed.

Originally the plan had been to offer the Vantage-spec engine as a conversion for standard saloon V8s, but soon the decision was taken to develop a new V8 Vantage model.

Revisions to the rest of the car were relatively minor. There were bigger Pirelli CN12 tyres and the rear springs were stiffened, while the front received a stiffer anti-roll bar on the development car, though it did not make it on to production Vantages. The most noticeable addition was a large air dam under the front bumper (together with a blanked-off grille and bonnet scoop) and a spoiler on the boot lid, which helped to cut aerodynamic drag by 10 per cent and reduced lift to negligible proportions front and rear – even at the very high speeds the new car could achieve. With the standard 3.54:1 final drive ratio Aston Martin claimed a top speed of 170mph (274km/h), while with the shorter 3.77:1 axle it could sprint from rest to 60mph in a fraction over five seconds – an extraordinary time for such a large and heavy machine. From its announcement in February 1977 the V8 Vantage was, for a while, the fastest accelerating production car on the planet.

Later the 'add-on' aerodynamic modifications were integrated more effectively into the existing bodywork, and the neat new tail that resulted was also adopted by the standard V8 saloon.

In 1986 the upgraded engine built for the new Zagato was offered in the Vantage, together with wider wheels and tyres, and flared wheel arches. These 'X-pack' cars (the name comes from the 'X' in the chassis number denoting the higher spec engine) were available with up to 432bhp.

The high-performance Vantage engine was a spin-off from development work on the Lagonda. Note the separate tail spoiler on this car, indicating that it is an early example.

■ 1977 V8 VANTAGE

Engine	V8, four Weber 48IDA carburettors
Valvegear	Twin overhead cam per cylinder bank
Bore and stroke	100 × 85mm
Capacity	5340cc
Power	380bhp @ 6,000rpm (approx)
Transmission	Five-speed ZF manual gearbox (some cars with Chrysler Torqueflite automatic transmission), rear-wheel drive
Chassis/body	Steel platform chassis, box-section body frame with aluminium alloy body
Suspension	Double wishbones and coil springs front, de Dion with trailing arms and Watt link rear
Brakes	Four-wheel Girling disc brakes, hydraulically operated
Performance	168mph (270km/h), 0–60mph in 5.4sec (approx) (with standard final drive ratio)

TOP: **The V8 Vantage evolved alongside the V8 saloon in the 1970s and 1980s, adopting BBS alloy wheels in 1986.**
ABOVE: **Late Vantages were available in 432bhp 'X-pack' guise, which included wider wheels and flared wheel arches.**

V8 VOLANTE

UNTIL THE DBS most Aston Martins had been available with drophead bodywork, but problems with the V8 engine, then reorganization following David Brown's disposal of the company in 1972, and then receivership just a couple of years later, had meant there was never time to develop a drophead DBS or Series 2 V8. In any case, US legislation was widely expected that would make true convertibles illegal, and most of the soft-top cars that had been launched around that time, such as Porsche's 911 Targa and the Triumph Stag, had featured fixed roll-over bars that improved safety but compromised the 'openness' of the car.

But the legislation banning convertibles never materialized, and once Aston Martin had been rescued from its mid-1970s nadir, it became clear that an open version of the V8 would find

LEFT: **It took Aston Martin until 1978 to offer the V8 in a convertible Volante form.**
BELOW: **The Volante hood was designed by George Mosely, who had designed the Rolls-Royce Corniche hood. The car was elegant with the hood raised or lowered.**

a ready market in the USA and elsewhere. Just how big that market might be was brought home to Aston managing director Alan Curtis when the company visited the Los Angeles Motor Show in 1977: although the striking new Lagonda took pride of place on the show stand, many of the enquiries taken by Aston Martin were asking when a convertible V8 would be available.

Development of a drophead was soon under way. Mechanically it was identical to the existing V8 saloon, but inside and out there were changes to the specification. At the front the Volante received a new bonnet with a bulge rather than a scoop, effectively a neater version of the bonnet introduced the previous year on the V8 Vantage (and it would later be adopted across the range). There was a neat rear deck with a new boot lid and a fully lined hood, which could be power operated only when the handbrake was engaged. Designed by George Mosely, who had previously designed the Corniche convertible hood for Rolls-Royce, the hood was elegant when erected and folded down until it almost disappeared from view – yet interior space was not compromised at all. The pay-off was the much reduced size of the boot, which was small enough on the saloon but was now reduced to just 5.1cu ft (144ltr). Inside, the dashboard was upgraded with walnut veneer facings. Underneath, the chassis was braced to restore the stiffness lost by removing the roof, which added around 70kg (155lb) to the overall weight.

The new V8 Volante was launched in June 1978. It was the last Aston worked on by Harold Beach, who had designed the platform chassis it used twenty years earlier for the DB4, and who retired that year after nearly forty years with Aston Martin. Initially Newport Pagnell made about three Volantes a week, all of them heading for export markets, but in 1981 the convertible became available in the UK. It received the same periodic updates as the saloon, adopting BBS wheels in 1983 and then switching to Weber-Marelli injection (and a flatter bonnet) in 1986. These cars are referred to as 'Series 2' Volantes by the Aston Martin Owners Club.

A restyled Vantage Volante was also announced in 1986, and there was also a rare 'Prince of Wales' specification with the Vantage engine but without Vantage Volante body modifications (see p.108). The last V8 Volantes were built in 1989.

■ 1978 V8 VOLANTE

Engine	V8, four Weber 42DCNF carburettors
Valvegear	Twin overhead cam per cylinder bank
Bore and stroke	100 × 85mm
Capacity	5340cc
Power	300bhp @ 6,000rpm (approx)
Transmission	Five-speed ZF manual gearbox, Chrysler Torqueflite automatic transmission optional, rear-wheel drive
Chassis/body	Steel platform chassis, box-section body frame with aluminium alloy body and power-operated hood
Suspension	Double wishbones and coil springs front, de Dion with trailing arms and Watt link rear
Brakes	Four-wheel Girling disc brakes, hydraulically operated
Performance	140mph (225km/h), 0–60mph in 8sec (approx)

The Volante was a consistently strong seller for Aston Martin, particularly in the US market.

JAMES BOND'S V8/VOLANTE

TIMOTHY DALTON TOOK over the role of James Bond for the 1987 film *The Living Daylights*. Part of director John Glen's strategy for positioning Dalton as a more traditional and less frivolous Bond than his predecessor, Roger Moore, was to have the character back behind the wheel of an Aston Martin.

Aston chairman Victor Gauntlett provided his own Vantage-engined Volante for scenes shot at Stonor House, then 007's car was 'winterized' – though in reality a V8 saloon took the Volante's place. Special equipment fitted to this car included skis which extended from the sills, rockets hidden behind the foglamps, a wheel hub-mounted laser, and a propulsion rocket hidden behind the rear number plate.

In its final scenes on a frozen lake in Austria, the rocket-powered Aston has to jump a wooden hut to escape pursuers. Dummy cars were built and launched using a compressed-air cannon, but on the first attempt the air valves had frozen up and the car didn't fly as far as planned, demolishing the hut instead of clearing it. A second attempt was more successful. In the story Bond then destroys the Aston using a self-destruct system – but happily the real car still survives.

◼ *THE LIVING DAYLIGHTS* VOLANTE

Engine	V8
Valvegear	Twin overhead cam per cylinder bank
Bore and stroke	100 × 85mm
Capacity	5340cc
Power	400bhp @ 6,000rpm (approx)
Fuel system	Four Weber 48IDA carburettors
Transmission	Five-speed ZF manual gearbox (some cars with Chrysler Torqueflite automatic transmission), rear-wheel drive
Chassis/body	Steel platform chassis, box-section body frame with aluminium alloy body
Suspension	Double wishbones and coil springs front, de Dion with trailing arms and Watt link rear
Brakes	Four-wheel Girling disc brakes, hydraulically operated
Performance	160mph (258km/h), 0–60mph in 5.5sec (approx)

ABOVE: **James Bond returned to Aston Martin in the 1987 film** *The Living Daylights*. **Modifications to the car included these sill-mounted skis.**
RIGHT: **This V8 was one of two Astons used in** *The Living Daylights*. **The other was Aston chairman Victor Gauntlett's own V8 Volante.**

DBS V8 RHAM1

MIDLANDS ASTON MARTIN specialist Robin Hamilton raced a DBS V8 in British events from 1974, gradually modifying the car more and more. The car was updated with a two headlamp nose, and after wind-tunnel work it was given a deep front air dam – Aston Martin shared the results of the tests, and used them to develop a similar (though less extreme) air dam for the V8 Vantage.

By 1977 the Aston had acquired a new chassis number, RHAM1, and Hamilton was aiming for Le Mans. Hamilton shared the car with David Preece at the Silverstone Six-Hours in May, where the Aston limped to the finish after heat soak from the rear brakes cooked the final drive oil seals – so brake and differential cooling were improved. At Le Mans there was trouble with the brakes, and third driver Mike Salmon suffered a broken gearlever, which he threw out of the window so it wouldn't roll around on the floor and get tangled in the pedals. Despite that the Aston soldiered on to finish seventeenth overall and third in its class.

Hamilton planned a return in 1978, with the car now sporting a turbocharged engine developing 800bhp. But it was dogged by heavy fuel consumption, and retired with a holed piston just three hours into the race. RHAM1's swansong was a world record for a car towing a caravan – 124.91mph (201.02km/h), set at RAF Elvington in 1980.

▮ 1977 DBS V8 RHAM1

Engine	V8, four Weber 50IDA carburettors
Valvegear	Twin overhead cam per cylinder bank
Bore and stroke	100 × 85mm
Capacity	5340cc
Power	520bhp @ 6,750rpm (approx)
Transmission	Five-speed ZF manual gearbox, rear-wheel drive
Chassis/body	Steel platform chassis, box-section body frame with aluminium alloy body
Suspension	Double wishbones, coil springs and anti-roll bar front, de Dion with trailing arms and Watt link rear
Brakes	Four-wheel Lockheed disc brakes, hydraulically operated
Performance	188mph (303km/h), 0–60mph in 5sec (approx)

Robin Hamilton's much modified V8 upheld Aston Martin honour in sports car racing in the 1970s.

NIMROD-ASTON MARTIN

ROBIN HAMILTON DECIDED that the RHAM1 project had achieved as much as it was going to, and laid plans to develop an entirely new racing car for the new Group C and IMSA regulations. The new car would use the relatively frugal normally aspirated Aston Martin V8 engine that had been developed for the RHAM1, but it would be installed in a purpose-built racing chassis.

A new company, Nimrod Racing Automobiles, was founded in September 1981 with Hamilton, Victor Gauntlett and Aston shareholder Peter Livanos as its principals. Its aim was to design, develop and then race this new car. Lola's Eric Broadley was engaged to design the chassis, an aluminium alloy tub with a tubular rear subframe that carried the rear suspension, engine and a Hewland transaxle.

Work on the new machine was already well advanced when regulation changes threatened to make the Nimrod obsolete before it had even turned a wheel. The IMSA regulations, which

had been expected to follow Group C rules, turned out to be very different, and when the FIA released the final Group C regulations, those too included significant changes from the draft around which the Nimrod had been designed. Key changes included a reduction in the minimum weight limit from 1,000kg to 800kg (2,205lb to 1,764lb) and the scrapping of the original requirement for a flat body underside to limit aerodynamic downforce. Because the Nimrod had been designed with the higher weight limit and flat-bottom regulations in mind, it was clear that the completed car would be overweight and would lack downforce compared with some of its rivals, and it was too late to make fundamental changes to the design. The team pressed on.

The finished prototype Nimrod was unveiled to the press at Goodwood in November, with a gaggle of current and former British racers there to see it including James Hunt, Derek Bell, Roy Salvadori, Nigel Mansell, Jack Fairman, Eric Thompson

Nimrod-Aston Martin in its later form. As originally built the car was hampered by a late change in the regulations, which left it overweight and aerodynamically inferior to the competition.

and Stirling Moss. Two race cars were built for a debut at the Silverstone Six Hours race in May 1982, the first to be run as a works car and the other owned by Viscount Downe and run by Richard Williams. Engine failures plagued the works car in testing and another engine problem ended its race, but using a lower rev-limit the Downe car avoided a major failure and overcame failing oil pressure to finish in an encouraging sixth place.

At Le Mans scrutineering both Nimrods were deemed to have windscreens that were a few centimetres below the regulation minimum height. Hamilton fixed the problem by raising the ride height on the works car, to the detriment of its handling. Williams solved the problem by fitting an extension 'bubble' on top of the Downe car that avoided handling problems but created additional aerodynamic drag, which reduced the top speed of the car by 7mph (11km/h). Come race day, the Downe car's bubble, which looked a bit like the roof light on a black cab, had acquired the legend 'TAXI'.

Three hours into the race the silver and green works car was eliminated by a tyre failure while Tiff Needell was driving. The red, white and blue Downe car soldiered on in the hands of Ray Mallock and Mike Salmon, despite a failing fuel pump allowing the mixture to go lean and burn the exhaust valves. It eventually limped home with only five of the eight cylinders in working order, recording a creditable seventh place overall behind five Porsches and a Ferrari, and fourth in its class. At Spa in September the works car was sidelined with another engine failure while the Downe car finished eleventh, and it followed that up with ninth place at Brands Hatch. As a result Nimrod finished third in the World Endurance Championship in 1982, behind Porsche and Rondeau.

Victor Gauntlett pulled out of the Nimrod project at the end of 1982 to concentrate on Aston Martin and his Pace Petroleum company. Hamilton continued, running two cars in American IMSA races and designing a new carbon-fibre car, the C3, but Nimrod ran out of money before the new car could be completed. The company closed at the end of 1983, but that was not quite the end of the Nimrod story.

For 1983 the Downe car had been revised by Ray Mallock and Richard Williams: it was 10 per cent lighter, and a new body gave it much more downforce. The Bovis-sponsored car could now lap Silverstone in the wet faster than the old Nimrod had managed in the dry. There were high hopes for the season after the 'evolution' Nimrod finished seventh on its debut in the Silverstone 1000km race, but a string of failures prevented any other finishes that year.

The Downe Nimrod was back in 1984, and it was joined by a second 'evolution' car which was built for Peter Livanos, with a Tickford turbo engine and Kevlar bodywork. Both cars failed to finish at Silverstone, then the Livanos car reverted to a normally aspirated engine for Le Mans. After early dramas the Nimrods ran fifth and thirteenth until Saturday evening, when John Sheldon suffered a rear tyre failure on the Downe Nimrod, which pitched the car into the barriers at 200mph (320km/h). Sheldon was lucky to escape injury, but flying wreckage killed a marshal and bits of disintegrated Nimrod were strewn all over the track. Moments later Drake Olsen arrived at the scene in the second Nimrod, together with Jonathan Palmer in a Porsche, and as the pair picked their way through the chaos Olsen put two wheels off the tarmac and the Nimrod spun into the barrier. The Nimrods never competed again in top-flight sports car racing.

Nimrod meets the Queen: this Nimrod took part in a parade of Astons at Windsor Castle in 2005.

■ 1982 NIMROD NRAC2/004

Engine	V8, Lucas mechanical fuel injection
Valvegear	Twin overhead cam per cylinder bank
Bore and stroke	100 × 85mm
Capacity	5340cc
Power	560bhp @ 7,000rpm (approx)
Transmission	Five-speed Hewland VG transaxle, rear-wheel drive
Chassis/body	Aluminium alloy tub with tubular rear subframe
Suspension	Inboard by coil springs, rocker arms and wishbones front, four-link with coil springs and anti-roll bar rear
Brakes	Four-wheel Lockheed disc brakes, hydraulically operated
Performance	203mph (327km/h), 0–60mph in 4.5sec (approx)

EMKA-ASTON MARTIN AND CHEETAH-ASTON MARTIN

TWO MORE ASTON-ENGINED cars competed in the World Endurance Championship alongside the Nimrods in the 1980s. Best known was the EMKA, run by Michael Cane Racing for Steve O'Rourke, manager of Pink Floyd. The name, shared with O'Rourke's production company, came from the name of his daughter, Emma Katheryne.

The EMKA was a Len Bailey design with an aluminium monocoque and a more compact version of the Aston Martin Tickford V8 used by the works Nimrods. At its debut in the Silverstone 1,000km in May the EMKA ran ninth, but was delayed by a detached wing and then stopped just a lap from the end by a failed wheel bearing. It finished seventeenth at Le Mans in 1983 driven by O'Rourke, Tiff Needell and Jeff Allam, then took a sabbatical in 1984 pending expected changes in the Group C regulations. The team reappeared at the 24-hour classic in 1985 with a revised car, which O'Rourke and Needell brought home in eleventh place, after Needell had led for a few minutes early in the race. On both occasions the EMKA was the first British car to finish.

The Aston Martin V8 also powered Swiss racing driver/constructor Chuck Graemiger's Cheetah G604, a carbon-monocoque car, which was considerably lighter than the Nimrod (at around 870kg/1,918lb). But the Cheetah project was always under-funded, and could never afford enough testing and development work to completely sort the suspension geometry or optimize the aerodynamic performance. It was dogged by poor reliability, and rarely finished a race.

■ 1984 CHEETAH G604

Engine	V8, Lucas mechanical fuel injection
Valvegear	Twin overhead cam per cylinder bank
Bore and stroke	100×85mm
Capacity	5340cc
Power	580bhp @ 7,000rpm (approx)
Transmission	Five-speed Hewland VG transaxle, rear-wheel drive
Chassis/body	Carbon-fibre composite monocoque
Suspension	Wishbones with coil springs and anti-roll bar front, wishbones with rocker-actuated coil springs rear
Brakes	Four-wheel Lockheed disc brakes, hydraulically operated
Performance	203mph (327km/h), 0–60mph in 4.5sec (approx)

Steve O'Rourke's EMKA-Aston Martin finished eleventh at Le Mans in 1985.

BULLDOG

THE BULLDOG WAS a fascinating 'one-off'. The Bulldog, project 'K9', started in 1976, but stalled under the pressure of other work and the departure of engineering chief Mike Loasby to DeLorean. Work restarted in 1979 under project manager Keith Martin, whose small team worked in an area of the factory that inevitably became known as 'the kennel'.

There they built up the Bulldog with its tubular spaceframe chassis, originally intended to have de Dion suspension at both ends but ending up with the standard Aston wishbones at the front. The V8 engine was mid-mounted and fitted with Bosch mechanical injection (which had been dropped from production V8s in 1973), apparently to reduce the engine's height. Forged Cosworth pistons reduced the compression ratio to 7.35:1, and there was a pair of massive Garrett turbochargers. Power was said to be 60 per cent more than the Vantage, implying around 600bhp. The two-seat body was a striking double wedge shape by William Towns, with electro-hydraulic gullwing doors and a drop-down flap at the front revealing five headlamps.

Bulldog achieved 192mph (309km/h) on the MIRA speed-bowl, so was probably capable of 200mph (320km/h) on the flat.

Aston Martin hoped for 230mph (370km/h) with a longer final-drive ratio, but the opportunity to test it never arose. Although a short production run was considered it never materialized, and the one and only Bulldog was sold to the Middle East in 1982.

▪ 1980 BULLDOG

Engine	V8, Bosch mechanical fuel injection, twin Garrett T04B turbochargers
Valvegear	Twin overhead cam per cylinder bank
Bore and stroke	100 × 85mm
Capacity	5340cc
Power	380bhp @ 6,000rpm (approx)
Transmission	Five-speed ZF manual transaxle, rear-wheel drive
Chassis/body	Tubular spaceframe chassis, aluminium alloy body
Suspension	Double wishbones and coil springs front, de Dion with trailing arms and Watt link rear
Brakes	Four-wheel disc brakes, hydraulically operated
Performance	200mph (322km/h), 0–60mph in 4sec (approx)

ABOVE: **Bulldog was another striking William Towns design, powered by a mid-mounted, twin-turbocharged V8 engine.**
RIGHT: **The Bulldog interior in its original form, trimmed in chocolate brown leather.**

VANTAGE ZAGATO

AT THE GENEVA show in March 1984 Aston Martin's stand was situated right next to that of a famous old Italian coachbuilder – Zagato. It was there that discussions began between Victor Gauntlett and new Aston shareholder Peter Livanos, and Elio and Gianni Zagato, about reviving the historic link between the two companies. The plan, announced exactly a year later at the 1985 Geneva show, was to create a new, limited edition two-seater, based on the V8 Vantage, with exceptionally high performance – it was to be capable of 300km/h (186mph) and 0–60mph in less than 5sec. By the summer of that year deposits had been taken for the full run of fifty production cars, which were expected to cost £70,000.

ABOVE: **The Vantage Zagato was born out of a chance meeting at the 1984 Geneva Motor Show.**
BELOW: **The Zagato was based on the V8 Vantage, but with more power, less weight and less drag it was significantly quicker.**

One of the unusual features of the Zagato design was these split door windows.

When Aston Martin and Zagato had worked together on the DB4GT Zagato in the 1990s, the wheelbase had been shortened, but this time the V8's standard 2,610mm wheelbase was retained, and instead the front and rear overhangs were reduced to the minimum. With lightweight bodywork the Zagato tipped the scales at 3,600lb (1,633kg), about 10 per cent lighter than the V8 Vantage.

At Newport Pagnell a well used V8 Vantage works development car, VNK 360S, became a 'mule' for the development of the Zagato chassis. The test car was lightened by removing the rear seats and much of the interior trim, the air-conditioning system and the spare wheel well, and by fitting perspex windows. The suspension was revised with variable-rate springs and Koni dampers, and there were new 16in wheels with Goodyear Eagle tyres.

The mule also had a tuned engine similar to that fitted to production Zagatos, and available, from 1986, on the V8 Vantage. Fuel injection had been planned, but development was delayed while Aston Martin worked on the injection for the Series 5 V8. So the Vantage Zagato was given a carburettored engine based on a specification developed for a South African customer, and generating 432bhp in its ultimate form – although most cars were strangled by emissions equipment and produced just 410bhp. The taller carburettor engine necessitated an unsightly bonnet bulge in the otherwise clean and purposeful Zagato shape, with its trademark 'double bubble' roofline. The body had recorded a drag coefficient of 0.29 in initial testing, although that slipped to 0.33 when a front air dam was added to reduce high-speed lift.

The first Vantage Zagato production car was delivered in July 1986, by which time the price had risen to £87,000 (by 1987

it was £95,000). Zagatos were built at the rate of two a month, Newport Pagnell dispatching complete rolling chassis to Milan, where Zagato removed the rear part of the chassis and added their bodywork.

Testing to prove the top speed had been planned to take place on a closed French autoroute, but when the Zagato arrived the road was still open – instead the local gendarmerie said they would look the other way. In less-than-perfect circumstances the Zagato recorded 298.75km/h, a fraction under 186mph. The 0–60mph sprint could be achieved in 4.8sec, significantly quicker than a V8 Vantage. At the time it was the fastest production car Aston Martin had ever built.

■ 1986 V8 VANTAGE ZAGATO

Engine	V8, four Weber 50IDA carburettors
Valvegear	Twin overhead cam per cylinder bank
Bore and stroke	100 × 85mm
Capacity	5340cc
Power	432bhp @ 6,000rpm (approx)
Transmission	Five-speed ZF manual gearbox or Chrysler Torqueflite automatic transmission, rear-wheel drive
Chassis/body	Steel platform chassis, box-section body frame with aluminium alloy body
Suspension	Double wishbones, coil springs and anti-roll bar front, de Dion with trailing arms and Watt link rear
Brakes	Four-wheel Girling disc brakes, hydraulically operated
Performance	186mph (300km/h), 0–60mph in 4.8sec

ZAGATO VOLANTE

ASTON MARTIN LAGONDA acquired 50 per cent of Zagato in July 1986, just as production of the Vantage Zagato was getting under way. Soon the two companies were working on the inevitable drophead version of the Zagato Aston, of course carrying the Volante name.

The Zagato Volante was signed off in November that year, and a prototype of the open-top Zagato made its public debut at the Geneva show in March 1987. Plans were announced for a production run of just twenty-five cars – and Aston Martin sold twenty-five before the first production car was built later that year.

The folding roof was not the only external change: the Zagato Volantes also featured a new front end with no radiator grille, and covers over the headlamps. Production Zagato Volantes were given the non-Vantage fuel-injected V8, which allowed for a flat bonnet but robbed the car of over 100bhp, and that reduction in power (plus a slight weight penalty) meant the Zagato Volante was significantly slower than the Vantage Zagato. That said, some cars were built with the Vantage engine, and a handful even had the Vantage Zagato front end.

Despite a price tag of £125,000, production went beyond the planned run of twenty-five, and thirty-seven Zagato Volantes were built by the end of 1988.

RIGHT: **Just twenty-five Zagato Volantes were built, and all of them were sold before the first customer car was built in 1987.**

■ 1987 V8 ZAGATO VOLANTE

Engine	V8, Weber-Marelli fuel injection
Valvegear	Twin overhead cam per cylinder bank
Bore and stroke	100 × 85mm
Capacity	5340cc
Power	305bhp @ 6,000rpm
Transmission	Five-speed ZF manual gearbox, rear-wheel drive
Chassis/body	Steel platform chassis, box-section body frame with aluminium alloy body
Suspension	Double wishbones, coil springs and anti-roll bar front, de Dion with trailing arms and Watt link rear
Brakes	Four-wheel Girling disc brakes, hydraulically operated
Performance	160mph (258km/h), 0–60mph in 6.5sec (approx)

The Zagato Volante used a lower-spec version of the V8 engine fitted with fuel injection, which meant there was no need for a bonnet bulge.

VANTAGE VOLANTE

SEVERAL VOLANTES WERE fitted with Vantage engines, including Victor Gauntlett's own example (which starred in the James Bond film *The Living Daylights* – see p.48), but it was not until 1986 that an official Vantage Volante model was introduced.

Announced at the Birmingham Motor Show in October 1986, the Vantage Volante was more than just a drophead body with the 400bhp Vantage engine (or even the 432bhp Zagato-spec unit): in addition to the more powerful engine and new 16in wheels, the Vantage Volante was given a bold bodykit with a bigger front air dam than the Vantage saloon, flared wheel arches, sill extensions and a big rear spoiler. In the context of the time this over-the-top style was appropriate, though it dated quickly and not everyone appreciated it – leading to the 'Prince of Wales' specification.

The Vantage Volante was in production for three years, soldiering on (alongside the regular Volante) for a while even after the V8 saloon had been replaced by the Virage. Despite a significantly higher price than the Volante (£135,000 versus £120,000 in 1989), 166 Vantage Volantes were built.

1986 V8 VANTAGE VOLANTE

Engine	V8, four Weber 48IDA carburettors
Valvegear	Twin overhead cam per cylinder bank
Bore and stroke	100 × 85mm
Capacity	5340cc
Power	400bhp @ 6,000rpm (approx)
Transmission	Five-speed ZF manual gearbox (some cars with Chrysler Torqueflite automatic transmission), rear-wheel drive
Chassis/body	Steel platform chassis, box-section body frame with aluminium alloy body
Suspension	Double wishbones and coil springs front, de Dion with trailing arms and Watt link rear
Brakes	Four-wheel Girling disc brakes, hydraulically operated
Performance	160mph (258km/h), 0–60mph in 5.5sec (approx)

The Vantage Volante combined the drophead body, a bold bodykit and the most powerful V8 engine. The wide-arch look dated quickly.

'PRINCE OF WALES' VANTAGE VOLANTE

THE BODYWORK MODIFICATIONS that were included in the Vantage Volante specification were clearly a step too far for some owners. HRH The Prince of Wales, a long-time Aston fan, ordered his Volante with the Vantage engine and larger wheels but without extensive bodywork changes – just small flares to the wheel arches to cover the fatter tyres. Prince Charles, a non-smoker, also specified an oddments compartment in place of the usual cigarette lighter and ashtray. This became known unofficially as the 'Prince of Wales' specification, though it was never marketed as such.

In all there were twenty-seven of these cars, most of them right-hand-drive cars with the full Vantage engine and manual gearbox, though there were a few 'cosmetic' Prince of Wales Vantage Volantes, with the wheels and flared arches but without the more powerful engine, which were built for the US market. Three more cars were built with the Vantage Volante 'flip' tail, but the Prince of Wales body. Aston Martin was keen to build cars to suit each customer's individual taste.

The Prince of Wales Volantes are highly sought-after, and on the rare occasions when they come up for sale they tend to make high prices. Inevitably replicas have been built, based on standard Volantes, so not every Volante with the 'Prince of Wales' flared arches is the real thing.

1989 'PRINCE OF WALES' VANTAGE VOLANTE

HRH Prince Charles ordered his Vantage Volante without the bodywork modifications, creating the 'Prince of Wales'-spec Volante, now a favourite with collectors.

Engine	V8, four Weber 48IDA carburettors
Valvegear	Twin overhead cam per cylinder bank
Bore and stroke	100 × 85mm
Capacity	5340cc
Power	400bhp @ 6,000rpm (approx)
Transmission	Five-speed ZF manual gearbox or Chrysler Torqueflite automatic transmission, rear-wheel drive
Chassis/body	Steel platform chassis, box-section body frame with aluminium alloy body
Suspension	Double wishbones and coil springs front, de Dion with trailing arms and Watt link rear
Brakes	Four-wheel Girling disc brakes, hydraulically operated
Performance	160mph (258km/h), 0–60mph in 5.5sec (approx)

NEWPORT PAGNELL'S
FORD ERA

**The Vanquish featured in some spectacular
stunts in the James Bond film *Die Another Day*.**

1987–2006

ABOVE: **Walter Hayes was the architect of Aston Martin's revival under Ford ownership.**
BELOW: **Aston Martin made a promising start in its return to sports car racing with the AMR1, but Ford politics killed the project.**

WALTER HAYES HAD been a Fleet Street newspaper editor before joining Ford of Britain to run its Public Affairs department in 1962. A shrewd judge of both people and projects, Hayes championed Ford's involvement in motor sport as a way of improving the image of the company's reliable, but pedestrian, products. He backed Ford's successful Indianapolis 500 campaign with Lotus, and the GT40 sports car project, which won the Le Mans 24-hours. He also persuaded Ford to back the Cosworth DFV Formula 1 engine in 1966, and it became the most successful in the history of the sport. Hayes was the driving force behind the development of several high-performance Ford road cars, including the Lotus-Cortina, the RS Escorts of the 1970s, and the Sierra RS Cosworth – all of which had successful competition histories. And it was Hayes who was central to the Ford takeover of Aston Martin. He had met Victor Gauntlett in Italy during the Mille Miglia retrospective early in 1987, where Gauntlett was running a DBR2. Hayes was a regular guest at Henry Ford II's house in Henley, and one day Ford casually remarked, 'What shall we do today, Walter?'. Hayes said he could always buy Aston Martin.

Development work on the Virage, the replacement for the long-running V8 saloon, was already well under way by the time Ford approached Victor Gauntlett with a proposal to buy the bulk of the Aston Martin equity. Gauntlett realized that the deal would put Aston Martin on a far more secure financial footing, and also give it the resources it desperately needed to develop new models – such as the Virage and the 'new DB4' or 'DP1999', a smaller and cheaper car to run alongside the V8-engined models that had often been discussed but which Aston Martin had never been able to develop. So in September 1987 Gauntlett and Livanos sold 75 per cent of Aston Martin to Ford, retaining the balance of the shares between them. Not everyone thought

Ford had struck a good deal: former team driver Carroll Shelby told *Autocar* that all Ford had bought was 'twelve blacksmiths and an obsolete engine'.

Most of Aston Martin's engineering team had been absorbed into a subsidiary company, Aston Martin Tickford, which had been sold off in 1983 (eventually becoming part of the Banbury-based Prodrive group) so Aston Martin needed help to develop the new car. While the chassis was largely carried over from the Lagonda, the engine was heavily reworked with 4-valve cylinder heads developed by Connecticut-based specialist Calloway Engineering. The much more modern styling was the work of John Heffernan and Ken Greenley, vehicle design tutors at the Royal College of Art, who beat competition from four other design teams.

The new era of Aston Martins arrived at the Birmingham International Motor Show in 1988, when the Virage was launched. A few months later, early in 1989, Aston Martin announced that it was teaming up with Écurie Écosse to develop a Group C1 car, the AMR1, which would be raced in the World Sportscar Championship and the Le Mans 24-hour race. The Max Boxstrom-designed AMR1 had a novel wasp-waisted appearance, with large ground-effect venturis front and rear for maximum downforce, and was powered by Callaway-

developed 4-valve versions of the Aston V8 engine, ultimately producing more than 700bhp.

The team recorded some good finishes that year – including eleventh place overall at Le Mans and a spirited fourth at Brands Hatch – but always struggled to come to terms with handling worries and the AMR1's lack of straight line speed, the result of excessive aerodynamic drag. In 1990 development of a low-drag AMR2 began, and in 1991 there were plans for a 3.5-litre car using a Cosworth F1 engine – but the political landscape changed when Ford bought Jaguar, already an established team in sports car racing. Early in 1990 Aston Martin's racing return was ended and the team disbanded.

On the road car front the news was happier. A Virage-based Volante was introduced in 1990, initially in two-seat form and later with two-plus-two seating and a roof that folded away more compactly. The Volante quickly became Aston Martin's most popular model, although sales of all cars were slow thanks to a worldwide recession. When Victor Gauntlett stepped down in 1991 he was succeeded as chairman by Walter Hayes, who came out of retirement to take on the job. Ford told him to 'sort out' Aston Martin, which meant closing down the loss-making company – but instead Hayes reorganized it, initiated the development of new models, and gave it a viable future. He

The Virage looked modern, but under the skin it shared much with the V8 and Lagonda.

ABOVE: **The Vantage was supercharged to produce 550bhp in original form, and 600bhp in later cars.**
BELOW: **The clay model for Project Vantage, which led to the Vanquish in 2000.**

also invited Sir David Brown to become the company's honorary life president.

Aston Martin Works Service then began to offer a 6.3-litre engine conversion, developed by Richard Williams and which offered a considerable increase in power. Virage-based four-door saloons and shooting brakes were also offered by Works Service, some of them with Lagonda badges – effectively replacing the William Towns Lagonda, which had been dropped in 1989. Then in 1992 Aston Martin introduced the extraordinary Vantage, based on the Virage but with revised bodywork, a 550bhp supercharged V8, and running gear that incorporated many of the lessons learned with the 6.3 project.

At the other end of the range Tom Walkinshaw's TWR Group created the 6-cylinder DB7, launched at the Geneva show in 1993 (see 'The Bloxham Cars', p.113). At the same show, Ford's in-house Ghia styling studio exhibited a Lagonda concept car, which it called the Vignale, though sadly it never reached production. For the time being, the Lagonda marque was seen on only a handful of Virages remodelled by Aston Martin Works Service.

In 1998 TWR developed Project Vantage, a concept car that heralded another new era for Aston Martin. Project Vantage was a preview of the production V12 Vanquish, which

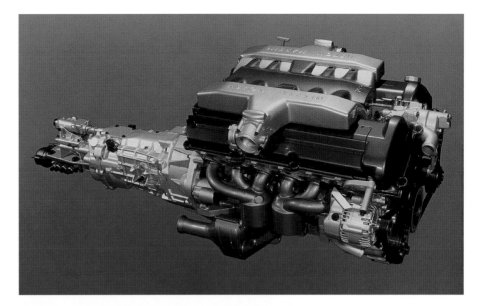

The V12 engine that powered the Vanquish had much in common with the Ford Taurus SHO V6.

Aston Martin boss Dr Ulrich Bez with the V12 Vanquish. Dr Bez arrived at Aston Martin partway through Vanquish development, and made important changes to the car.

used a very advanced bonded and riveted structure made from extruded aluminium and composite materials, clothed in aluminium panels using a new process called Superforming. Power came from a slightly more powerful development of the Cosworth-built V12 engine which had first been seen in mock-up form in 1994, and had gone into the DB7 Vantage in 1999. Ford invested £2 million in refitting the Newport Pagnell factory in preparation for the Vanquish, which replaced the V8 cars in 2001. That marked the end of the Tadek Marek V8 engine, which had powered the majority of Astons and Lagondas since 1969, and of Harold Beach's platform chassis, which could trace its lineage back to the DB4 of 1958.

Aston Martin's most famous customer, James Bond, was back behind the wheel of a DB5 in the 1990s films *GoldenEye* and

Tomorrow Never Dies, the first two films starring Pierce Brosnan as the secret service agent. In the twentieth Bond film, *Die Another Day*, Aston Martins were more heavily featured and it was the Vanquish that took centre stage. Three standard cars were supplied for close-ups and interior shots, and four ex-development cars were rebuilt with four-wheel-drive transmissions for an action sequence shot on a glacier in Iceland.

While the Bloxham-built DB7 and later the Gaydon-built DB9 became Aston Martin's bread-and-butter cars, the Vanquish continued to be hand-built in small numbers at the Newport Pagnell factory until 2007. Production of the Vanquish ended with fifty black-painted 'Ultimate Edition' examples – and these were the last cars that Aston Martin would build at Newport Pagnell.

VIRAGE

IN AUGUST 1986 five designers were invited to compete for the job of designing a new Aston Martin. The winning quarter-scale model came from John Heffernan and Ken Greenley, both vehicle design tutors at the Royal College of Art. William Towns' sharp-edged Lagonda had dated quickly, but the Heffernan/Greenley Virage shape was a more timeless design, which successfully blended traditional Aston Martin styling cues such as the grille shape and the front wing vents into a sleek fastback devoid of excessive exterior decoration. To reduce costs, existing lamps were used at the front (from the Audi 200) and rear (Volkswagen Scirocco). The final shape of the car closely echoed the original styling sketches except at the rear, where the tail was slightly raised to reduce rear-end lift. The Virage was a little longer than the V8 it replaced, helping to reduce aerodynamic drag.

The chassis was a short-wheelbase version of the Lagonda's. The front supension was the usual double wishbone layout, with revised geometry. At the rear the suspension used a cast light-alloy de Dion 'tube', and was located fore and aft by cast-alloy arms that met at a rubber-mounted ball joint. A two-door Lagonda 'mule' registered D972MKX was built to test the new suspension on the roads around Newport Pagnell and at test

ABOVE: **The Virage was shaped by John Heffernan and Ken Greenley. The rear lights were from the Volkswagen Scirocco.**
LEFT: **The Virage's nose retained the classic Aston Martin grille shape, yet was far more modern than that of the cars it replaced.**

venues such as Bruntingthorpe Proving Ground. The truncated wedge shape was rather out of proportion, but Victor Gauntlett liked it enough to wonder whether it should go into production.

Revisions to the engine for the Virage included 4-valve cylinder heads developed by Reeves Calloway's Calloway Engineering company in Connecticut. Hydraulic valve lifters were incorporated to reduce maintenance requirements. The bottom end of the V8, which had always been reliable in service, was essentially unchanged.

Two Virages were on Aston Martin's stand at the British International Motor Show in 1988 on the car's launch, one in silver and another in dark green. Reaction to the new shape was favourable, and the Virage proved to be more comfortable and more refined than the car it replaced. But there were some complaints about vague handling: the rubber in the rear suspension, which soaked up vibration and noise, also promoted instability and squat under-acceleration. A revised rear suspension layout introduced on the Vantage in 1992 was adopted soon after by the Virage. This reverted to the twin radius arms used on the old V8, and adopted a chassis-mounted Watt link for lateral location.

Works Service offered a variety of Virage conversions including a performance package based around a 6.3-litre engine (see p.121) and a three-door shooting brake. From 1993 Works Service could turn a Virage into a long-wheelbase four-door saloon or a five-door, seven-seat shooting brake, both of which were given Lagonda badges.

The final Virage-badged cars were the limited edition models announced in October 1994, featuring British Racing Green paint and a wire-mesh grille, anti-lock brakes and a more powerful engine.

■ 1989 VIRAGE

The final Virage cars were the limited edition models of 1994, which had more power, anti-lock brakes and bright mesh grilles.

Engine	V8, Weber/Marelli engine management
Valvegear	Twin overhead cam per bank, 4 valves per cylinder
Bore and stroke	100 × 85mm
Capacity	5340cc
Power	335bhp @ 5,300rpm
Transmission	Five-speed ZF manual gearbox, rear-wheel drive
Chassis/body	Steel platform chassis, steel box-section body frame with aluminium alloy panels
Suspension	Wishbones with coil springs and anti-roll bar front, de Dion with coil springs, A-frame and Watt linkage rear
Brakes	Discs all round (outboard rear)
Performance	Top speed 157mph (253km/h), 0–60mph in 6.8sec

THE AMR1

ASTON MARTIN ANNOUNCED in August 1987 that it was planning to race a Group C1 race car, the AMR1. A new team called Proteus Technology (or Protech) was set up as a joint venture between Aston Martin and the established Écurie Écosse operation. Richard Williams ran the team, while the car itself was designed by Max Boxstrom. Power would come from a Callaway-developed, 6-litre, 32-valve version of the Aston Martin V8 engine designated RDP87. A quarter-scale model of the car was ready for aerodynamic testing at Southampton University that September, just as Ford was taking control of Aston Martin. The new owners made it clear that they would not be funding the racing programme: instead, Peter Livanos picked up the bill.

Boxstrom's AMR1 design had full-width ground-effect venturis at the front and rear, generating plenty of downforce. The mid-mounted Calloway engine was tipped forwards to clear

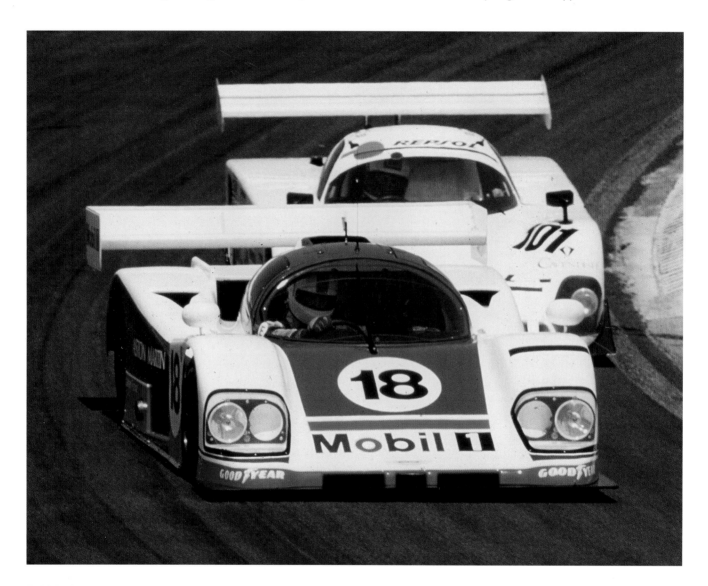

THIS PAGE:
The AMR1 was designed by Max Boxstrom and used a Calloway-developed V8 engine. The first cars took to the track in 1988.

OPPOSITE PAGE:
TOP: **Reeves Calloway developed 4-valve cylinder heads for the V8 engine, which went into the Virage and the AMR1 racer. This shot also shows the massive cross-drilled and internally ventilated rear brake discs.**
BOTTOM: **The AMR1 powered Aston Martin to sixth place in a hotly contested 1989 World Sports Prototype Championship.**

the rear venturi and the final drive was offset to the left. Power was fed through a bespoke transaxle, which also provided mounting points for the rear suspension and rear wing.

The first chassis, AMR1/01, took to the track in November 1988, four months later than planned, powered by a 5.3-litre, 530bhp engine. The second car, AMR1/02, was shortlived: at Donington in January David Leslie crashed the car after a hub failure, damaging the chassis beyond repair. Soon after, Aston Martin announced that it would enter the 1989 World Sports Prototype Championship.

The team started badly, with a £250,000 fine for missing the first round of the championship at Suzuka in Japan. Despite two unexpected engine failures in testing, AMR1/01 appeared alone for the second championship round at Dijon, wearing a 'black armband' over the left front wing out of respect for former Aston Martin team boss John Wyer, who had died a few weeks earlier. Driven by David Leslie and Brian Redman, the AMR1 finished in seventeenth place despite handling problems and the team's understandable reluctance to push too hard in its first race. Even so, the Aston was the first British car home, both the TWR Jaguars having retired.

Three weeks later AMR1/01 was joined by a new chassis, AMR1/03 for the (non-championship) Le Mans 24-hours, both cars sporting revised noses and smaller rear wings. Brian Redman shared with Michael Roe and Costas Los, while David Leslie was partnered by Ray Mallock and David Sears. Excessive drag and inadequate handling held the Astons back in qualifying, but they picked up places in the race until one AMR1 suffered an engine failure early on Sunday morning. The remaining Aston worked its way up through the field despite a scare when a suspension joint failed on the Mulsanne straight with Redman at the wheel, eventually finishing eleventh.

A new chassis, AMR1/04, was the sole Aston at Brands Hatch for the next race. Lighter and better handling than the earlier AMR1s, it recorded a fine fourth-place finish in the hands of Leslie and Redman. Carbon fibre brakes were fitted for the next round at the Nürburgring, where Leslie/Redman finished eighth, then at Donington in September Redman and Sears finished seventh in AMR1/04 just behind Leslie and Roe in the new, even lighter, AMR1/05.

At Spa two weeks later the Aston struggled with misfires and more handling problems in the wet practice session. In the race the Leslie/Roe car retired with a broken conrod while running eighth, while Redman and Le Mans winner Stanley Dickens in AMR1/04 recovered from thirty-second on the grid to finish seventh. A single AMR1, fitted with a 'Version II' 6.3-litre engine developing over 700bhp, was entered in the final round of the championship at the Rodriguez circuit in Mexico, where Leslie and Redman finished eighth despite being held up in traffic. Aston Martin ended the year sixth in the championship, a point ahead of Toyota.

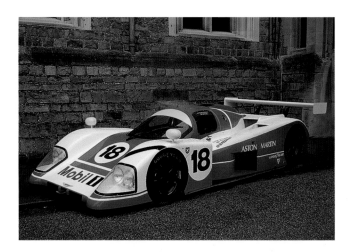

AMR1 in 2005, still wearing the 'black armband' across the front left wing in memory of former Aston Martin team manager John Wyer.

Work began on AMR2 for 1990, which would have been lighter and faster thanks to cleaner aerodynamics and a more powerful 'Version III' Callaway engine. Then came the shock news: Aston Martin was withdrawing from competition and the team was being disbanded. Officially the reasons were that the important Le Mans race looked to be in jeopardy for 1990 because of wrangles over television rights, and that regulation changes due the following year would outlaw the big Aston engine. There had been plans for Aston Martin to adopt Ford's Cosworth-designed HB F1 engine and adapt it for endurance racing in a new Tony Southgate-designed car, but then Ford bought Jaguar and suddenly the Cosworth engine was being pencilled in for a sports car from Coventry. It went into the Ross Brawn-designed XJR-14, which would go on to win the 1991 World Sportscar Championship. But for a quirk of history, a 3.5-litre Aston Martin AMR3 might have won that year.

■ 1989 AMR1

Engine	V8, Zytek electronic engine management
Valvegear	Twin overhead cam per bank, 4 valves per cylinder
Bore and stroke	Not revealed
Capacity	6000cc
Power	Approx 700bhp @ 8,000rpm
Transmission	Aston Martin transaxle
Chassis/body	Carbon/Kevlar monocoque tub
Suspension	Wishbones with coil springs and anti-roll bar all round
Brakes	AP ventilated discs all round
Performance	Top speed 217mph (349km/h), 0–60mph in 4sec (approx)

VIRAGE VOLANTE

ALMOST EVERY CAR Aston Martin has ever made has been available in open-top form, and the Virage was to be no different to the seventy-five years of Astons that preceded it. The latest Volante had been planned right from the start of the Virage project in 1986 and made its public debut at the Birmingham International Motor Show in 1990, exactly two years after the debut of the Virage saloon.

The first Virage Volantes were well received, not least because the Virage shape lent itself very well to the drophead style. Despite that, these early cars had some notable drawbacks: there were only two seats, with a carpeted luggage area aft of the driver's and passenger's seats, and the hood stowed in an unsightly lump at the back of the cabin. Solutions to both problems came with a revised Volante in 1992, which offered two-plus-two seating and a neater hood arrangement. That year Aston Martin sold fewer than fifty cars thanks to a worldwide recession, and the Volante was its mainstay.

■ 1990 VIRAGE VOLANTE

Engine	V8, Weber/Marelli engine management
Valvegear	Twin overhead cam per bank, 4 valves per cylinder
Bore and stroke	100×85mm
Capacity	5340cc
Power	335bhp @ 5,300rpm
Transmission	Five-speed ZF manual gearbox, rear-wheel drive
Chassis/body	Steel platform chassis, steel box-section body frame with aluminium alloy panels
Suspension	Wishbones with coil springs and anti-roll bar front, de Dion with coil springs, A-frame and Watt linkage rear
Brakes	Discs all round (outboard rear)
Performance	Top speed 157mph (253km/h), 0–60mph in 6.8sec

RIGHT: **A neater hood and two tiny rear seats were added to the Virage Volante in 1992.**
BELOW: **Early Volante versions of the Virage were strictly two seats only.**

DB4GT ZAGATO SANCTION II

ASTON'S DB4GT ZAGATO, of which just nineteen were built between 1959 and 1962, has always been one of the rarest and most revered classics. They rarely come up for sale, and when they do they command the highest auction prices of any Aston.

In the 1980s, collector's car prices rose to record levels and supercar makers were quick to build limited edition cars to reap the rewards. In 1987 Victor Gauntlett and Peter Livanos decided to build four brand new DB4GT Zagatos, using chassis numbers allocated in the 1960s but never built. Aston specialist Richard Williams built four chassis to DB4GT spec, then sent them to Zagato – along with his own original Zagato, which acted as a pattern for the new bodies. These 'Sanction II' bodies were returned to England for completion, though they were not finished until 1991 as the build was put on hold during the AMR1 project.

The new cars looked almost identical to 1960s Zagatos, though they were fitted with 15in wheels instead of 16in, and radial tyres rather than crossplies. The suspension was revised to suit the new tyres, and adjustable anti-roll bars fitted at both ends. The Sanction II cars used the correct 6-cylinder engine, complete with DB4GT twin-plug cylinder head, but the engines were bored out to 4.2 litres and given modern electrics.

Two extra bodyshells were built up as spares, but were never needed. After they had lain in storage for several years Richard Williams obtained permission to build them into two 'Sanction III' Zagatos, which were completed in 1996.

It looked like a car of the 1960s, but the DB4GT Zagato Sanction II was built in 1991. A further two 'Sanction III' cars were built in 1996.

■ 1991 DB4GT ZAGATO SANCTION II

Engine	In-line 6-cylinder, triple Weber 50DCO1SP carburettors
Valvegear	Twin overhead cam
Bore and stroke	98 × 92mm
Capacity	4212cc
Power	352bhp @ 6,000rpm
Transmission	Four-speed manual, rear-wheel drive
Chassis/body	Steel platform chassis, tubular steel body frame with aluminium alloy panels
Suspension	Wishbones with coil springs and anti-roll bar front, coil-sprung live axle with twin trailing arms and Watt linkage rear
Brakes	Discs all round
Performance	Top speed 153mph (246km/h), 0–60mph in 5.5sec

VIRAGE 6.3

ASTON MARTIN SPECIALIST Richard Williams ran Viscount Downe's racing Nimrods and would later manage the works AMR1s. In between he developed a 6.3-litre conversion for the V8 engine, and began work on a 7-litre, 500bhp version of the venerable Marek V8. The rights to the 6.3 conversion were taken over by Aston Martin Works Service, which offered it as part of a comprehensive package of upgrades for the Virage. The extra capacity was created by widening the bores to 103.1mm and fitting a new forged-steel crankshaft with a 95mm stroke, together with Cosworth pistons and H-section Carillo conrods. With gas-flowed cylinder heads by Tickford and a remapped engine management system, the 6.3-litre V8 delivered 130bhp more than the standard 5.3, with a maximum of 460lb ft available at 4,250rpm.

The standard car's five-speed ZF gearbox was swapped for a six-speed unit of similar origin, which it shared with the Corvette ZR1 and Lotus Carlton. The suspension was uprated with stiffer springs and Koni dampers, and the rubber-cushioned spherical bearing built into the rear suspension was replaced by a solidly mounted ball joint to sharpen the handling. Braking was by enormous AP Racing discs, which sat inside 10 × 18in OZ Racing split-rim wheels, covered by widened wheel arches, which gave it a muscular stance. The result was the fastest Aston since the Vantage Zagato.

1992 VIRAGE 6.3

Aston Martin Works Service offered a 6.3-litre engine upgrade, which took the Virage to 465bhp.

Engine	V8, Weber Alpha engine management
Valvegear	Twin overhead cam per bank, 4 valves per cylinder
Bore and stroke	103.1 × 95mm
Capacity	6347cc
Power	465bhp @ 5,750rpm
Transmission	Six-speed ZF manual, rear-wheel drive
Chassis/body	Steel platform chassis, steel box-section body frame with aluminium alloy panels
Suspension	Wishbones with coil springs and anti-roll bar front, de Dion with coil springs, A-frame and Watt linkage rear
Brakes	Discs all round (outboard rear)
Performance	Top speed 174mph (280km/h), 0–60mph in 5.3sec

IT WAS ALMOST inevitable that a higher-performance Vantage version of the Virage would follow in due course, though the car that would emerge was more comprehensively modified than had been the case in the past: it was not just a Virage with a tuned engine.

While the Works Service 6.3 conversion had generated more power through extra engine capacity, the Virage-based Vantage, introduced at the Birmingham International Motor Show in 1992, employed a different tactic. The V8 engine in the Vantage retained the 5340cc capacity of the Virage and most of the V8 models before it, but added a pair of Roots-type Eaton superchargers delivering up to 10psi boost. To cope with the extra

boost the compression ratio was reduced to 8.2:1. An air by-pass system was incorporated to reduce parasitic losses at low engine speeds, a common problem with supercharged engines, and twin alloy intercoolers were added to reduce intake temperatures to improve power and maintain reliability. The supercharged V8 used a Ford EEC IV engine management system and Bosch injection in place of the Virage's Weber/Marelli systems, and enabled the Vantage to produce 550bhp yet still pass all existing and planned emissions regulations.

The supercharged engine went into a heavily revised body and chassis. New styling by John Heffernan smoothed out the front end and extended the wheel arches to cover massive wheels and tyres, the same size as seen on the Works Service 6.3. The tail was raised to improve the aerodynamics, the Vantage being said to generate positive downforce at speed. Only the roof and door skins were shared with the Virage.

Under its skin the new car dropped the Virage's rubber-mounted linkage and instead reverted to the system used on the old V8 cars, with twin trailing arms on both sides. A chassis-mounted Watt linkage provided lateral location. Brakes followed 6.3 practice, with huge 14in discs up front and Bosch ABS.

The new Vantage certainly had the performance to live up to its illustrious name. Despite an all-up weight approaching 2 tonnes it could despatch the 0–60mph acceleration benchmark in just 4.6sec, would hit 100mph (160km/h) from rest in a little over 10sec, and would continue accelerating to more than 186mph (300km/h).

If that wasn't enough – and for some Aston customers there was no such thing as enough – Works Service was soon

ABOVE: **The Vantage was easy to spot from the rear thanks to its higher tail with circular rear lights. The V600 spec produced by Works Service boosted the engine to 600bhp.**
RIGHT: **Inside the Vantage was trimmed in leather and walnut, as were all Aston Martins of that era.**

offering a £43,000 V600 conversion which provided 600bhp thanks to higher boost pressure, bigger intercoolers and a less restrictive exhaust system. Other options included Dymag magnesium alloy wheels, race-style Stack instrumentation, AP Racing brakes and uprated suspension with stiffer springs and anti-roll bars and adjustable dampers. With the 600bhp engine the Vantage's top speed was around 200mph (320km/h).

In 1999 Aston Martin announced a special edition Le Mans Vantage, celebrating the fortieth anniversary of the company's win in the Le Mans 24-hours. A bigger front air dam, blanked-off grille and DBR1-style wing vents were the visual clues to the Le Mans Vantage, which was available with either the standard 550bhp Vantage engine or the 600bhp 'works prepared' unit. Just forty were built, one for each year since Aston's Le Mans success.

ABOVE: **The twin Eaton superchargers were mounted high up on either side of the Vantage engine.**
BELOW: **The Vantage Le Mans was announced in 1999 to celebrate the fortieth anniversary of Aston Martin's Le Mans win. Just forty were made.**

■ 1993 VANTAGE

Engine	V8, twin Eaton superchargers, Bosch fuel injection and Ford EEC IV engine management
Valvegear	Twin overhead cam per bank, 4 valves per cylinder
Bore and stroke	100 × 85mm
Capacity	5340cc
Power	550bhp @ 6,500rpm
Transmission	Six-speed ZF manual
Chassis/body	Steel platform chassis, steel box-section body frame with aluminium alloy panels
Suspension	Wishbones with coil springs and anti-roll bar front, de Dion with coil springs, trailing arms and Watt linkage rear
Brakes	Discs all round, outboard rear, ABS
Performance	Top speed 186mph (300km/h), 0–60mph in 4.6sec

V8 COUPÉ AND VOLANTE

THE VIRAGE LIMITED Edition of 1994 was the last car to carry the Virage name (for the time being), but a direct successor did not appear until 1996. In the meantime Aston Martin concentrated on the Vantage, the Volante and the DB7. The car that replaced the Virage arrived at the Geneva Motor Show in March 1996: it was known simply as the V8 Coupé.

New cylinder heads, camshafts and pistons, a higher compression ratio and Weber Alpha Plus engine management all helped to raise engine output to 350bhp. The revised engine went into a slightly more conservative version of the Vantage body with the same triple headlamps (with heated plastic covers) but narrower wings, as the wheels and tyres were smaller than on the supercharged car.

The Volante was updated to the Vantage/V8 Coupé body style in 1998. At the same time it was given a 200mm wheelbase stretch, which allowed greater rear legroom. In 2000, Newport Pagnell built a run of eight Vantage V600 Volantes using the shorter standard wheelbase, and which were the ultimate development of the line: that year both the V8 and the Volante made way for the Vanquish.

RIGHT: **The V8 Coupé of 1996 was essentially a Vantage body with a normally aspirated V8 engine.**
BELOW: **In 1998 the Volante was updated to the V8 Coupé body style, and given a longer wheelbase to increase rear legroom.**

◼ 1996 V8 COUPÉ

Engine	V8, Weber Alpha Plus engine management
Valvegear	Twin overhead cam per bank, 4 valves per cylinder
Bore and stroke	100 × 85mm
Capacity	5340cc
Power	350bhp @ 6,500rpm
Transmission	Five-speed ZF manual or four-speed automatic
Chassis/body	Steel platform chassis, steel box-section body frame with aluminium alloy panels
Suspension	Wishbones with coil springs and anti-roll bar front, de Dion with coil springs, trailing arms and Watt linkage rear
Brakes	Discs all round, outboard rear, ABS
Performance	Top speed 'over 150mph' (241km/h), 0–60mph in 'under 6sec'

PROJECT VANTAGE

T HE FIRST SIGHT of the successor to the Virage family came in January 1998, when Aston Martin unveiled a metallic green concept called Project Vantage at the New York International Auto Show. Like the DB7 it was designed by Ian Callum, but it was altogether more muscular than the Bloxham-built Aston, with pronounced 'haunches' at the rear. The body was clothed in aluminium panels, as was traditional for Aston Martin, but underneath was a very modern aluminium and carbon-fibre bonded structure. Inside, Project Vantage eschewed traditional wood veneer trim, instead using modern finishes such as aluminium and carbon fibre.

The new car was powered by the 5.9-litre V12 engine as seen in the 1996 Ford Indigo concept car, and which had a lot in common with the Ford 'SHO' V6 used in the high-performance Taurus. The engine drove through a six-speed gearbox operated by an electro-hydraulic system developed by Ford and Magneti Marelli: the driver commanded gearchanges using paddles behind the steering wheel.

The 1998 Project Vantage concept car paved the way for the V12 Vanquish production machine in 2000.

Traditional wood trim found no place in the Project Vantage interior, which instead employed high-tech materials such as aluminium alloy and carbon fibre.

■ 1998 PROJECT VANTAGE

Engine	V12, Ford Visteon EEC V engine management
Valvegear	Twin overhead cam per bank, 4 valves per cylinder
Bore and stroke	89 × 79.5mm
Capacity	5935cc
Power	About 450bhp @ 6,000rpm
Transmission	Six-speed sequential with paddle shift
Chassis/body	Bonded carbon fibre and aluminium structure with aluminium outer panels
Suspension	Wishbones with coil springs and anti-roll bar all round
Brakes	Cross-drilled ventilated discs all round, with anti-lock
Performance	Top speed 200mph (320km/h) estimated, 0–60mph (97km/h) in 4sec estimated

V12 VANQUISH

ALTHOUGH ASTON MARTIN officially claimed that Project Vantage had been built with no production aim in mind, the rumours were that it would go into production to replace the existing 'V-car' range, and that it would be called the DB8 or DB9. Those prophecies came partly true, as a production version did indeed follow late in 2000 – but it did not carry a DB name: instead it was called the V12 Vanquish. Externally it was very similar to Project Vantage, though there were in fact detail differences all over the car. The most noticeable change was at the rear, where the rear light clusters were tidier.

TOP: **The Vanquish used an advanced bonded and riveted aluminium structure with carbon-fibre A-pillars and transmission tunnel.**

ABOVE: **The Vanquish was Ian Callum's second major production car design for Aston Martin, after the DB7.**

Although less avant garde than the Project Vantage cabin, the interior of the Vanquish was still much more modern in style than that of the Virage family.

The innovative composite structure on Project Vantage was carried forwards to the production car, with a strong carbon-fibre transmission tunnel bonded and riveted to extruded aluminium alloy members that formed the front and rear bulkheads. The A-pillars were composite structures made from braided carbon fibre around an aluminium honeycomb centre, developed with the help of Nottingham University. A carbon/steel/aluminium subframe bolted to the front bulkhead carried the engine and front suspension and, right at the front, a deformable composite crash structure. At the back of the car the panels around the boot made up another crash structure.

Underneath, the Vanquish was completely flat as far back as the rear axle, to reduce aerodynamic drag. At the rear the underbody formed a venturi shape to help generate downforce at high speed. The structure was said to be strong enough to meet all existing or planned safety legislation, and compared to the V-cars it was both stiffer and lighter.

Although the Vanquish was clothed with aluminium panels like most previous Astons, the panels were shaped using a hot forming process called 'Superforming', which Aston Martin had first used for some parts of the Lagonda in the late 1970s. The panels were fitted and finished by Newport Pagnell's skilled craftsmen.

Power for the Vanquish came from the 5.9-litre, 60-degree V12 which had made its debut in the DB7 Vantage in 1999. A new crankshaft, inlet manifolds, camshafts and valvegear helped raise power from the DB7 Vantage's 420bhp to 460bhp. That was fed through a 'robotized' manual gearbox, as on Project Vantage, which replaced the conventional manual gearlever with gearchange paddles behind the steering wheel.

Customers could choose between a two-seat interior with a rear luggage platform and a two-plus-two configuration with a pair of tiny rear seats. The production Vanquish was available with either modern brushed metal finishes (giving a flavour of the Project Vantage interior) or more traditional wood veneers, both coupled with the usual swathes of Connolly leather and Wilton carpet. The eyeball vents, which had been fitted on the top of the dashboard in Project Vantage and the early Vanquish prototypes, were apparently vetoed by incoming Aston Martin chief executive Dr Ulrich Bez, as they were from the Ford Ka. Their replacement was one of the factors that caused the Vanquish debut to slip from the Birmingham Motor Show in October 2000 to the Geneva show in March 2001.

■ 2001 V12 VANQUISH

Engine	V12, Ford Visteon engine management
Valvegear	Twin overhead cam per bank, 4 valves per cylinder
Bore and stroke	89 × 79.5mm
Capacity	5935cc
Power	460bhp @ 6,500rpm
Transmission	Six-speed manual transmission with paddle shift
Chassis/body	Bonded carbon fibre and aluminium structure with aluminium outer panels
Suspension	Wishbones with coil springs and anti-roll bar all round
Brakes	Cross-drilled ventilated discs all round, with Teves anti-lock
Performance	Top speed 190mph (306km/h), 0–60mph (97km/h) in 5sec

JAMES BOND'S VANQUISH

JAMES BOND HAS been inextricably linked with Aston Martin since the appearance of the DB5 in *Goldfinger* in 1964. Although the film makers had given Bond lesser cars in some subsequent films, Aston Martins continued to appear more often than any other marque. For *Die Another Day*, the twentieth Bond film and the last to star Pierce Brosnan, Ford signed a deal with Eon Productions to supply all the major cars and a good deal of technical support. Bond was to drive an Aston Martin Vanquish, while the lead female character Jinx (played by Halle Berry) would drive a Ford Thunderbird and Bond's adversaries were equipped with another Ford-family vehicle, Jaguar's XKR. Volvos and Land Rovers were also used in the film.

Bond was introduced to his Vanquish by the new Q, played by John Cleese, in a Q-branch laboratory located in a disused underground station. As with that iconic DB5, the Bond Vanquish was fitted with a host of special features: machine guns appeared from the bonnet vents, the grille was fitted with heat-seaking missiles and shotguns, and the tyres featured retractable ice spikes. The Vanquish was even equipped with a 'stealth' capability, which could make it all but disappear.

Aston Martin provided a total of seven cars for *Die Another Day*, all of them sharing the registration number KE02EWW while on screen. Three were standard Tungsten silver Vanquish production cars, which were used for close-ups and interior shots – known variously as the 'hero' or 'pretty' cars. The other cars were four of the seventy pre-production Vanquish prototypes, which, together with a handful of Jaguar XKR convertibles, were substantially modified for action sequences to be shot on the Vatnajökull glacier in south-east Iceland and at Pinewood Studios in the UK.

The film's stunt team specified four-wheel drive, so both the Astons and Jaguars had to be equipped with new drivetrains by special effects engineer Andy Smith. The Vanquish V12s were removed and replaced by 5-litre Ford V8s, which were mounted as far back in the engine bay as possible to leave space for the grille-mounted weapons systems and the driven front axle, which came from a Ford Explorer SUV. Power was taken through an automatic gearbox, which was set up to lock in gear until the driver moved the selector, and a transfer box split drive to the front and rear axles and allowed the modified Vanquish to drive as fast in reverse as it could forwards. A hydraulic handbrake was fitted to allow the stunt drivers to lock the rear wheels, which proved useful in the 'Ice Hotel' sequence filmed at Pinewood. Tests on dry tarmac in the UK proved the reliability of the transmission, but to be on the safe side the team took a vast stock of spares on the month-long Iceland shoot, including engines, axles, driveshafts and tyres. Nothing broke, though two cars were damaged – one skidded into an iceberg, while another ended up sliding along on its roof as part of the plot.

After filming was complete the cars were used to promote the film, then two of the standard cars were sold off – one making £190,000 at auction in 2003 and another selling for £144,500 in 2004, both surprisingly good value. The remaining 'hero' car was retained by MGM/Eon, while the two surviving special effects cars remained with Aston Martin.

James Bond actor Pierce Brosnan with V12 Vanquish in 2002. Brosnan drove the Vanquish in his last Bond film, *Die Another Day*.

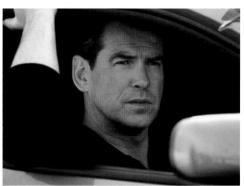

LEFT: **John Cleese as the new Q introduces James Bond to his latest Aston Martin.**
BELOW: **Pierce Brosnan in one of the standard Vanquishes used in filming *Die Another Day*. Two of these cars were sold at auction, one of them making £190,000.**

■ 2002 *DIE ANOTHER DAY* SPECIAL EFFECTS VANQUISH

Engine	Ford V8, Holley four-barrel carburettor
Valvegear	Overhead valve, 2 valves per cylinder
Bore and stroke	89 × 79.5mm
Capacity	4949cc
Power	325bhp @ 6,000rpm
Transmission	Three-speed automatic transmission, four-wheel drive
Chassis/body	Bonded carbon fibre and aluminium structure with aluminium outer panels
Suspension	Wishbones with coil springs and anti-roll bar all round
Brakes	Cross-drilled ventilated discs all round
Performance	Top speed 120mph (190km/h) (approx), 0–60mph in 7sec (approx)

Four-wheel-drive Vanquishes and Jaguars were built for the stunt sequences in *Die Another Day*, which were shot on a glacier in Iceland.

VANQUISH ZAGATO ROADSTER

THE ITALIAN COACHBUILDER Zagato has been associated with Aston Martin since the DB4GT Zagato in 1960, renewing its association with Astons in the 1980s (with the V8 Vantage Zagato) and 2000s (with the DB7 Zagato and DB AR1). Once production of the DB7-based Zagato cars had come to an end, Zagato turned its attention to the other family of Aston Martin cars – the Vanquish.

At the Geneva show in March 2004 Zagato showed a very stylish Vanquish Roadster concept, finished in a bright metallic blue with a deep red interior. The car was styled by Zagato's chief designer Nori Harada, who had been responsible for the DB7 Zagato and the DB AR1, with cooperation from Aston

Martin's design manager Peter Hutchinson. Zagato's previous Astons had always been completely new body designs based on existing mechanical components, but the Vanquish Roadster was different. This time the familiar Vanquish front end and doors were retained, and only the roof and tail were new. At the back there was a new bumper, boot lid and rear panel with circular tail lights reminiscent of those on the DB AR1. The Roadster was designed to be fitted with a hard top in winter, then in summer that was to be replaced by a double-curved glass cover over the rear of the cabin. There was also said to be a removable soft top.

Although there were reports that Zagato would build a run of ninety-nine Vanquish Roadsters – as that had been previous Zagato practice with the DB7-based cars – no production cars were ever built, and the Vanquish Roadster remained a one-off. After touring the major auto shows and being featured in numerous articles in magazines, it was sold to a private owner in the USA.

ABOVE: **Aston Martin never made a convertible Vanquish, but Zagato did. This is designer Nori Harada's styling sketch.**
RIGHT: **The most noticeable feature of the Vanquish Roadster was the double-humped rear glass cover over the rear of the cabin.**

**Only the roof and tail of Zagato's Vanquish Roadster were new –
the front end and doors were the same as the Vanquish coupé.**

VANQUISH BERTONE JET 2

BERTONE IS ONE of the greatest of all the Italian styling houses, but it has only rarely applied its talents to Aston Martins. The best known Bertone Aston is the DB4GT Jet (*see* p.56) of 1961, and when Bertone built a Vanquish-based concept car in 2004 it was named the Jet 2 as a tribute to the earlier car.

Unveiled at the Geneva show in 2004 (the same show that saw the debut of Zagato's Vanquish Roadster) the Jet 2 was not a rakish coupé like the original Jet, but instead was a four-seat, estate-bodied version of the Vanquish. The front of the Jet 2 was much the same as a regular Vanquish, though there were extra cooling ducts in the nose to channel air to the brakes, but the rear was all new, with a vertical tailgate, the shape of which echoed the classic Aston Martin grille shape.

Unlike the Zagato Roadster, which was built on a standard Vanquish platform, the Jet 2 had 8.3in (210mm) added to the wheelbase to provide space for a pair of rear seats. In keeping with the multi-purpose nature of the car, the rear seats were arranged to fold into the floor to increase the luggage area. The interior was trimmed in embossed leather and matt-finished pear wood, apparently inspired by classic Italian motorboats, with a new centre console derived from that in the DB9.

In addition to showing how a different Vanquish body style might work, the Jet 2 was intended to demonstrate Bertone's skill in producing specialist variations on existing vehicles, with the practicalities of production firmly in mind. Jet 2 was designed so that the main points of the structure underneath were unaltered, making it relatively cheap and easy to build as a production car. Even so, the Bertone Jet 2 never went into production.

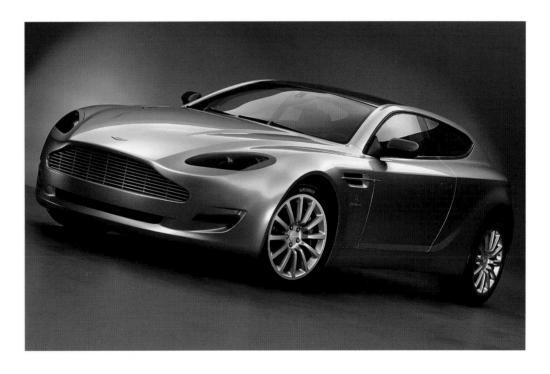

Bertone unveiled the Jet 2 concept in 2004. It was a four-seat, estate-bodied version of the V12 Vanquish.

2004 V12 VANQUISH BERTONE JET 2

Engine	V12, Ford Visteon engine management
Valvegear	Twin overhead cam per bank, 4 valves per cylinder
Bore and stroke	89 × 79.5mm
Capacity	5935cc
Power	460bhp @ 6,500rpm
Transmission	Six-speed manual transmission with paddle shift
Chassis/body	Bonded carbon fibre and aluminium structure with aluminium outer panels
Suspension	Wishbones with coil springs and anti-roll bar all round
Brakes	Cross-drilled ventilated discs all round, with Teves anti-lock
Performance	Top speed 190mph (306km/h), 0–60mph (97km/h) in 6.0sec (approx)

VANQUISH S

ANNOUNCED AT THE Paris show in September 2004, the Vanquish S was at the time the fastest-ever Aston Martin production car, with a top speed 'in excess of 200mph (320km/h)'.

The Vanquish S had a revised body with a reshaped grille to improve cooling, and a raised tail to reduce lift. The steering geometry was revised, with shorter steering arms, and Sports Dynamics suspension and braking systems (stiffer springs and dampers, and bigger brake discs and calipers) were fitted to sharpen response. The engine was a development of the existing 5935cc V12 with new cylinder heads, revised engine management mapping, and new fuel injectors to improve power to 520bhp. There were also detail improvements to the interior.

The Ultimate Edition built in 2007 marked the end of Vanquish production. A run of forty cars was planned, but in the end fifty were built, all in a unique 'Ultimate black' with semi-aniline leather interiors and dark chrome fittings. Mechanically they are the same as the Vanquish S. The Ultimate Edition cars were the last Aston Martins to be made at Newport Pagnell. The final car, which came off the line in July 2007, was retained by Aston Martin and went on display at the Heritage Motor Centre at Gaydon, just down the road from Aston Martin's new headquarters.

2004 V12 VANQUISH S

Engine	V12, Ford Visteon engine management
Valvegear	Twin overhead cam per bank, 4 valves per cylinder
Bore and stroke	89 × 79.5mm
Capacity	5935cc
Power	520bhp @ 7,000rpm
Transmission	Six-speed manual transmission with paddle shift
Chassis/body	Bonded carbon fibre and aluminium structure with aluminium outer panels
Suspension	Wishbones with coil springs and anti-roll bar all round
Brakes	Cross-drilled ventilated discs all round, with Teves anti-lock
Performance	Top speed 200mph (320km/h) (approx), 0–60mph (97km/h) in 4.8sec

Aston Martin unveiled the 520bhp Vanquish S at the Paris show in 2004. It was said to be the fastest Aston Martin built up to that time.

THE BLOXHAM
CARS

**The DB7 saved Aston Martin from oblivion in the
mid-1990s. This is the DB7 Vantage introduced in 1999.**

1993–2003

STON MARTIN'S CHAIRMAN in the 1980s, Victor Gauntlett, often talked of his desire to add a second model line alongside the company's hand-built V8s – a 'new DB4', sometimes referred to cryptically as 'DP1999', which would be lighter and cheaper and sell in far greater numbers than the existing cars. Although William Towns produced drawings for an angular 6-cylinder coupé – very much in the style of his 1976 Lagonda – in the early 1980s, the project was never seriously pursued. It was not until 1991, with Aston Martin now owned by Ford, and Walter Hayes behind the chairman's desk, that the idea of a second model line began to gain real impetus.

At about the same time another member of the Ford family, Jaguar, was making plans for its own future sports cars. Development of a new coupé and drophead – officially called XJ41 and XJ42 respectively, but known to everyone as the 'F-type' – had been going on since 1980. It had suffered numerous delays, first because the important XJ40 saloon took precedence, and later due to uncertainty over the car's specification and reorganization of the project management. As the brief evolved and the performance targets were raised the F-type became progressively more complex, heavier, and more expensive to build. When Ford took over Jaguar in 1989 the F-type project was one of the first casualties of the company's reorganization. But it was the first in a series of key decisions within Ford, Jaguar and Aston Martin that would ultimately lead to the creation of the DB7.

Jaguar's very successful racing efforts were being run by Tom Walkinshaw's TWR group, which also built tuned JaguarSport XJ-S models and the XJ220 supercar. When the F-type died, TWR came up with a proposal to use the well liked F-type body style on a development of the existing XJ-S platform. Jaguar turned down this 'Project XX', believing it to be too expensive to build in the required numbers. But Walter Hayes saw potential in Project XX for Aston Martin.

Not only did TWR have the makings of the long-awaited 'new DB4' in Project XX, they also had a factory to build it. The existing Aston Martin production facilities at Newport Pagnell, which could build only a handful of cars a week, certainly could not cope with the rate of production that would be essential for the new car. But TWR's factory at Wykham Mill near Bloxham, where the XJ220 had been made, would soon be available. Everything came together at the right time: Hayes' vision for a new Aston, Project XX, and the Bloxham factory.

Soon the TWR team was working on turning the Project XX idea into a reality, and chief designer Ian Callum was working on the shape of what became known as NPX, the 'Newport Pagnell Experimental'. Apart from the revised shape, the biggest change was under the bonnet. Neither the F-type's twin-turbo Jaguar XJ6 engine nor TWR's preferred unit, its own 48-valve version of the Jaguar V12, would power the new car: instead Walter Hayes pushed through the idea of a straight six, again Jaguar-based, fitted with an Eaton supercharger to boost power and performance.

The result was the definitive DB7, launched at the Geneva Salon in 1993. At the same show Ford's in-house Ghia styling studio exhibited a Lagonda concept car, which it called the Vignale. Styled by Moray Callum, brother of DB7 designer Ian, the Vignale was a running car with a Ford V8 engine. It was hoped that a revised version might go into production, but sadly the project never progressed that far, and for the time being, the Lagonda marque was seen on nothing more than a handful of Virages remodelled by Aston Martin Works Service.

The DB7 was well received by the motoring media, which praised the car's effortless elegance and robust performance – even if there was some concern about the inevitable cost-cutting compromises, such as the parts-bin switchgear and the Jaguar parentage of the chassis and engine. The customers who flocked to buy DB7s did not worry about these details, and

TWR built a working prototype to convince Ford that the DB7 was a viable car – and the tactic worked.

ABOVE: **DB7s were built at the Bloxham factory, previously occupied by JaguarSport, which had built the XJ220.**

RIGHT: **Ian Callum's DB7 shape was widely admired, and the car sold in unprecedented numbers.**

the DB7 sold in record numbers. It put Aston Martin back on a sound financial footing for the first time in many years.

The 6-cylinder DB7 spawned a series of limited editions, beginning with the Alfred Dunhill car that was offered in 1998. In 1999 the DB7 'i6' was joined by a DB7 Vantage, with comprehensively revised body and running gear and powered by a new engine – a 5.9-litre V12 engine developed by Ford's Core and Advanced Powertrain team in Detroit and related to the 3-litre Ford Duratec V6. But sales of the 6-cylinder DB7 dwindled to almost nothing once the much more powerful DB7 Vantage was on sale, and it was phased out in 2000.

In 2002 the DB7 GT was introduced, offering a slightly more powerful 435bhp V12 engine, revised suspension for crisper handling, better brakes and aerodynamic tweaks. There was also a GTA model with a ZF five-speed automatic transmission, which shared the GT's body and chassis upgrades but retained the DB7 Vantage's 420bhp engine specification.

The DB7 Vantage provided the basis for three Italian Astons. The first was built by Italdesign in 2001 and styled by Giorgetto Giugiaro and his son Fabrizio. Called the Twenty Twenty, this 'research prototype' was intended to suggest what an Aston Martin roadster might be like in the year 2020. The Twenty

ABOVE: **The DB7 started life as a Jaguar project, and under the skin it shared much with the XJ-S.**
LEFT: **The DB7 Vantage was powered by a Ford-derived V12 engine. This is the even more powerful DB7 GT of 2002.**

ABOVE: **The DB7, seen in coupé and Volante convertible forms, quickly became Aston Martin's biggest seller.**
RIGHT: **The DB7 spawned a number of special editions. This is Zagato's DB American Roadster 1.**

Twenty was a complete running vehicle, and has been demonstrated in recent years at events such as the Goodwood Festival of Speed, but it remained a one-off.

The other two Italian DB7s were production cars, though they were only available in strictly limited numbers. Both were built by Zagato, and arose after a conversation between new Aston Martin CEO Ulrich Bez and Andrea Zagato at the Pebble Beach Concours d'Élégance in 2001. The DB7 Zagato, which was unveiled in 2002, was 8.3in (211mm) shorter than the DB7 Vantage, most of that coming out of the rear overhang. It was a taut and muscular shape, which incorporated classic Aston styling cues such as the grille shape wing vents, together with Zagato's 'double bubble' roof line. The Zagato used the same 435bhp V12 as the DB7 GT, mated to the GT's gearbox.

It was no surprise that the Zagato coupé was followed by a roadster, though the DB American Roadster 1, as it was called, was a little more than just a DB7 Zagato with the roof removed. The DB AR1 was built on the standard DB7 wheelbase and had a new rear deck incorporating a proper boot lid (the Zagato had only a drop-down flap), and buttresses behind the seats that echoed the 'double bubble' Zagato roof. There was no hood, as the DB AR1 was designed for the sunnier American states where a roof was unnecessary.

Just ninety-nine production versions of the DB7 Zagato and DB AR1 were built, the last of them in 2004 – by which time the DB7 Vantage had been phased out in favour of the Gaydon-built DB9. That would be the start of a whole new era for Aston Martin.

NPX PROTOTYPE

CAR COMPANY MANAGEMENT will generally sign off a new car for production based on a full-size clay model, but Tom Walkinshaw was keen to make a bigger impression on the Aston Martin and Ford bigwigs than a mere clay model could achieve. Ian Callum told him a glassfibre model, though more expensive, was more impressive as it would have a more realistic surface finish and see-through windows. When Walkinshaw asked if there was anything better than a glassfibre model, all Callum could think of was to build a real car – and that's what the TWR team did. When Ford management gathered at Aston Martin's sales office in Knightsbridge in March 1992 they were expecting to see a mock-up of the proposed new Aston – and were amazed when the car was driven into the showroom.

The complete running prototype had been built in just three months. The shape was very close to the full-size clay model built by Ian Callum and Andrew Miles at TWR's Kidlington design studio, and would change only in detail for the production car that would arrive a year later – the clamshell bonnet was swapped for a conventional item, and the lift-out roof panel was deleted. Details such as the door mirrors and wheels were changed. The NPX prototype was also powered by a different engine – a twin-turbo version of the 4-litre Jaguar AJ6 straight six which had been developed for the stillborn Jaguar XJ41/42 project in 1989, rather than the supercharged 3.2-litre version that would be seen in the definitive DB7. While the XJ41/42 had eventually been given four-wheel drive, NPX was rear drive only.

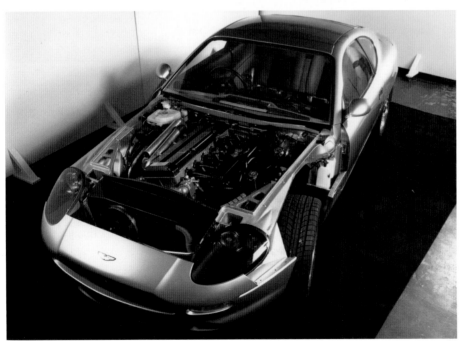

ABOVE: **Ian Callum's clay model of Project NPX, which became the DB7. The car was styled at TWR's studios in Kidlington, near Oxford.**
LEFT: **The original NPX prototype had a clamshell bonnet and twin-turbo Jaguar engine, as seen here.**

The impact created by the NPX prototype had exactly the effect Walkinshaw and Walter Hayes were hoping for. Ford management gave the project their approval, and allocated a £1m budget for the construction of a series of prototypes, about thirty in all, which would be used to develop the DB7 production car.

NPX was taken to Tom Walkinshaw's home at Broadstone Manor, near Oxford, for a photo session.

TWR developed NPX into the production DB7 using 'fully engineered vehicles' or FEVs like this one.

◼ 1992 NPX PROTOTYPE

Engine	In-line six, fuel injection, twin turbochargers
Valvegear	Twin overhead cam, 4 valves per cylinder
Bore and stroke	91 × 102mm
Capacity	3980cc
Power	330bhp @ 5,000rpm
Transmission	Getrag five-speed manual gearbox, rear-wheel drive
Chassis/body	Steel monocoque with composite bumpers, sills, clamshell bonnet and boot lid
Suspension	Wishbones with coil springs and anti-roll bar front, wishbones with longitudinal control arms, coil springs and anti-roll bar rear
Brakes	Ventilated discs all round, with Teves anti-lock
Performance	Top speed 160mph (258km/h), 0–60mph in 6sec (approx)

DB7

THE LONG-AWAITED 'NEW DB4', project NPX, was unveiled to the press and public at the Geneva show in March 1993. It was a show full of new stars – including the Lagonda Vignale concept – but it was the DB7 that stole the limelight. The show car, painted a restrained BMW silver grey and trimmed in oxblood and parchment leather, was hand-built with minute care to ensure it looked its best. The Geneva car still exists, incidentally, and has been on display at the Coventry Transport Museum for the last few years.

One of the biggest surprises about the specification of the DB7 was its engine, which was taken neither from an existing Aston Martin unit nor (as some Aston diehards had feared) a Jaguar. It was based on Jaguar's all-alloy AJ6 straight six, but although the DB7 engine shared its block casting with the Jaguar unit, there were detail differences in the machining. On top sat a bespoke 4-valve cylinder head, and a new cam cover that proudly carried the maker's name. More importantly, the DB7 had benefited from a particular interest of Walter Hayes – supercharging.

Ford had been working with the Eaton Corporation on supercharged engines for its US models, the first fruit of the collaboration being the Thunderbird SC in 1989. So it was no surprise that the supercharger installation on the DB7 had an Eaton blower, a Roots-type unit that used a pair of counter-rotating three-lobed rotors to compress air into the cylinders and generate more power.

Driven by a poly-vee belt from the nose of the crankshaft, the supercharger provided up to 14psi of boost through an air/

ABOVE: **The DB7 that announced the arrival of the new car at the Geneva show in 1993, on display at Coventry Transport Museum.**
LEFT: **The flush wheel covers originally fitted to the DB7 were later deleted, and many early cars have now had them removed.**

RIGHT: **The DB7 interior blended modern shapes with traditional wood and leather trim.**
BELOW: **The DB7 was the most thoroughly developed Aston Martin yet made, undergoing thousands of miles of testing in the UK, Europe and the USA.**

water intercooler, which helped to keep intake charge temperatures down to manageable levels. Unlike the twin superchargers on the Vantage V8, which were mounted in prominent positions in the engine bay, the DB7's blower was mounted low down to the left of the engine. The engine itself was a short-stroke 3.2-litre unit, with shorter pistons than the equivalent normally aspirated Jaguar unit to lower the compression ratio to 8.5:1. With 335bhp and 36lb ft, the DB7 engine had higher maximum power and torque than the naturally aspirated, 5.3-litre V8 in the contemporary Virage, and more than the 6-litre V12 in the Jaguar XJ-S on which the DB7 was based.

Testing of the new car took full advantage of Ford's facilities, including the hot-weather test facility in Arizona. Tom Walkinshaw himself took an active part in the development driving, and three-times Formula 1 champion Jackie Stewart was also brought in to advise on the DB7's handling.

The first DB7 production cars left the Wykham Mill factory in Bloxham in June 1994, six weeks later than planned, the factory averaging a car a week for the first few months. But within a year the total number of DB7s surpassed the total number of Virages, which had been in production for six years. The 1,000th DB7 was built in 1996, and the 2,000th in 1998.

LEFT: **A DB7 on test in the wind tunnel at the Motor Industry Research Association (MIRA) in Warwickshire. The smoke lance helps testers to visualize the air flow over the car.**
BELOW: **Though the NPX prototype had a clamshell bonnet, the production DB7 was given a conventional bonnet panel with separate wings. The wings were made of a composite material, which meant they were very light.**

Bloxham was where final assembly took place, but sub-assemblies were built by specialists elsewhere. The steel bodies were built by Mayflower Vehicle Systems in Coventry, each one taking five days to produce. At first the DB7 bodyshells were painted by Rolls-Royce at its Crewe factory, but in October 1996 a £1m paint shop was opened at Bloxham so the cars could be painted on site. The 6-cylinder engines were built and tested by TWR Engines in Kidlington and supplied to Bloxham with their transmissions already fitted. Inserting the engine/transmission assembly into the cars using a hoist caused some headaches, the process often resulting in damage to the engine bay or the engine itself, which then had to be rectified. A custom-designed hoist was later introduced, reducing the time taken to fit the engine and also virtually eliminating damage.

A Volante was added to the range in 1996, the coupé receiving a number of improvements at the same time: the damping was softened, the brakes and steering revised, and the original composite bonnet was swapped for a steel one. Safety standards were rising, so the new DB7s were fitted with driver and passenger airbags – which necessitated a change to a Jaguar-sourced steering wheel with a rather ugly crash pad. There were also new column stalks and repositioned electric seat controls. The seat backs had already been modified after reports that they could move about during hard cornering. A more noticeable change was the deletion of the 'aero' hubcaps in favour of small 'pope's hat' knave plates for the wheels – because most people preferred the looks of the twelve-spoke alloy wheels.

When the V12-engined DB7 Vantage was introduced in 1999, the original 6-cylinder car continued in production, but it was the V12 that took the lion's share of sales. The original DB7 was phased out in 2000.

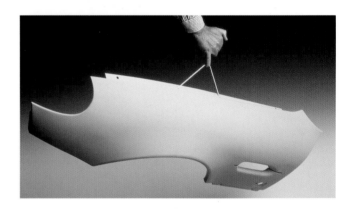

■ 1993 DB7

Engine	In-line six, Zytek (later Ford EEC V) fuel injection, Eaton M90 supercharger with air/water intercooler
Valvegear	Twin overhead cam, 4 valves per cylinder
Bore and stroke	91 × 83mm
Capacity	3239cc
Power	335bhp @ 5,750rpm
Transmission	Five-speed manual gearbox, GM (later ZF) four-speed automatic transmission optional, limited slip differential rear-wheel drive
Chassis/body	Steel monocoque with composite bumpers, sills, front wings, bonnet and boot lid
Suspension	Wishbones with coil springs and anti-roll bar front, wishbones with longitudinal control arms, coil springs and anti-roll bar rear
Brakes	Ventilated discs all round, with Teves anti-lock
Performance	Top speed 165mph (266km/h), 0–60mph in 6sec

DB7 WORKS PREPARED

A PROPOSAL FOR a DB7 racing series led Aston Martin Works Service at Newport Pagnell and Banbury-based automotive engineering group Prodrive to develop a racing version of the car, known as the DB7 GT (not to be confused with the V12 production car with the same name – see p. 158). The race car had upgraded brakes and suspension, and ran on slick racing tyres. Sadly the race series never happened, but the race car suspension was later adapted by Works Service into a series of upgrades for DB7 road cars.

Upgrades included AP Racing ventilated brake discs: these were so big they would not fit inside the standard wheels, so Newport Pagnell supplied larger five-spoke OZ Racing magnesium rims – though later on a big-brake kit was developed, which did fit inside the standard wheels. The more robust brakes were a useful addition to the spec when the engine was treated to a Works Service tuning programme, which offered larger intercoolers and freer-flowing exhaust systems to boost power to 385bhp.

Newport Pagnell also offered a Visual Dynamics body kit with a new nose, sill extensions and a rear aerofoil – though the end result was not universally admired. V8 Vantage-style twin circular rear lamps were also offered.

Works Service was also happy to take on more extreme modifications, including a DB7 with a 450bhp, 6.3-litre Aston Martin V8 engine.

Aston Martin Works Service soon found itself busy with orders for upgrades to DB7s, and produced a range of 'Works Prepared' options.

■ 1999 DB7 WORKS PREPARED (Typical Specification)

Engine	In-line six, Ford EEC V fuel injection, Eaton M90 supercharger with air/water intercooler
Valvegear	Twin overhead cam, 4 valves per cylinder
Bore and stroke	91 × 83mm
Capacity	3239cc
Power	385bhp @ 5,750rpm
Transmission	Five-speed manual gearbox, limited slip differential rear-wheel drive
Chassis/body	Steel monocoque with composite bumpers, sills, front wings, bonnet and boot lid
Suspension:	Wishbones with coil springs and anti-roll bar front, wishbones with longitudinal control arms, coil springs and anti-roll bar rear
Brakes	Ventilated discs all round, with Teves anti-lock
Performance	Top speed 180mph (290km/h), 0–60mph in 5sec (approx)

LAGONDA VIGNALE

ASTON MARTIN AFICIONADOS remember the Geneva Motor Show in March 1993 for the launch of the DB7, the car that saved Aston Martin from oblivion. But that same show also saw the debut of a concept car that almost led to a mid-1990s revival of Lagonda.

The Lagonda Vignale was designed by Ghia, a famous Italian carrozzeria which had come under the control of Ford in 1970. Ghia continued to operate as an in-house design studio for Ford, as well as lending its name to Ford's upmarket road cars. In the Lagonda's case it was thought important to avoid any confusion with Ghia-badged Fords, so the concept was badged Vignale – the name of another Italian coachbuilder, long since defunct. The Vignale's exterior was shaped by Moray Callum (younger brother of DB7 designer Ian Callum), who went on to lead Mazda design and is now director of design for Ford in North America. The soft curves and short overhangs gave it a fresh and distinctive shape, and it was beautifully detailed: exterior brightwork, for instance, was in nickel rather than chrome because of its subtler shine.

The Art Deco-inspired interior was the work of David Wilkie, who went on to become design chief at Stile Bertone. Soft aniline-dyed leather swathed the cabin, which was dominated by an oval dashboard in dark-stained beech flanked by polished metal air vents.

The Vignale show car was based on a Lincoln chassis with independent front suspension and a live rear axle, but it was expected that a production car (to be built at an expanded Bloxham factory) would either employ the modular aluminium frame structure unveiled on the 1991 Ford Contour concept, or the more conventional Jaguar X300 (XJ saloon) platform. While the show car was fitted with a rather anaemic 190bhp Ford V8 engine, the production version was expected to use a V12, probably the 'double SHO' Ford V12 unveiled in mock-up form the following year and which would later power a generation of Astons, beginning with the DB7 Vantage.

Two Vignales were built by Ghia in 1993, one in silver and one in Sorrento blue. The silver Vignale was probably broken up, while the blue car was sold in a charity auction in 2002 for more than $400,000 – far in excess of its estimate. Meanwhile a third

ABOVE: **The Lagonda Vignale appeared at the Geneva Motor Show in 1993, the show where the DB7 made its debut. Sadly it never reached production.**
LEFT: **The Vignale, styled by DB7 designer Ian Callum's brother Moray, was a compelling blend of art deco and modern style.**

Vignale was built at Newport Pagnell, based on a Ford-family (possibly Jaguar) platform and powered by a V12 engine. DP2138, as it was known inside the factory, was very different under the skin to the first two Vignales, and its shape was not as convincing – no doubt due to the compromises necessary when using a production platform. It may have been built to explore the possibility of production, or it may just have been a one-off commission – it is reported to be one of the dozens of Aston Martin Lagonda cars now owned by the Brunei royal family.

RIGHT: **The Vignale's spectacular interior included a full-width wooden dashboard and sumptuous leather trim.**
BELOW: **Though the Vignale never became a production car, two were built by Ghia and a replica was made by Aston Martin Works Service for a private customer.**

■ 1993 LAGONDA VIGNALE (speculative production specification)

Engine	V12, Ford Visteon EEC V engine management
Valvegear	Twin overhead cam per bank, 4 valves per cylinder
Bore and stroke	89 × 79.5mm
Capacity	5935cc
Power	420bhp @ 6,000rpm
Transmission	Five-speed automatic
Chassis/body	Chemically bonded modular aluminium frame with composite panels
Suspension	Wishbones with coil springs and anti-roll bar front and rear
Brakes	Ventilated discs all round, cross-drilled at front, with anti-lock
Performance	Top speed 175mph (282km/h), 0–60mph in 6sec

DB7 VOLANTE

A VOLANTE DROPHEAD version of the DB7 was inevitable, but to ensure there were no compromises in the shape of the coupé, designer Ian Callum deliberately waited until its styling was signed off before beginning work on a Volante.

Rather than build a new clay model from scratch, Callum and his team modified the coupé clay model – by taking an axe to the roof. Visually the coupé and convertible models were the same from the nose to the rear edge of the doors, roof excepted, but the tail of the Volante was entirely new. The boot lid

ABOVE: **The DB7 Volante clay model outside the TWR styling studio in Kidlington. Cars look different in natural light, so styling models were often brought outside for review.**

LEFT: **The TWR design team began work on the DB7 Volante clay model by taking an axe to the coupé model. Note the US licence plate, indicating the Volante's key market.**

was longer and flatter, and the rear wheel arches were smoother and flatter to suit the 'notchback' shape. The fuel filler, which on the coupé was situated at the bottom of the rear pillar, was repositioned into the top of the wheel arch.

The folding roof was designed around a number of conflicting requirements: it had to make the interior as warm and comfortable as possible when erected, to fold away as neatly as possible, but also to reduce interior and boot space as little as possible. Ian Callum worked closely with the trimmers at Newport Pagnell to understand the constraints imposed by the soft-top material and the roof mechanism. For maximum comfort and refinement the roof had a multi-layer mohair construction and a glass rear window. It could not fold away entirely out of sight without stealing boot space, so a compromise was reached, which traded a slightly more prominent folded roof for a bigger boot. The shape of the top when raised was fine-tuned in BMW's wind tunnel to reduce wind noise to a minimum.

One of the biggest problems in the design of a drophead is to ensure that the body is stiff enough despite the lack of a fixed roof – to resist vibration, and to avoid distortion of the body that might alter the suspension geometry, leading to imprecise handling. Reinforcing tubes were inserted into the sills, and a cruciform stiffening structure was added under the floor. The windscreen frame was also strengthened, to provide roll-over protection. As a result of the stiffening work, the Volante was around 330lb (150kg) heavier than the mechanically similar coupé.

The DB7 Volante was launched in January 1996 at the Detroit and Los Angeles motor shows. It marked the re-emergence of Aston Martin in the USA, which the company had all but abandoned by the 1990s due to the enormous cost of emissions certification – which was simply not justifiable when Aston Martin was selling only a few dozen cars a year. The DB7 was a different story, and both coupé and Volante were designed from the outset to pass emissions standards across the world. With the arrival of the DB7 Volante the USA would quickly become Aston Martin's biggest export market.

■ 1993 DB7 VOLANTE

Engine	In-line six, Ford EEC V fuel injection, Eaton M90 supercharger with air/water intercooler
Valvegear	Twin overhead cam, 4 valves per cylinder
Bore and stroke	91 × 83mm
Capacity	3239cc
Power	335bhp @ 5,750rpm
Transmission	Five-speed manual gearbox, ZF four-speed automatic transmission optional, limited slip differential rear-wheel drive
Chassis/body	Steel monocoque with composite bumpers, sills, front wings, bonnet and boot lid, folding mohair roof
Suspension	Wishbones with coil springs and anti-roll bar front, wishbones with longitudinal control arms, coil springs and anti-roll bar rear
Brakes	Ventilated discs all round, with Teves anti-lock
Performance	Top speed 155mph (249km/h), 0–60mph in 6sec

The Volante was an elegant car, though the roof could have stowed more neatly.

DB7 V12 TWR PROTOTYPE

THE FIRST V12 DB7 was built in 1996, though it was a very different car to the production DB7 Vantage that would follow in 1999. That first V12 was built as a showcase for TWR's engineering skill, and also as a bespoke personal car for the founder of the group, Tom Walkinshaw.

The engine that powered it was derived from the TWR involvement in the Jaguar racing programme. Many of the TWR-designed Jaguar racing cars built between 1985 and 1991 used production-based V12 engines, usually with single overhead-cam valvegear and 2 valves per cylinder. Al Melling designed a 4-valve version with twin chain-driven cams on each cylinder bank in 1988, but it raced only once. The 4-valve V12 was proposed for TWR's Project XX, but dropped in favour of a supercharged straight six when XX became NPX, the prototype XB7. It was a 475bhp version of this V12 that went into Walkinshaw's DB7, mated to a Borg Warner six-speed manual gearbox.

Externally the car was treated to styling and aerodynamic changes, including a deeper air dam and large low-level air intake, deep sills, a new rear bumper moulding and a boot lid-mounted wing. There were no sheet metal changes – despite which the new car had its own distinct character. Walkinshaw's DB7 V12, now in the hands of a collector, remained a one-off.

Tom Walkinshaw's original plan for Project XX, which became the DB7, included a 4-valve V12 engine. This is his own DB7, which had such an engine fitted.

The Walkinshaw DB7 V12 had some body modifications, including a deeper front air dam and a rear aerofoil.

▌ 1996 DB7 V12 PROTOTYPE

Engine	V12, Zytek engine management
Valvegear	Twin overhead cam per bank, 4 valves per cylinder
Bore and stroke	90 × 84mm (estimated)
Capacity	6413cc (estimated)
Power	475bhp @ 6,000rpm
Transmission	Six-speed Borg Warner T56 manual gearbox, limited slip differential
Chassis/body	Steel monocoque with composite bumpers, sills, front wings and boot lid
Suspension	Wishbones with coil springs and anti-roll bar front, wishbones with longitudinal control arms, coil springs and anti-roll bar rear
Brakes	Ventilated discs all round, with Teves anti-lock
Performance	Top speed 182mph (293km/h), 0–60mph in 4.8sec (approx)

DB7 DUNHILL LIMITED EDITION

THE DUNHILL DB7 was originally unveiled as a one-off concept vehicle in June 1996, when the DB7 had been on sale for little more than two years. It was developed as a joint project between Aston Martin and the famous English luxury clothing and accessory specialist Alfred Dunhill, and was intended to show off some of the latest items in the Dunhill accessories collection.

Interest in the original car proved strong enough for Aston Martin to turn the Dunhill into a limited edition production model, available either as a coupé (at a list price of $138,580) or as a Volante drophead ($148,580). The planned production run was 150 cars, but it appears that only about half that number was actually made in 1998–9 before the DB7 Vantage arrived – rapidly killing off any interest in 6-cylinder DB7s.

The Dunhill cars were mechanically and bodily the same as a regular production DB7, the differences being in the details and the interior appointments. All the cars were finished in a special metallic silver colour, different to the standard DB7 silver, which was chosen to match the polished steel finish of the Dunhill Millennium watch set into the dashboard. The wheels were painted the same metallic silver, and their 'aero' hubcaps were replaced by small knave plates whose shape was based on that of the watch. The exterior door handles and boot release surround were etched with a distinctive 'tri-line' motif, which was a feature of the Dunhill AD2000 watch collection.

The Dunhill DB7s were trimmed in charcoal Connolly hide with silver highlights throughout the cabin to match the exterior – including silver-grey piping on the seats, brushed steel panels on the dashboard in place of wood veneer, and a brushed metal gearknob instead of the standard leather item. The gearknob was another component etched with the Dunhill 'tri-line' motif. The instrument panel graphics were redesigned to match the Dunhill watch inset into the dash.

Hidden under the armrest between the front seats was a humidor – a constant-humidity box designed for storing cigars – with a cedar-wood lining and ebony trim. A silver cigar cutter and cigar lighter were also provided. Non-smokers, who might have felt rather left out by all this attention to the needs of the dedicated cigar puffer, could order their Dunhill DB7 with a personal grooming kit in place of the humidor. In either case the ashtray was the standard, rather small, DB7 item. Each of these limited edition DB7s was supplied with a pair of Dunhill AD2000 carbon-fibre pens and a set of Dunhill CityScape luggage.

The Dunhill DB7 was the first of several limited editions. About seventy-five were made before the DB7 Vantage made it effectively obsolete.

Dunhill described these cars as the 'ultimate masculine indulgence', while the press noted the elaborate cigar-related paraphernalia and quickly dubbed the Dunhill DB7 the 'ultimate accessory' for smokers. The success of the Dunhill DB7 – in terms of the interest and press attention it generated, if not in its sales performance – paved the way for a number of other special editions based on the 6-cylinder DB7, as the model entered its twilight years.

The Dunhill's interior had a Millennium watch mounted on the dashboard and a humidor for cigars built into the centre armrest.

■ 1993 DB7 DUNHILL LIMITED EDITION

Engine	In-line six, Ford EEC V fuel injection, Eaton M90 supercharger with air/water intercooler
Valvegear	Twin overhead cam, 4 valves per cylinder
Bore and stroke	91 × 83mm
Capacity	3239cc
Power	335bhp @ 5,750rpm
Transmission	Five-speed manual gearbox, or ZF four-speed automatic transmission, limited slip differential rear-wheel drive
Chassis/body	Steel monocoque with composite bumpers, sills, clamshell bonnet and boot lid
Suspension	Wishbones with coil springs and anti-roll bar front, wishbones with longitudinal control arms, coil springs and anti-roll bar rear
Brakes	Ventilated discs all round, with Teves anti-lock
Performance	Top speed 165mph (266km/h), 0–60mph in 6sec

DB7 16 LIMITED EDITIONS

FOLLOWING THE DUNHILL Limited Edition (see p.149) there were a number of other special DB7s, first of them being the Beverly Hills, of which just six were made – two coupés and four Volantes. All were finished in midnight blue (with blue hoods on the Volantes) with silver alloy wheels and stainless steel grilles. The interiors were two-tone leather, blue over parchment, and the dashboard was given special wood polished veneer trim including a veneered instrument panel. This special edition DB7 was only available through Aston Martin's dealer in Beverly Hills.

The Dallas, Texas-based department store Neiman Marcus, known for supplying extravagant gifts, offered its own limited edition Volante in its 1998 Christmas gift catalogue. The cars were black with a black mohair roof, chromed mesh grille and chrome-plated wheels. The interiors were in grey Connolly hide with black piping, and there were carbon-fibre dash inserts in place of the standard wood. The Neiman Marcus cars were supplied with a set of black Swaine Adeney

Brigg luggage and a monogrammed car cover, and listed at $148,580.

Stratstone of Mayfair built a limited edition of nineteen customer cars in 1999: nine coupés and ten Volantes. Manual and automatic transmission was offered, most of the cars being automatics. The Stratstone cars had black bodywork and chrome grilles, and interiors in grey hide with charcoal piping, carbon-fibre trim and white instruments.

Stratstone was also behind the GTS and GTS II packages, which were available on new DB7s and as conversions for a customer's own car. The conversion work was carried out at Car Care Works in Bovingdon – also known as Chiltern Aston Centre, a well known DB7 specialist. As the cars were built to order, specifications varied, but typically the cars were fitted with Speedline split-rim wheels, bulged and vented bonnets, an interior with more wood trim and a Garrard analogue clock, and on the GTS II, V8 Vantage-style rear lamps. More than fifty DB7s were converted.

The Neiman Marcus limited edition Volante was offered in the department store's 1998 Christmas gifts catalogue.

DB7 VANTAGE

THE HEART OF the DB7 Vantage, unveiled in 1999, was a V12 engine, which had first been seen in public in mock-up form at the Turin show in 1994. The first prototype engines ran in September 1995, and then the V12 went into the Ford Indigo show car in 1996. It was first seen with Aston Martin badges in 1998 when it appeared alongside Project Vantage at the Detroit show.

The new engine shared much with Ford's light, compact Duratec 3-litre V6, which powered the Ford Taurus/Mercury Sable. Effectively the 5.9-litre V12 was two of these engines siamesed together, though that meant a new block, cylinder heads, camshafts and crankshaft. Cosworth designed the heads

and the block, both of which were quite different to the V6 designs. The V12 block proved to be stiffer than the much shorter V6, a significant engineering feat. Cosworth built the production engines at its factory in Wellingborough, which had first been used to build the famous turbo YB engines for the Sierra Cosworth in the 1980s. In its initial form the V12, which Cosworth knew as the SGA engine, developed 420bhp and 400lb ft from its 5935cc and powered the DB7 Vantage to 185mph (298km/h).

Ian Callum reworked the styling for the DB7 Vantage, enlarging the front grille and inserting combination indicator/fog lamp clusters in the front valance – the lamps being inspired by those

LEFT: **The DB7 Vantage was introduced in 1999 and quickly made the 6-cylinder DB7 redundant.**
BELOW: **In addition to the much larger and more powerful engine, the DB7 Vantage had revised styling and a tidier interior.**

LEFT: **Though superficially similar to the 6-cylinder DB7's interior, the DB7 Vantage cabin included a number of detail enhancements, including new seats and a tidier dashboard.** BELOW: **The DB7 Vantage was powered by a V12 engine that was related to the Ford Taurus SHO V6, first seen in mock-up form in 1994.**

on the 1960s Project cars. The valance itself was reshaped to form a deep skirt, matching the more prominent sills, which made the DB7 Vantage appear closer to the ground. The rear valance was restyled to suit, and housed larger bore exhaust tailpipes. Inside there were numerous detail improvements, notably new seats and a neater dashboard with new switchgear and a red 'engine start' button on the centre console.

The coupé was given stiffer suspension, new front uprights to reduce steering offset, and bigger Brembo brakes with four-piston calipers. A cruciform brace was added under the final drive unit to reduce axle tramp under hard acceleration, and there were bigger wheels with ten blade-like spokes. When the DB7 Vantage entered production in 1999 it was the most comprehensively tested Aston ever, with a two-year development programme during which prototypes covered more than half a million miles.

A year after the DB7 Vantage's debut Aston Martin introduced the option of Touchtronic control for the automatic transmission, which provided steering wheel-mounted gearchange buttons. Developed in conjunction with the German transmission specialist ZF, the system was monitored by a transmission computer, which was linked to the engine management system. It was programmed to detect misuse – such as an attempt to change down into a low gear and too high a speed – and ignore the input.

Although the 6-cylinder DB7 continued in production alongside the DB7 Vantage for a few months, the V12 car quickly took over as the focus of Bloxham production. It was in production for four years, during which time just over 4,000 were built – making it, in sales terms, the most successful Aston Martin the company had yet built.

▪ 1999 DB7 VANTAGE

Engine	V12, Visteon EEC V fuel injection
Valvegear	Twin overhead cam per bank, 4 valves per cylinder
Bore and stroke	89 × 79.5mm
Capacity	5935cc
Power	420bhp @ 6,000rpm
Transmission	Six-speed manual gearbox, or ZF five-speed automatic transmission, limited slip differential rear-wheel drive
Chassis/body	Steel monocoque with composite bumpers, sills, front wings and boot lid
Suspension	Wishbones with coil springs and anti-roll bar front, wishbones with longitudinal control arms, coil springs and anti-roll bar rear
Brakes	Ventilated discs all round, with Teves anti-lock
Performance	Top speed 185mph (298km/h), 0–60mph in 5sec

DB7 VANTAGE VOLANTE

VOLANTE DROPHEAD VERSIONS of previous Astons were usually unveiled months or even years after the appearance of the saloon. It had taken Aston Martin nearly three years following the launch of the 6-cylinder DB7 in 1994 to launch the DB7 Volante that everyone knew would be coming. But with the DB7 Vantage it was a different story, and the Volante was launched alongside the coupé at the Geneva show in 1999.

The DB7 Vantage Volante shared the coupé's Cosworth-built V12 engine and the choice of a six-speed manual or a five-speed automatic gearbox, the latter with the option of Touchtronic control from 2000. The Volante also benefited from the interior improvements and the exterior changes that made all the V12 DB7s look more aggressive – though in the process they perhaps lost a little of the purity and elegance of the original car.

Although the coupé was given stiffer suspension settings, the Volante retained slighter softer springs thus giving a more forgiving ride, a feature that was expected to have greater appeal to a Volante customer. The Volante also lacked the high top

speed of the coupé, not because it developed less power, but because it was electronically limited to 165mph (266km/h) to avoid sealing and reliability issues with the folding roof – but that still made it one of the fastest convertibles money could buy.

The DB7 Vantage Volante was launched at the same time as the saloon in March 1999.

1999 DB7 VANTAGE VOLANTE

Engine	V12, Visteon EEC V fuel injection
Valvegear	Twin overhead cam per bank, 4 valves per cylinder
Bore and stroke	89 × 79.5mm
Capacity	5935cc
Power	420bhp @ 6,000rpm
Transmission	Six-speed manual gearbox or ZF five-speed automatic transmission, limited slip differential rear-wheel drive
Chassis/body	Steel monocoque with composite bumpers, sills, front wings and boot lid
Suspension	Wishbones with coil springs and anti-roll bar front, wishbones with longitudinal control arms, coil springs and anti-roll bar rear
Brakes	Ventilated discs all round, with Teves anti-lock
Performance	Top speed 165mph (266km/h), 0–60mph in 5sec

RDS DB7 GRAND TOURER

IN 2002 WARWICKSHIRE-BASED RDS Automotive built a prototype long-wheelbase DB7 Volante. Designed and built in just five months, the so-called DB7 Grand Tourer had a 6in (150mm) longer wheelbase, the new metal going into the panel behind the doors. This increased rear legroom without making any changes to the rear suspension pick-up points or the fuel tank location.

New rear quarter glasses were needed, along with longer composite sill covers and a redesigned rear bench seat. The exhaust system was extended using original type parts, and there was a new propshaft, both longer and of wider diameter. Otherwise the car was mechanically identical to a DB7 Vantage.

The prototype's bodywork was constructed by Park Sheet Metal in Coventry, and the car was painted by QCR in Nuneaton. RDS offered the conversion for any DB7 – 6-cylinder or V12, Volante or coupé – at a cost of £75,000, which was said at the time to be more per extra centimetre than it had cost to dig the Channel Tunnel!

Although the extra length made a welcome improvement to the rear seat legroom of the DB7, and the overall cost was competitive alongside other four-seat premium coupés and convertibles – such as the £230,000 Bentley Azure – it is believed that the prototype, in black with a grey interior, was the only example of the RDS Grand Tourer to be built.

ABOVE: **RDS built this prototype long-wheelbase DB7 Vantage Volante in 2002. It had a 6in (150mm) increase in wheelbase, which provided much better rear legroom.**
RIGHT: **The long-wheelbase RDS offered much improved interior accommodation, but apparently not one was sold.**

ITALDESIGN TWENTY TWENTY

GIORGETTO GIUGIARO, ONE of Italy's greatest car designers and the creative genius behind the Italdesign company, unveiled his vision for an Aston Martin roadster of 2020 in 2001.

The Twenty Twenty, designed by Giugiaro and his son Fabrizio, was considerably shorter than a standard DB7, most of the

ABOVE: **The Twenty Twenty blended interior leather and wood with aluminium.**
BELOW: **ItalDesign's Twenty Twenty of 2001 was the company's idea of an Aston Martin for 2020.**

difference being taken from the front and rear overhangs. It built on the themes of exposed technical components that Giugiaro had previously explored in his Alfasud Capsula in 1982 and VW V12-engined Structura in 1998. The car was built around an exposed extruded aluminium frame with a brushed finish, which contrasted with the painted composite body panels. The engine, an Aston V12 said to develop 500bhp, was clearly visible through grilles in the bonnet. Even the metal strip over the wing vent, which could easily be dismissed as no more than a visual feature, had a real function: it formed the exposed top hinge for the door.

The Twenty Twenty was a two-plus-two, with a pair of tiny rear seats hidden under a cover. It had a removable roof panel that slotted in between the fixed roll-over bar and the top of the windscreen surround, which was fitted with air deflectors to minimize turbulence around the passengers' heads during fast open-top motoring. The interior blended traditional leather and wood with aluminium elements in an unusual and attractive mixture.

The motoring press was quick to spot the connection between Giugiaro and Aston Martin CEO Ulrich Bez – Italdesign had worked on a number of projects for Daewoo when Bez was technical director – and to suggest that the Twenty Twenty could offer clues to the future direction of Aston Martin design. But in the decade since the Twenty Twenty was unveiled there have been no more Italdesign Astons.

DB7 V12 SPECIALS

L IKE THE DB7 i6 before it, the V12 spawned a number of special editions and a series of in-house upgrades from Works Service.

First of the special editions was the Jubilee of 2002, produced to celebrate the fiftieth year of Queen Elizabeth II's reign. All twenty-four were Touchtronic autos, eleven saloons and thirteen Volantes, most of them supplied in right-hand drive. Each one was finished in a unique Jubilee blue with wide-mesh stainless steel grille, chromed mirrors, clear indicator repeaters and silver brake calipers, with a magnolia leather interior. There were white-faced instruments, and special Italian walnut veneer dashboard panels. Each one was supplied with a limited-edition chronograph watch, an electric watch winder and even a special umbrella.

The Keswick was created for the Lancaster dealer group (of which Henry Keswick was chairman). Just ten of these metallic black cars were made, all with black interiors trimmed with silver piping and aluminium dash panels.

The Anniversary Edition of 100 cars marked the tenth anniversary of the DB7's Geneva show debut in 1993. Available in Caspian blue and Arctic blue, the Anniversary had Touchtronic automatic transmission, fluted leather seats, powerfold mirrors, satellite navigation (satnav) and a premium sound system.

Works Service at Newport Pagnell continued to offer some of the enhancements it had developed for the 6-cylinder DB7, and created some new ones specifically for the V12 car. The rear seats could be replaced by either a luggage platform (complete with retaining straps and cargo net) or a secure storage box. White instruments and alternative wood trim were offered, along with a satellite navigation system, front and rear parking sensors, and V8 Vantage-style circular rear lamps. There was an alternative design of 19in, nine-spoke alloy wheel, and Works Service could also offer DB7 GT-style bodywork, brake, wheel and gearshift enhancements. DB7s with these modifications often carried discreet 'Works Prepared' badges.

Like the 6-cylinder DB7 before it, the V12 spawned a series of special edition cars, and bespoke specifications were built by Works Service.

DB7 GT AND GTA

THE DB7 GT was introduced, Aston Martin said, because some customers were asking for 'more performance, increased driver involvement and improved road handling'. This car was a DB7 Vantage with the emphasis more on perform-ance and driver appeal than civility and refinement, and the changes included aerodynamic revisions, suspension changes and uprated brakes, plus a little more power.

The GT's performance mien was obvious from the revised body shape. The grille and lower air intake gained bright mesh stone guards, though that was just for show. More significantly there were air exit vents in the bonnet to allow hot air out of the engine bay and, at the back, the boot lid had been reshaped to provide a pronounced spoiler lip. The aerodynamic changes extended to unseen parts of the car such as the wheel arch liners (which were extended) and the undertray (which was reshaped). The aero tweaks cut the rear end lift by almost 50 per cent at high speed, making the DB7 GT much more stable.

The suspension changes were carried out in conjunction with John Miles, a respected ride and handling engineer who had worked for Lotus for many years, and had been involved with the development of the Vanquish. Miles also raced for Lotus in sports cars and, briefly, in Formula 1. One of the most signif-icant changes wrought on the GT suspension was a move to digressive damping, where the rate of increase in damping force

The DB7 GT of 2002 had more power, and revised attention to both the running gear and the aerodynamics.

was reduced at higher speeds of wheel movement. This meant the GT could use stiffer damper settings for excellent body control without the harshness that a stiff linear-rate damper would have induced. Further suspension changes included relo-cated damper mountings and bump stops, stiffer bushes, and improved wishbone location. The steering-rack mounting was beefed up for more positive steering with better feel.

The GT used the same diameter wheels as the DB7 Vantage, but they had new five-spoke rims that took wider Bridgestone tyres. Inside these were Brembo brake discs that were grooved rather than cross-drilled, and which were acted on by silver calipers carrying Pagid RS42-1 brake pads, as these were said to offer better resistance to fade and judder when braking from high speeds.

The V12 engine in the GT was largely the same as in the DB7 Vantage, but there was a new 'active' exhaust system like that fitted to the Vanquish, which bypassed the rear silencers above 3,500rpm to reduce back pressure. The engine was given recal-ibrated fuel and ignition mapping to take advantage of the freer-breathing exhaust, resulting in an increase of power from 420bhp to 435bhp, and a rise in maximum torque from 400lb ft to 410lb ft. A new twin-plate AP Racing clutch ensured that the extra power could be handled reliably, and also offered a reduction in pedal effort compared to the DB7 Vantage. The six-speed manual gearbox was the same, but a lower final drive ensured that the gearing was shorter. A 'quick shift' gear linkage was fitted to reduce the throw of the lever. A GTA automatic was also available, but this retained the 420bhp Vantage engine.

Just over 300 DB7 GT/GTA models were built in 2002/3.

ABOVE: **The reprofiled tail of the DB7 GT helped to cut rear-end lift by 50 per cent, making it much more stable at speed.**

RIGHT: **The cabin of the DB7 GT, with six-speed manual gearbox. A GTA automatic was offered with the same body and running gear enhancements, but a lower-rated engine.**

■ 2002 DB7 GT/GTA

Engine	V12, Visteon EEC V fuel injection
Valvegear	Twin overhead cam per bank, 4 valves per cylinder
Bore and stroke	89 × 79.5mm
Capacity	5935cc
Power	GT: 435bhp @ 6,000rpm, GTA: 420bhp @ 6,000rpm
Transmission	GT: Six-speed manual gearbox; GTA: ZF five-speed automatic transmission with Touchtronic control. Limited slip differential, rear-wheel drive
Chassis/body	Steel monocoque with composite bumpers, sills, front wings and boot lid
Suspension	Wishbones with coil springs and anti-roll bar front, wishbones with longitudinal control arms, coil springs and anti-roll bar rear
Brakes	Ventilated discs all round, with Teves anti-lock
Performance	GT: Top speed 185mph (298km/h), 0–62mph in 5sec

DB7 ZAGATO

LIKE THE V8 Vantage Zagato of the 1980s, the DB7 Zagato was the result of a chance meeting between Zagato and Aston Martin principals. This time the venue was the Pebble Beach Concours d'Élégance in 2001, where Aston Martin CEO Dr Ulrich Bez and Andrea Zagato, grandson of company founder Ugo, were both acting as judges. Soon the two men formulated a plan for a new Zagato Aston, based on the DB7 platform.

The new Aston/Zagato partnership was officially announced at the Geneva show in March 2002, by which time work was already well advanced on the shape of the new car: Zagato designer Nori Harada was working with the new Aston Martin design director Henrik Fisker on a lithe, two-seater coupé with more muscular lines than the standard DB7. It was built on a wheelbase 2.4in (60mm) shorter than standard, and thanks to short overhangs front and rear, the Zagato was 8.3in (211mm) shorter overall.

The twin intakes of the DB7 nose were replaced by a single large grille, which still had a recognizable Aston Martin shape. Early drawings showed 'stacked' headlamps, but the final car reverted to standard DB7 Vantage headlamps and auxiliary light clusters. The glass area was smaller than the standard DB7, and

ABOVE: **The DB7 Zagato marked a new chapter in the relationship between Aston Martin and Zagato. It was lighter and more powerful than the regular DB7, and had a little more power.**
LEFT: **The DB7 Zagato had its own quilted leather trim, but was otherwise similar to the regular DB7.**

the window line, particularly where the corner of the rear quarter window met the corner of the rear window, had a distinctly DB4GT Zagato feel.

The Zagato was based on the heavier but stiffer Volante structure, with largely unstressed bodywork hand-made in aluminium, though the sill covers and aprons front and rear were composite. As a result it was only about 130lb (60kg) lighter than the standard DB7, when a greater weight advantage might have been expected. The most eye-catching feature of the Zagato was the double-bubble roof – which was steel – and a matching compound, curved rear window. In place of a conventional boot lid there was a simple drop-down flap in the tail. The interior was much the same as the standard DB7, but usually trimmed in dark brown aniline leather with a quilted pattern and embossed Zagato 'Z' motifs.

The running gear for the new car was much the same as the DB7 Vantage, with revised damping, which was said to optimize the handling, and uprated Pagid brake pads as used on the DB7 GT. The engine also came from the DB7 GT, with 15bhp more than the DB7 Vantage fed through an AP Racing twin-plate clutch to the usual six-speed manual gearbox, which was fitted with GT-style quick-shift linkage. There was no auto option.

Initially a run of seventy-five cars was planned, with up to ninety-nine to be built if the reaction was positive. After a sneak preview at the Pebble Beach concours in August 2002 and an official launch at the Paris show the following month, Aston Martin received more than 200 serious enquiries, and the full production run was sanctioned. In fact 100 production cars were built, although only ninety-nine were customer cars – the last one was retained by Aston Martin, and has been displayed at the Heritage Motor Centre in Gaydon.

■ 2002 DB7 ZAGATO

Engine	V12, Visteon EEC V fuel injection
Valvegear	Twin overhead cam per bank, 4 valves per cylinder
Bore and stroke	89 × 79.5mm
Capacity	5935cc
Power	435bhp @ 6,000rpm
Transmission	Six-speed manual gearbox, limited slip differential, rear-wheel drive
Chassis/body	Steel monocoque with aluminium and composite panels
Suspension	Wishbones with coil springs and anti-roll bar front, wishbones with longitudinal control arms, coil springs and anti-roll bar rear
Brakes	Ventilated discs all round, with Teves anti-lock
Performance	Top speed 185mph (298km/h), 0–62mph in 4.8sec (approx)

The DB7 Zagato featured the classic Zagato 'double-bubble' roof, and the shape extended backwards into the rear window.

DB AMERICAN ROADSTER I

WHEN ANDREA ZAGATO and Ulrich Bez met again at the Pebble Beach Concours in 2002, where the prototype DB7 Zagato made its first public appearance, Bez enthused about driving an Aston DBR1 at Le Mans in the summer. From that conversation came the idea to create not a convertible Aston but a genuine no-compromise roadster, based on the DB7 Zagato.

It was called the DB American Roadster 1, and was aimed at customers in the dry states of the USA. Although it looked much the same as the DB7 Zagato from some angles, it had certain major differences. To start with, it was built on the standard DB7 wheelbase, not the shortened wheelbase used for the Zagato. It had a longer, reshaped tail with a proper boot lid, longer doors and reshaped front wings. The nose was also different, with cooling ducts added under the main grille. There was no roof, just a double-cowled rear deck which echoed the shape of the Zagato's roof.

The DB AR1 was available with the 435bhp GT/Zagato engine and six-speed Tremec manual gearbox, or with the standard 420bhp engine and five-speed ZF automatic with Touchtronic control. Again, a run of ninety-nine customer cars was built, each one costing about $230,000 (£136,000 at the time).

The DB AR1 appeared to be little more than a DB7 Zagato with the roof removed – but there were subtle changes to the rest of the body, too.

■ 2002 DB AR1

Engine	V12, Visteon EEC V fuel injection
Valvegear	Twin overhead cam per bank, 4 valves per cylinder
Bore and stroke	89 × 79.5mm
Capacity	5935cc
Power	manual 435bhp @ 6,000rpm; auto 420bhp @ 6,000rpm
Transmission	Six-speed manual gearbox, or ZF five-speed automatic transmission with Touchtronic control, limited slip differential, rear-wheel drive
Chassis/body	Steel monocoque with composite bumpers, sills, front wings and boot lid
Suspension	Wishbones with coil springs and anti-roll bar front, wishbones with longitudinal control arms, coil springs and anti-roll bar rear
Brakes	Ventilated discs all round, with Teves anti-lock
Performance	Top speed 185mph (298km/h), 0–62mph in 5sec

THE GAYDON ERA

The 2011 Aston Martin Virage shows off its V12 engine.
The Virage plugged a gap between the DB9 and DBS.

2000–2012
AND BEYOND

A new factory at Gaydon in Warwickshire, next door to Jaguar and Land
Rover, took over from Newport Pagnell as Aston Martin's headquarters.

ROYAL AIR FORCE Gaydon was one of the hundreds of airfields established across Britain during World War II. In the 1950s it was remodelled, with a 2-mile (3km) runway for the new generation of V-bombers, and acted as a training base until the 1970s. In 1978 it became the home of BL Technology, which developed the site as a vehicle test track and built a number of test facilities, including a wind tunnel. In 1994 control of Gaydon passed to BMW, and the site was sold to Ford along with Land Rover in 2000.

Later that year Aston Martin – now led by a new chief executive, the ex-Porsche, ex-BMW Dr Ulrich Bez – announced its intention to build a new factory at Gaydon. There were plans for a third Aston Martin model line, and there was not enough space at either Newport Pagnell or Bloxham to establish a factory of the size required. The Gaydon site ultimately became Aston Martin's headquarters, providing the company's main production facility and accommodating the engineering team, which had swelled to more than 200 people, along with all the other functions of a car company. The Wykham Mill factory at Bloxham was closed when DB7 production ended, but Newport Pagnell continued as home to Works Service, and as the production base for the V12 Vanquish.

The first Aston Martin to be made at Gaydon was the DB7's successor, the DB9, launched in 2003. This was also the first Aston to use the 'vertical/horizontal' or 'VH' platform, a bonded aluminium structure that would form the basis for the next generation of Aston Martins. The VH structure was seen again in 2005, when that third Aston model – the V8 Vantage – was revealed at the Geneva show. The 4.3-litre V8 engine (related to a Jaguar unit, but comprehensively re-engineered) was built alongside the V12s at a new engine plant at Niehl in Cologne, which had opened in October 2004.

At about the same time Aston Martin announced a return to sports car racing with the DBR9 GT1 car, based on the DB9: this won its class first time out at the Sebring 12-hours in March 2005. At Le Mans that year, where the DBR9 finished third in class, Aston Martin announced a less extreme DBRS9 car for GT2-class competition.

By then, Aston Martin's owner, Ford, was sustaining heavy losses and coming under increasing pressure to concentrate on its core businesses. Under new chairman Alan Mulally, Ford sought to divest itself of the expensive, high-profile brands it had formed into the Premier Automotive Group: Volvo, Jaguar, Land Rover, Lincoln and Mercury in addition to Aston Martin. In

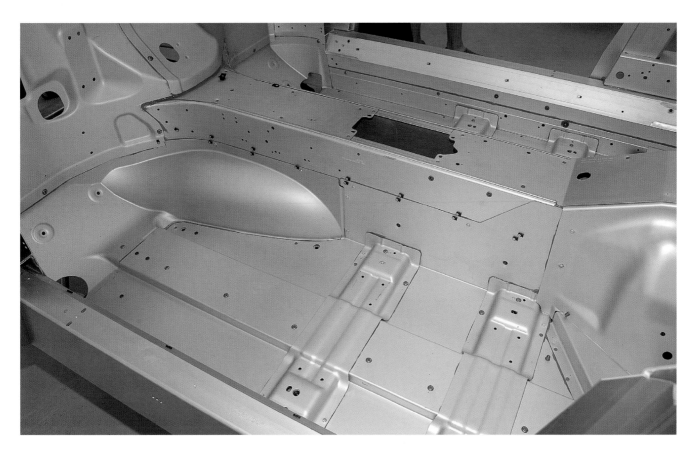

Aston Martin's new family of cars used the 'VH' platform – a highly
adaptable structure made from bonded and riveted aluminium.

Aston Martin returned to racing as a works team with the **DBR9**
GT1 car in 2005. The car won its class first time out at Sebring.

In early 2007 Ford sold Aston Martin to a consortium led by David Richards (*left*). Ulrich Bez (*right*) stayed on as CEO.

early 2007 Ford sold Aston Martin to a consortium of investors led by Prodrive founder David Richards, who became the company's chairman.

Once again, therefore, Aston Martin was a tiny independent company instead of a division of a global conglomerate. But in contrast to previous changes of ownership, Aston Martin went into this new era with a strong image and a competitive and growing range. In 2007 the DBS was announced: a high-performance derivative of the DB9, it quickly became the latest in a long line of Aston Martins to become the preferred transport for the silver screen secret agent James Bond. The DBS took over as Aston Martin's most exclusive, and expensive, model when production of the Vanquish ended in July 2007 – bringing to an end more than forty years of Aston Martin production at Newport Pagnell.

The model range expanded further in 2009 when the biggest Aston engine – the 5.9-litre V12 – was dropped into the smallest body, that of the V8 Vantage, to create a new V12 Vantage. A new four-door Aston Martin – not Lagonda – called the Rapide was announced the same year. Rapide became the first production Aston Martin to be built outside the UK: it was assembled in Austria by the specialist manufacturer Magna Steyr as there was no spare capacity at Gaydon. Although the Rapide carried an Aston badge, the Lagonda marque did make a reappearance, albeit in concept form, when a four-wheel-drive

vehicle was shown at the Geneva salon in 2009. It seems likely that the Lagonda marque will return as a fully fledged production car in the future.

Meanwhile, Aston Martin has expanded its range still further with cars that have taken it into brand new market areas. The most unlikely and most controversial car in Aston Martin's history was the Cygnet, which went on sale in 2011 – a restyled and retrimmed Toyota iQ city car. The Cygnet polarized opinion: some saw it as a necessary and praiseworthy step for a premium car maker in an environmentally conscious age, others as the cynical exploitation of the brand, which could only do long-term harm.

At the other end of the scale Aston Martin introduced a car that caused far less debate: the breathtaking £1m One-77 was a carbon monocoque supercar, which became the fastest road-going Aston Martin ever made. It was also destined to be one of the rarest, with a production run of just seventy-seven.

As Aston Martin heads into its centenary year it faces the task of refreshing its core model range, but without having the resources of Ford to back up its development plans. And like every other supercar manufacturer, it will have to deal with rising fuel and ownership costs, and the impact of a range of new automotive technologies. But in its new guise it is a bold independent, not afraid to take risks – and that might be just what Aston Martin's future needs.

AMV8 VANTAGE CONCEPT (AM305)

IAN CALLUM HAD been working on a possible mid-engined Aston before he moved to Jaguar full time in 1999, but the arrival of new CEO Ulrich Bez at Aston Martin in 2000 heralded a change of direction. The development of a new small Aston Martin, codenamed AM305, began that year, with the emphasis on a traditional front engine/rear drive layout.

The result was revealed in January 2003 in the form of a concept car known as the AMV8 Vantage. The new car blended classic curves and traditional Aston styling cues into a crisp Noughties shape, which Aston Martin described as a 'muscular athlete wearing a tailor-made suit'. Drawn up by new Aston design director Henrik Fisker, the AMV8 Vantage was 12in (300mm) shorter than Aston's existing models and considerably lighter. It had only two seats, plus a useful boot accessed through a hatchback rear door. Inside, the attractive interior of the concept was swathed in leather and featured bright metal finishes for a modern look. The switchgear and instrumentation were influenced by the design of contemporary high-end watches and hi-fi.

Power came from a 4.3-litre V8, though at this stage Aston Martin declined to reveal any further details of the engine – including its power output. The engine was mounted as far back as possible in the engine bay for a 'front/mid-engined' layout, said to provide almost exactly fifty/fifty weight distribution. The gearbox was at the back of the car in unit with the rear axle, and connected to the engine by a torque tube. The whole car was based on the new 'VH' platform, which it was said would feature in all future Aston Martins.

The AMV8 concept led directly to the V8 Vantage production car, though that would not make its debut until 2005.

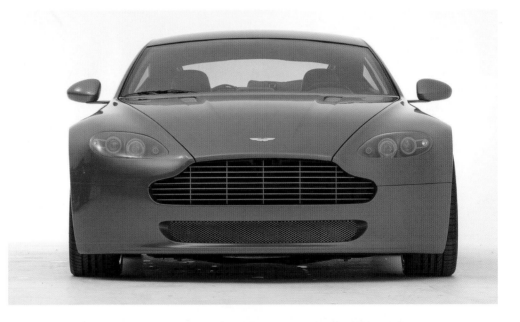

RIGHT: **The AMV8 concept, styled by Henrik Fisker, was unveiled in 2003.**
BELOW: **The AMV8 concept was the forerunner of the V8 Vantage production car, which followed two years later.**

DB9

THE REPLACEMENT FOR the DB7 Vantage was the DB9, which was announced at the Frankfurt show in 2003 and went on sale the following spring. In some ways it was a very familiar machine, carrying over the V12 engine from the DB7 Vantage and incorporating the traditional Aston Martin styling cues into its shape. But the DB9 was also a very different car to the Astons that had come before: it introduced an entirely new structure, and it was built in a brand new factory.

The first Gaydon-built Aston was also the first to use the company's 'vertical/horizontal' or VH platform, a structure adaptable enough to be used for all Aston Martin's future models. The new structure was fabricated using die-cast, extruded and stamped aluminium alloy components, which were bonded together using structural adhesives, and mechanically fixed using self-piercing rivets. The aluminium roof and rear wings were bonded to this structure, the adhesive being applied by Aston

The DB9 replaced the DB7 in 2004. It used a similar V12 engine to the older car, but a new aluminium structure based on the VH platform.

The DB9 continued the styling themes begun by Ian Callum with the Vanquish, incorporating classic Aston Martin elements such as the grille shape and side vents.

The 'swan wing' doors of the DB9 were designed to rise as they opened, to avoid high kerbs.

Martin's only robot – quickly nicknamed the 'James Bonder'. The two-part C-pillar was joined using an ultrasonic welding process, which was much stronger than conventional spot welding and used less energy, a motor-industry first for Aston Martin.

The bonnet was aluminium, but like the DB7, the DB9 had composite front wings. The boot lid was another composite panel, while the windscreen surround was an aluminium casting – another technological first for the new Aston. Aluminium castings were also used for the subframes, which carried the suspension; the latter had forged aluminium wishbones and aluminium-bodied dampers front and rear. 'Flow-formed' alloy wheels saved 1kg (2.2lb) per corner compared to conventional cast-alloy wheels. The brakes used grooved discs with monobloc calipers, supplemented by electronic anti-lock, brake-assist and brake-distribution systems connected by a state-of-the-art multiplex electrical system.

The V12 engine was largely the same as that in the DB7 Vantage and Vanquish, but was retuned for a broader spread of torque throughout the engine speed range at the expense of a little top end power – not that its 450bhp could be thought of as inadequate. The V12 drove through a carbon-fibre propshaft inside an aluminium torque tube to a transaxle – the gearbox was mounted in unit with the final drive, its rearward position helping to deliver near-perfect weight distribution. DB9 customers could choose from two six-speed transmissions, a Graziano manual and a ZF Touchtronic automatic: this had no control lever, instead being operated by buttons and magnesium-alloy gearchange paddles behind the steering wheel.

The two-plus-two interior was an attractive mixture of traditional wood and leather with aluminium accents, hand crafted with Aston Martin's typical care and attention to detail. There was more evidence of careful detailing in the design of the 'swan

Ulrich Bez presents the DB9 Volante to the press at its launch early in 2004.

LEFT: **In the event of a rollover, roll hoops automatically extended from the rear head-restraints, improving passenger protection without compromising the DB9 Volante's looks.**
BELOW: **The DB9 Volante had a tidier hood arrangement than its predecessor, making it a much more stylish machine when the roof was lowered.**

wing' doors, which had angled hinges so they rose up at an angle of 12 degrees to avoid kerbs. Once the doors were open beyond 20 degrees an 'infinite door-checking' function held them wherever they were released. LEDs incorporated into the door handles lit up when the car was unlocked so the handles were easy to find in the dark.

The rest of the exterior followed lines similar to the Vanquish, with the emphasis on fuss-free elegance: cut lines were minimized, the front lamps were all set in a single cluster, and there was no separate nose cone as there had been on the DB7 – instead the bonnet stretched to the very front of the car, emphasizing the length of the nose.

Aerodynamic testing in Ford's environmental test lab at Dunton was just one example of Aston Martin making the most of the resources available to it. Volvo engineers contributed to the design of the car's structure to improve crash performance, and carried out crash tests on DB9 prototypes in Sweden. Aston Martin built ninety-three DB9 prototypes, which were tested all over the world – including at Ford's test facility in Lommel, Belgium.

The DB9 was a vital new car for Aston Martin, as it would have to be one of the company's mainstay models for the following decade. It proved to be one of the stars of the Frankfurt show in 2003, and was received very positively by the motoring press. Just a few weeks later, at the Detroit show in early 2004, there was more big DB9 news with the launch of a Volante drophead. Despite the increasing popularity of folding metal roof systems for open cars, Aston Martin stuck to a traditional cloth roof, which was lighter and folded more compactly. In the DB9 the roof folded out of sight in just seventeen seconds, leaving an uncluttered rear deck, which added to the Volante's elegant look. In the event of a rollover, roll hoops automatically extended from the rear head-restraints.

If there was any criticism at all of the DB9 it was that it lacked the fine edge of sharpness to its handling that some customers were looking for – a deliberate choice when the car was developed, of course, as the DB9 was intended to be a grand tourer rather than the ultimate race-track machine. But for those who wanted a sharper DB9, Aston Martin introduced the Sports Pack in 2006, with stiffer suspension and lighter wheels. It could be applied to new cars or retro-fitted to older DB9s by Works Service; it was not, however, available on the Volante. The Sports Pack was standard on the Le Mans Special Edition DB9 (which celebrated the DBR9's GT1 class win at Le Mans in 2007), along with special Magnum silver paint and red interior trim highlights.

For the 2009 model year the DB9 was given an 'emotion control unit' in place of the conventional starter button, a stiffer structure, revised suspension using Bilstein dampers, and a retuned engine with 470bhp. A Premium Sports Pack with adaptive damping from the DBS was offered until 2010, when adaptive damping was adopted as standard, along with a host of other detail changes – the biggest single upgrade the DB9

had been given since production began. Included in the new specification was a revised valance with reshaped air intakes and hexagon mesh stone guards, new sill panels, new lights, new wheels, silver brake calipers, a tyre-pressure monitoring system and new Bang & Olufsen hifi options.

The revisions helped to keep the DB9 fresh as it entered the final few years of production. In sales terms it will be remembered as one of the most successful Aston models ever, with more than 14,000 built to date. It was the car that established Aston Martin in its new era at Gaydon as a serious player in the bespoke sports car market.

■ 2004 DB9

Engine	V12, fuel injection
Valvegear	Twin overhead cam per bank, 4 valves per cylinder
Bore and stroke	89 × 79.5mm
Capacity	5935cc
Power	450bhp @ 6,000rpm
Transmission	Six-speed manual transmission, or six-speed Touchtronic automatic, limited slip differential, rear-wheel drive
Chassis/body	Extruded aluminium 'VH' structure with aluminium alloy and composite panels
Suspension	Double wishbones, coil springs, anti-roll bar and monotube dampers front and rear
Brakes	Ventilated discs all round, with anti-lock
Performance	Top speed 190mph (306km/h), 0–60mph in 4.8sec

The DB9 was a fast touring car rather than an extreme sports car, which meant its ride and handling balance erred towards the side of comfort. Suspension upgrades were later made available for drivers who wanted sharper handling.

DBR9

ASTON MARTIN HAD been absent from its traditional motor sport arena, sports car racing, since the death of the AMR project in 1989. In 2004 it announced a return with a new car, the DBR9, based on the road-going DB9 and developed by Aston Martin Racing, a joint venture between Gaydon and the Banbury-based Prodrive group.

The DBR9 was built to the FIA GT1 racing regulations, using the DB9's VH aluminium structure augmented by a strong steel roll cage. The roof was aluminium alloy, but the rest of the body panels were in lightweight carbon-fibre composite materials, with a flat underside and massive carbon-fibre rear wing. The

DBR9 was 100mm wider than its roadgoing cousin thanks to extended wheel arches covering massive forged magnesium alloy OZ Racing wheels, the front pair having carbon brake discs and six-pot Brembo calipers. Power came from a V12 engine based on the road car unit and developing 600bhp and well over 500lb ft of torque, despite the mandatory twin 31.2mm air restrictors. Power was fed via a four-plate carbon clutch to a six-speed Xtrac transaxle. The whole machine weighed in at 1,100kg (2,425lb), about a third lighter than a DB9 road car.

The DBR9 made its race debut at the Sebring 12-hours in March 2005, where the leading Aston finished fourth overall and

LEFT: **The DBR9 battled the mighty Corvettes at Le Mans from 2005 onwards, but had to settle for second best until 2007.**
BELOW: **Johnny Herbert doughnuts a DBR9 for the crowd at a Prodrive open day. The DBR9 was developed by Aston Martin Racing, a partnership between Aston Martin and Prodrive.**

LEFT: **Detail of the DBR9's engine bay. The production-based V12 engine produced around 600bhp.**
BELOW: **In 2008 the DBR9 ran in the famous blue and orange colours of Gulf Oil, and repeated its class win at Le Mans.**

beat the GT1 Corvettes to win its class in the hands of Darren Turner, David Brabham and Stéphane Ortelli. Peter Kox, Pedro Lamy and Stéphane Sarrazin were fifteenth overall in the sister car. In May, Aston Martin went to Silverstone for the RAC Tourist Trophy, which Kox and Lamy won outright, heading an Aston one-two ahead of Brabham and Turner, and a gaggle of privately entered Maseratis. Spirits were high ahead of the Le Mans 24-hours, where the Astons led their class for most of the race before hitting trouble late on, though Brabham, Sarrazin and Turner did claim third in class for the DBR9. At Spa the Astons finished fifth and sixth behind Maseratis and Ferraris, then in October they competed in two American Le Mans Series (ALMS) races, finishing behind Corvettes on both occasions.

In 2006 the DBR9 was campaigned by several customer teams in addition to the Prodrive-operated works team. Le Mans was the most important event, but again the Astons were beaten by the Corvettes. In 2007 the works team put all its efforts into the Sarthe classic and were rewarded with a famous class win, Brabham and Turner teaming up with Rickard Rydell to finish first overall ahead of the leading Corvette. The DBR9 won its class at Le Mans again the following year, this time in Gulf colours, finishing ten laps down on the Aston-engined Charouz Lola.

While Aston Martin Racing now concentrates on the Lola-based LMP1 cars, the DBR9 is still campaigned in a variety of series by private entrants. Thanks to the DBR9 and its cousin the DBRS9, there have been more Astons in sports car racing over the last few years than at any time since the 1950s.

■ 2005 DBR9

Engine	V12, fuel injection with Pectel ECU
Valvegear	Twin overhead cam per bank, 4 valves per cylinder
Bore and stroke	Not quoted
Capacity	5935cc
Power	600bhp (approx)
Transmission	Xtrac six-speed manual transmission with four-plate carbon clutch, limited slip differential, rear-wheel drive
Chassis/body	Extruded aluminium 'VH' structure with aluminium roof and composite panels, steel roll cage
Suspension	Double wishbones, coil springs, anti-roll bar and monotube dampers front and rear
Brakes	Ventilated discs all round, with anti-lock
Performance	Top speed 196mph (313km/h), 0–60mph in 3sec (approx)

V8 VANTAGE

TWO YEARS ELAPSED between the AMV8 Vantage show car and the final production car – which, despite suggestions that it might be called DB8, was given the name V8 Vantage. The Cool Yellow car was unveiled at the Geneva show in 2005, and then made its first British public appearance at the St George's Day Aston Martin parade at Windsor. Its styling closely followed that show car, which had been very warmly received, and there was already a waiting list stretching into years for the new £83,000 two-seater.

Based on the same all-aluminium VH structure as the DB9, the V8 Vantage used a combination of aluminium alloy, steel and composites for its body panels. The front wings were composite mouldings, made using a resin transfer moulding (RTM) process developed by Ford Research and Nottingham University. The process provided an excellent surface finish and optimum strength for the weight of the panel. The body sides were pressed in steel because that material allowed the use of a single panel rather than several, and this meant the rear quarter area looked neater. The doors had cast magnesium alloy frames, while the windscreen frame was a single aluminium alloy casting, as on the DB9. It all added up to a lightweight car, but one that Aston Martin claimed had class-leading rigidity.

The Vantage was powered by a new V8 engine, based on the Jaguar AJ-V8 design but sharing no major parts with the Jaguar unit. The Aston V8 featured race-style dry-sump lubrication, which allowed the height of the engine to be reduced and ensured perfect delivery of lubricant even under hard cornering. The four-cam, 32-valve V8 featured variable cam phasing, adjusting the timing of the inlet camshaft to optimize gas flow throughout the engine speed range. As a result the 4.3-litre engine developed 380bhp at 7,000rpm and a healthy 302lb ft at 5,000rpm. The new V8 was mounted a long way back in the engine bay – Aston Martin described it as a 'front mid-engine' configuration – and drove through a carbon-fibre propshaft and an alloy torque tube to a gearbox mounted in unit with the final drive, which incorporated a limited slip differential. The combination of the set back engine location and rear-mounted transmission gave the V8 Vantage almost perfect fifty/fifty weight distribution.

Suspension was the same layout at all four corners: double wishbones with coil springs wrapped around aluminium monotube dampers. There were anti-roll bars front and rear, and ventilated steel disc brakes all round: 355mm grooved discs at the front and flat-faced 330mm discs at the rear. The parking brake used separate calipers, operating on the rear discs. The V8 Vantage also had a Teves stability control system, which incorporated anti-lock braking, electronic brake force distribution, traction control, brake assist and dynamic stability control.

A smiling Ulrich Bez climbs into the V8 Vantage on its British public debut, at the 2005 St George's Day parade of Aston Martins at Windsor Castle.

As standard the car wore ten-spoke, 18in wheels that were 8.5in wide at the front and 9.5in wide at the rear, but there was the option of seven-spoke 19in wheels in the same widths, all wrapped in Bridgestone Potenza high-performance tyres.

Minor changes were made early in 2006, the start of a busy year for the V8 Vantage. At the Los Angeles show Aston Martin unveiled the inevitable convertible version, known as the Roadster (not Volante), which used thicker gauge aluminium alloy and extra strengthening webs in its chassis to ensure that it still had good torsional stiffness despite lacking a fixed roof. The Roadster also had detail changes to its suspension. Later that year Aston Martin announced the option of a Prodrive-developed Sportshift robotized manual transmission, which offered clutchless manual shifting using paddles behind the steering wheel or fully automatic operation.

■ 2005 V8 VANTAGE 4.3

Engine	V8, fuel injection
Valvegear	Twin overhead cam per bank, 4 valves per cylinder
Bore and stroke	89 × 86mm
Capacity	4280cc
Power	380bhp @ 7,000rpm
Transmission	Six-speed manual transaxle, limited slip differential, rear-wheel drive
Chassis/body	Extruded aluminium 'VH' structure with steel, aluminium alloy and composite panels
Suspension	Double wishbones, coil springs, anti-roll bar and monotube dampers front and rear
Brakes	Ventilated discs all round, with anti-lock
Performance	Top speed 175mph (280km/h), 0–62mph in 5sec

RIGHT: **Like all modern Astons, the V8 was painstakingly developed. It was the first Aston to use a new V8 engine, based on a Jaguar design – although the two engines shared no major parts.**
BELOW: **Aston Martin unveiled a convertible V8 Vantage – known as the Roadster, not Volante – in Los Angeles early in 2006.**

DBRS9

UNVEILED DURING THE Le Mans weekend in 2005, the DBRS9 was built for club and national GT racing, and potentially as a machine for well heeled track-day enthusiasts.

'There are many people who want to race Aston Martins competitively in everything from the occasional track day to weekend club or national series races,' said David Richards at the time. 'The DBRS9 opens up GT racing to more enthusiasts, and with its levels of performance will offer aspiring racing drivers the experience of a GT racing car without the complexity associated with running a full GT1 car.'

Although the DBRS9 shares much with the hardcore DBR9 racing car, it costs considerably less at around £200,000 compared with the £500,000-plus of its big brother. The DBRS9 shares its VH structure and aluminium roof with the DBR9 and DB9, and is fitted with a full roll cage similar to that in the DBR9. The DBR9 had fixed steering wheel and seat positions to save weight, but in the DBRS9 both could be adjusted easily to suit different drivers. The DBRS9 could also be supplied with a passenger seat for demonstration drives.

The bodywork is also similar to the GT1 car, every panel except the roof being a carbon-fibre composite moulding. The body panels were designed to be removable to make servicing and damage repair quicker and easier. The side and rear windows were polycarbonate to save weight. Overall the DBRS9 was a substantial 450kg (990lb) lighter than the DB9 road car, but still 180kg (397lb) heavier than the DBR9.

Power came from a tuned version of the DB9's 5.9-litre V12 engine, delivering 550bhp and 457lb ft of torque, substantially more than the DB9 but inevitably less than the heavily reworked V12 in the DBR9. Even so, the DBRS9 was said to hit 60mph (96km/h) from rest in four seconds and 100mph (160km/h) in nine, thanks in part to short gear ratios in the conventional H-pattern manual gearbox. A full sequential racing transmission was available as an optional extra, which benefited performance and reliability at the same time.

The DBRS9 competed in the new FIA European GT3 championship from 2006. The car's first win came when a pair of DBRS9s, run by BMS Scuderia Italia, finished first and second in the second race at Oschersleben, and there were more good performances by that team and Barwell Motorsport at Spa and Dijon later in the year. BMS Scuderia Italia won again with the DBRS9 in the last race of the 2007 season in Dubai, while Barwell Motorsport ran its car in the British GT championship and notched up wins at Donington, Snetterton and Thruxton, giving Barwell the team championship. The DBRS9 continued to win races in the FIA European GT3 championship in 2008 and 2009, and gained numerous points placings.

For the 2011 season Barwell entered a new DBRS9, now with Petronas backing, in the Belgian Belcar GT series. The car was to be driven by Tim Verbergt and Jeffery van Hooydonk, with the team targeting outright victory in the most prestigious race of the series, the Spa 24-hours.

The DBRS9 was a customer racing and track-day car, which Aston Martin unveiled during the 2005 Le Mans weekend.

RIGHT: **Although it looked similar to the DBR9, the DBRS9 was much easier and cheaper to run.**
BELOW: **DBRS9s were seen in sports-car racing championships in several countries. This Barwell Motorsport car competed in the British GT Championship.**

■ 2005 DBRS9

Engine	V12, fuel injection
Valvegear	Twin overhead cam per bank, 4 valves per cylinder
Bore and stroke	89 × 79.5mm
Capacity	5935cc
Power	550bhp (approx)
Transmission	Six-speed manual transmission or six-speed sequential, limited slip differential, rear-wheel drive
Chassis/body	Extruded aluminium 'VH' structure with aluminium roof and composite panels, steel roll cage
Suspension	Double wishbones, coil springs, anti-roll bar and monotube dampers front and rear
Brakes	Ventilated discs all round, with anti-lock
Performance	Top speed 190mph (307km/h), 0–60mph in 4sec (approx)

V8 VANTAGE RALLY GT

ASTON MARTINS MIGHT seem unlikely cars for modern-day rallying, but there are still rallies that are run entirely on twisty ribbons of asphalt rather than unmade forest tracks. It was for these tarmac events that the V8 Vantage Rally GT was made.

Built by Prodrive for Frédéric Dor, a millionaire enthusiast who had previously run Prodrive-developed Ferrari 550 Maranello race cars and a pair of DBR9s, the Rally GT used a tuned 4.3-litre V8 engine with 420bhp and 320lb ft of torque, fed to a standard six-speed manual gearbox. A competition-style fly-off handbrake was fitted, and there was a safety cut-out switch on the dashboard – which, incongruously, was trimmed in grey leather. There were no carpets, and the seats were replaced by Sparco competition buckets. The Rally GT was said to be 250kg (550lb) lighter than the standard Vantage, despite the fitment of a full roll cage.

The Dor car competed in French tarmac rallies in 2006 and appeared at the Race of Champions event in 2007, where it was driven by a host of famous names including rally champions Sebastien Loeb and Colin McRae, and F1 stars Jenson Button and David Coulthard.

Prodrive offered replicas for sale, but it seems only four cars were built.

2006 V8 VANTAGE RALLY GT

Engine	V8, fuel injection
Valvegear	Twin overhead cam per bank, 4 valves per cylinder
Bore and stroke	89 × 86mm
Capacity	4280cc
Power	420bhp @ 7,200rpm
Transmission	Six-speed manual transmission, limited slip differential, rear-wheel drive
Chassis/body	Extruded aluminium 'VH' structure with aluminium alloy, magnesium alloy and composite panels
Suspension	Double wishbones, coil springs, anti-roll bar and monotube dampers front and rear
Brakes	Ventilated discs all round, with anti-lock
Performance	Top speed 189mph (305km/h), 0–60mph in 4sec (approx)

The V8 Vantage made an unlikely rally machine, but Prodrive built a handful of rally-spec cars. This one is on display at a Prodrive open day in 2007.

RAPIDE CONCEPT

FOUR-DOOR ASTON MARTINS have been few and far between. A very small number of four-door saloons were built in the 1930s, and the one-off Atom built during the war had four doors. The wedge-shaped Lagonda was originally badged 'Aston Martin Lagonda', and one or two of the rare Works Service Virage saloons may have had an Aston, rather than a Lagonda, badge. But that was about it, until the advent of the Rapide.

Aston Martin's new director of design, Marek Reichman, made the first Rapide sketches in the summer of 2005 and the car quickly took shape at Gaydon, making its public debut in January 2006 at the Detroit Motor Show. It also appeared at the Geneva show and London motor shows.

The Rapide was 300mm (12in) longer than the DB9, all the extra length going into the wheelbase. The extra length provided space for a second pair of doors, and increased legroom inside for the rear passengers. The Rapide concept was 40mm (1.5in) taller than the two-door car and around 140kg (308lb) heavier. Its specification was lavish, and included full-length polycarbonate roof panels that could turn from clear to opaque at the flick of a switch, a chilled cabinet fitted in the luggage area that concealed two magnums of champagne, a chess set, and even playing cards for the amusement of rear seat passengers.

The Rapide was powered by the usual 5.9-litre V12, though the engine carried a legend which described it, inaccurately, as a '6.0 V12'. It was tuned to give 480bhp, and fitted with a ZF Touchtronic automatic gearbox. The combination was said to provide similar performance to the 450bhp DB9 despite the Rapide's extra weight. The brakes were carbon ceramic discs, the first time Aston Martin had used them.

Such was the reception given to the Rapide by the press and public that Aston Martin pressed ahead with a production version, though it would be more than two years before the definitive Rapide would make its debut.

ABOVE: **The Rapide concept made its debut at the Detroit show early in 2006.**
RIGHT: **The cocktail cabinet in the boot of the Rapide concept was not an idea that was likely to reach production.**

V8 VANTAGE N24

ASTON MARTIN ENTERED a V8 Vantage in the Nürburgring 24-hour race in 2006. The car was driven by Aston CEO Dr Ulrich Bez, the company's vehicle engineering manager Chris Porritt, test driver Wolfgang Schuhbauer and German journalist Horst von Saurma. It finished twenty-fourth overall in a field of 220, most of the other cars being purpose-built for racing. The Vantage, meanwhile, was a prototype car that had been stripped of its interior trim and fitted with polycarbonate windows to save weight. A full roll cage, racing seat, air jacks, fire extinguishers and a racing fuel tank were then added, along with slick racing tyres.

The Nürburgring car was back in action later in the year at the inaugural 24-hours of Bahrain, where it finished eighth overall. In 1,600 miles (2,575km) of high-speed racing it ran faultlessly, needing pit stops only for fuel, tyres and brake pads. By then Aston Martin had announced that it would build the N24, a replica of the Nürburgring car, as an upmarket track-day car, or a machine to use in National GT racing championships.

ABOVE: **The Vantage N24 was a replica of the Vantage prototype that Aston Martin entered in the Nürburgring 24-hour race in 2006.**
BELOW: **The Vantage finished twenty-fourth overall in the 2006 Nürburgring 24-hours and returned in 2007 and 2008, winning its class on its third appearance.**

Production of N24s began in January 2007 in a dedicated facility within the Gaydon factory. Based on the European specification (left-hand-drive) V8 Vantage, the N24 was given a package of modifications that saved weight, improved power and engine response, and made the car more suitable for track use. The engine internals were lightened and balanced, and the cylinder-head ports were reprofiled. Free-flow ITG air filters and low-loss catalytic converters were fitted, and the engine management system was remapped to suit. The V8 Vantage's standard dry-sump lubrication system was ideal for track use as it prevented oil surge under heavy cornering forces, so it was retained. The revised engine produced 410bhp, 30bhp up on the standard V8. The power was fed through a Valeo twin-plate cerametallic clutch to a six-speed manual gearbox.

Larger anti-roll bars were fitted front and rear, and there were aluminium dampers with adjustable spring platforms so the ride height could be varied, together with new linear-rate springs and separate helper springs. The front subframe was modified to increase camber and castor to suit the Yokohama A048-R tyres, which were fitted to Speedline five-spoke magnesium alloy wheels. The brakes were upgraded with Pagid RS29 race-spec pad material.

Inside, the N24 was devoid of all interior trim save for a simple Alcantara-covered dashboard and lightweight door trims. A Recaro race seat and Schroth six-point harness were provided for the driver, but the air conditioning and airbags were removed to save weight. Despite the addition of a full steel roll cage, the N24 weighed in at 1,350kg (2,980lb), 250kg (550lb) lighter than the standard V8 Vantage.

The N24 prototype returned to the Nürburgring 24-hour race twice more, winning its class in 2008. It was joined by customer N24s on both occasions. In 2008, twenty production N24s competed in the Aston Martin Asia Cup, a one-make series, which was won by Japanese driver Kota Sasaki.

■ 2006 V8 VANTAGE N24

Engine	V8, fuel injection
Valvegear	Twin overhead cam per bank, 4 valves per cylinder
Bore and stroke	89 × 86mm
Capacity	4280cc
Power	410bhp @ 7,500rpm
Transmission	Six-speed manual transaxle, six-speed Sportshift automated manual optional, limited slip differential, rear-wheel drive
Chassis/body	Extruded aluminium 'VH' structure with steel, aluminium alloy and composite panels
Suspension	Double wishbones, coil springs, anti-roll bar and monotube dampers with adjustable ride height, front and rear
Brakes	Ventilated discs all round, with anti-lock
Performance	Top speed 175mph (280km/h), 0–62mph in 4sec (approx)

The N24 had a blueprinted engine and stripped interior, and was designed with racing and track days in mind.

DBS

WITH THE DEMISE of the Vanquish in July 2007, a gap opened up at the top of the Aston Martin range for a 'hero car', with the accent very much on performance. That gap was filled by the DBS, which had been announced early in 2006 and made its public debut at the Pebble Beach Concours in August 2007. Based on the DB9, it had changes to the engine, transmission, brakes, suspension and bodywork, which made it a car for the altogether more serious driver.

The engine was the familiar 5.9-litre V12, in 510bhp form (the same as the outgoing Vanquish S). At first only the six-speed manual gearbox was offered, though the Touchtronic 2 automatic became available from 2008. In both cases the ratios in the gearbox were the same as in the DB9, but the DBS was given a shorter 3.70:1 final drive ratio – trading a little cruising refinement and fuel economy for greater in-gear acceleration.

To cope with the extra performance the DBS was fitted with new carbon ceramic matrix (CCM) brake discs, the first time they had been used on a road-going Aston. The CCM brakes saved 12.5kg (28lb) of unsprung weight, improving performance and handling while at the same time shortening stopping distances and providing remarkable resistance to fade in repeated heavy use. The tracks were wider and the suspension lower. A new 'adaptive damping system' (ADS) allowed the driver to set the damping to one of five firmness presets, and then monitored the throttle, brakes, steering and vehicle speed, altering the damping to suit the prevailing conditions. This meant the DBS could respond more effectively when the driver was using the car's prodigious performance, but without compromising ride quality when cruising. The system included a 'track' mode, which firmed up the dampers for circuit use. The stability control system also had a track mode, which allowed an experienced driver to explore the handling of the DBS while still providing a back-up for extreme situations – or the brave could disengage it entirely.

The revised mechanicals were clothed in a more muscular body reminiscent of the DBR9, with enlarged air intakes and a pair of air vents in the bonnet, through which hot air was exhausted. A new nose with a carbon-fibre splitter helped to direct air around the wheels, while at the rear there was a carbon-fibre diffuser and a reshaped boot lid, which worked together to reduce lift at high speeds.

Most of the bodywork was made from carbon-fibre to save weight. To ensure the carbon panels still had the fine surface finish expected of an Aston Martin, a patented 'Surface Veil' process was used to apply a 200 micron layer of epoxy resin and glass to the surface of each panel before it was painted.

The lightweight approach extended to the interior, with carbon-fibre door pulls saving a further few grams, and light-

The DBS filled the gap left when production of the Vanquish ended in 2007.

TOP: **The DBS was also available as a Volante convertible.**
ABOVE: **The UB-2010 special edition DBS celebrated the tenth year of Ulrich Bez's tenure as Aston Martin CEO.**

weight semi-aniline leather saving a few more. Originally the DBS shaved away still more weight by deleting the rear seat, but 'plus two' seating was made available as an option from 2008. At the same time twenty-spoke, forged alloy wheels were offered, saving a further 8kg (17.6lb), while the DBS was given a Bang & Olufsen BeoSound audio system as standard. In 2010 a special edition DBS with a 'metallic' leather interior, the UB-2010, was unveiled to celebrate Ulrich Bez's tenth anniversary as Aston Martin CEO. Dr Bez signed off each car personally.

The DBS remains, for the moment, the pinnacle of Aston Martin's mainstream range – though its place as the ultimate Aston has been taken by the incredible limited-edition One-77.

■ 2007 DBS

Engine	V12, fuel injection
Valvegear	Twin overhead cam per bank, 4 valves per cylinder
Bore and stroke	89 × 79.5mm
Capacity	5935cc
Power	510bhp @ 6,000rpm
Transmission	Six-speed manual or six-speed Touchtronic automatic transmission, limited slip differential, rear-wheel drive
Chassis/body	Extruded aluminium 'VH' structure with aluminium alloy and composite panels
Suspension	Double wishbones, coil springs, anti-roll bar and adaptive dampers front and rear
Brakes	Carbon ceramic matrix discs all round, with anti-lock
Performance	Top speed 191mph (307km/h), 0–60mph in 4.3sec

JAMES BOND'S DBS

EARLY IN 2006 Aston Martin announced that in the next James Bond feature film a new Aston Martin would make its debut, alongside a new leading actor – Daniel Craig. Though few details were released at the time, the new car turned out to be the DBS, which appeared with Craig in *Casino Royale*, released in November 2006.

Although *Casino Royale* marked a break with previous Bond films and reintroduced 007 as a younger, less experienced agent, there was at least one echo of the past as far as Aston Martin enthusiasts were concerned: as on so many previous occasions, Bond's Aston ended up rather worse for wear. This time it met its end in a road accident in which it rolled over. In fact, stunt driver Adam Kirley made the DBS flip eight times in mid-air, a world record for that kind of stunt.

The DBS returned in the next Bond film, *Quantum of Solace*, in 2008 – and was equally badly treated. This time 007's Aston is chased by villains in Alfa Romeos along the shores of Lake Garda in Italy. It loses a door before being chased into a quarry – where, naturally, Bond evades his pursuers. At least six DBSs were used in filming, one of which was written off before shooting even began – on the way to the location it left the road and ended up in the lake, though fortunately the driver was unhurt.

TOP: **The DBS appeared alongside Daniel Craig in the film *Casino Royale* in 2006.**
ABOVE: **The DBS was the latest in a long line of 007 Aston Martins – and was as badly treated as most of its predecessors.**

The DBS is unlikely to return in the twenty-third Bond film, as yet unnamed, which is due for release late in 2012. If Bond again uses an Aston Martin – which is far from certain – it is more likely to be a One-77.

V8 VANTAGE N400

ASTON MARTIN WAS rightly proud of the fine performances of the V8 Vantage in the Nürburgring 24-hour races. To celebrate, a special edition Vantage, the N400, was unveiled in 2007. It was available as a coupé and a roadster, and incorporated a mildly reworked version of the V8 engine, which still had a capacity of 4.3 litres, but now produced 400bhp and 309lb ft of torque. Buyers could choose from a six-speed manual gearbox or six-speed Sportshift automated manual. Uprated springs were fitted, and coupé models were given a stiffer rear anti-roll bar, while both models received lightweight forged alloy wheels with a graphite and diamond-turned finish.

Other obvious external changes were reshaped sills, clear rear lamps and a Magnum Silver grille. The N400 was only available in three special body colours: Karrussell Orange, Bergwerk Black and Lightning Silver. Inside there was a unique 'micro-spin' alloy facia, and the seats and dash were trimmed in black leather, with perforated seat facings and coarse stitching in either orange or silver. An outline of the Nürburgring Nordschleife race circuit was stitched into the centre armrest.

Gaydon built 480 N400s, 240 coupés and 240 roadsters, the total apparently representing the car's 480sec (8min) Nürburgring lap time.

■ V8 VANTAGE N400

The N400 celebrated the Vantage's fine performances in sports car races at the Nürburgring.

Engine	V8, fuel injection
Valvegear	Twin overhead cam per bank, 4 valves per cylinder
Bore and stroke	89 × 86mm
Capacity	4280cc
Power	400bhp @ 7,300rpm
Transmission	Six-speed manual transaxle or six-speed Sportshift automated manual, limited slip differential, rear-wheel drive
Chassis/body	Extruded aluminium 'VH' structure with steel, aluminium alloy and composite panels
Suspension	Double wishbones, coil springs, anti-roll bar and monotube dampers
Brakes	Ventilated discs all round, with anti-lock
Performance	Top speed 177mph (285km/h), 0–60mph in 4.85sec (approx)

V8 VANTAGE AND ROADSTER 4.7

V8 VANTAGE BUYERS looking for more power had the option of a Prodrive upgrade package from 2006, which provided them with a 425bhp engine, revised exhaust system, Bilstein/Eibach suspension, carbon-fibre spoilers front and rear, and fourteen-spoke, 19in forged alloy wheels. But in May 2008 both the coupé and roadster V8 Vantages were given an enlarged engine as standard, which provided a similar power output, together with a package of detail upgrades that made improvements to the rest of the car.

The V8 engine switched from cast-in to pressed-in cylinder liners, allowing the liners to be thinner and the bore to be increased from 89mm to 91mm. At the same time the stroke was increased from 86mm to 91mm, giving a capacity of 4735cc. There were new forged steel conrods and aluminium pistons, revised cylinder heads with improved porting and larger intake valves, and a more efficient dry-sump system. The changes resulted in an increase in maximum power to 420bhp, while maximum torque rose to 347lb ft.

ABOVE: **In 2008 the V8 Vantage was given a 4.7-litre engine and a host of detail improvements.**
LEFT: **The new engine was bigger in both bore and stroke; power climbed to 420bhp.**

A new flywheel and clutch saved weight, reduced pedal effort and improved engine response. The Sportshift transmission was given a revised control strategy with Comfort and Sports modes, the latter providing a more aggressive response to throttle inputs to deliver a more sporting feel. The Sportshift system also now had extra data inputs, giving it more sophisticated automatic control of gearchanges. It could recognize when the Vantage was cornering, in which case it delayed a gearchange that might otherwise unsettle the car. It could also detect a hill descent, hanging on to a lower gear to make maximum use of engine braking.

All Vantages were upgraded to low-friction Bilstein dampers, which were said to improve the ride, and the revised damper mountings and bump stops introduced on the Volante were carried over to the coupé. The front springs were stiffened by 11 per cent and the rears by 5 per cent. There were 22 per cent stiffer front lower wishbone bushes and revised steering geometry to enhance steering response.

There were also changes inside the V8 Vantage, including revised switchgear and a new centre console, die cast in zinc alloy with a graphite silver finish. The original key was replaced by an Aston Martin 'emotion control unit' made from glass,

Interior changes on the 2008 cars included a new centre console and the addition of an 'emotion control unit'.

stainless steel and polycarbonate – a touch first seen on the DBS in 2006. The revised Vantage was also given a hard-disc navigation system, which had better graphics and was faster at processing routes.

A new twenty-spoke 19in alloy wheel design was fitted as standard, but a lighter five-spoke wheel was available as part of the Sports Pack upgrade, which also included uprated springs and rear anti-roll bar (on the coupé only), and revised damping. Aston Martin said the pack offered better dynamic performance, and was aimed at 'the most enthusiastic of drivers'.

■ 2008 V8 VANTAGE 4.7

Engine	V8, fuel injection
Valvegear	Twin overhead cam per bank, 4 valves per cylinder
Bore and stroke	91 × 91mm
Capacity	4735cc
Power	420bhp @ 7,000rpm
Transmission	Six-speed manual transaxle, Sportshift automatic optional, limited slip differential, rear-wheel drive
Chassis/body	Extruded aluminium 'VH' structure with steel, aluminium alloy and composite panels
Suspension	Double wishbones, coil springs, anti-roll bar and monotube dampers front and rear
Brakes	Ventilated discs all round, with anti-lock
Performance	Top speed 180mph (290km/h), 0–62mph in 4.8sec

V8 VANTAGE GT2

WITH THE INTRODUCTION of the Vantage GT2 in 2007, Aston Martin Racing became the only constructor to offer customer cars for all four classes of GT racing.

The GT2 retained the V8 Vantage's VH aluminium structure and added a steel roll cage to enhance crash safety and to stiffen the structure. The roof was aluminium, but the rest of the body panels were carbon-fibre, and there was a sophisticated aerodynamic package including a carbon splitter, rear diffuser and rear aerofoil. The GT2 could meet the FIA GT2 minimum weight of 1,150kg (2,536lb).

The engine was a 4.5-litre version of the V8, designed specifically for use on E85 bio-ethanol. It drove through a six-speed sequential manual transmission with a 'flat shift' or full-throttle gearshift function, and a competition clutch.

Drayson Racing ran the GT2 in the IMSA Cup in 2008 and the American Le Mans Series (ALMS) in 2009, with a best finish of seventh place at Spa. The team also took the car to Le Mans in 2009, where their race ended after twenty-two hours following electrical problems. At least seven GT2 cars have been built in Banbury, and the cars continue to compete in GT2 events.

■ 2008 V8 VANTAGE GT2

Engine	V8, Pectel SQ6 engine management
Valvegear	Twin overhead cam per bank, 4 valves per cylinder
Bore and stroke	Not quoted
Capacity	4500cc (approx)
Power	475bhp (approx)
Transmission	Six-speed sequential manual transaxle with 'flat shift' and competition clutch, limited slip differential, rear-wheel drive
Chassis/body	Extruded aluminium 'VH' structure with steel, aluminium alloy and composite panels
Suspension	Double wishbones, coil springs, anti-roll bar and monotube dampers front and rear
Brakes	Ventilated discs all round, with anti-lock
Performance	Top speed 190mph (305km/h), 0–60mph in 4sec (approx)

Built specifically for sports car racing, the Vantage GT2 had a 4.5-litre V8 engine developing around 475bhp.

V8 VANTAGE GT4

ASTON MARTIN REPLACED its Vantage N24 GT4-class contender with a new car in 2009. Simply called the Vantage GT4, it took advantage of the 4.7-litre engine upgrade that had been made to the V8 Vantage road cars. The increased capacity provided greater torque throughout the rev range, making the GT4 considerably quicker than the N24. The car was available with either a manual transmission or the Sportshift system. Both versions were fitted with a Valeo twin-plate cerametallic racing clutch and lightweight flywheel.

Changes were also made to the suspension to improve handling, including the use of modified front uprights to increase negative camber for more front-end grip. The brakes were also improved, with larger diameter front discs and better brake cooling to reduce fade.

The rest of the specification was much the same as the N24. The body was fitted with polycarbonate windows and was prepared for the fitment of on-board jacks. The stripped-out interior was protected by a full steel roll cage and Lifeline fire extinguisher system, and there was a gel battery and racing cut-out switch. The road-car suspension was retuned to suit Yokohama racing tyres, and there were Pagid competition brake pads to cope with repeated heavy braking.

The first GT4s were delivered in January 2009 and cost £96,645. Once GT4s hit the tracks the N24 became practically obsolete, and some N24 owners have had their cars upgraded to GT4 spec.

◼ 2009 V8 VANTAGE GT4

Engine	V8, fuel injection
Valvegear	Twin overhead cam per bank, 4 valves per cylinder
Bore and stroke	91 × 91mm
Capacity	4735cc
Power	450bhp (approx)
Transmission	Six-speed manual transaxle, Sportshift automatic optional, limited slip differential, rear-wheel drive
Chassis/body	Extruded aluminium 'VH' structure with steel, aluminium alloy and composite panels
Suspension	Double wishbones, coil springs, anti-roll bar and monotube dampers front and rear
Brakes	Ventilated discs all round, with anti-lock
Performance	Top speed 180mph (290km/h), 0–62mph in 4sec (approx)

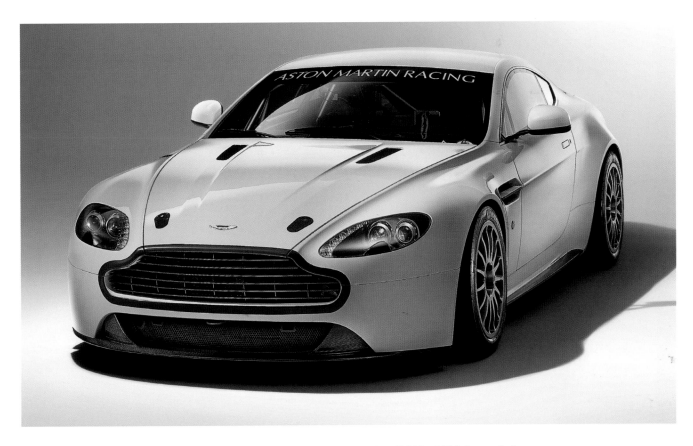

**The N24 was replaced by the Vantage GT4 in 2009. It used the
4.7-litre engine with either a manual or Sportshift transmission.**

V8 VANTAGE N420

YET ANOTHER VARIATION on the V8 Vantage theme, the N420, was unveiled in 2010. It was based on the revised 4.7-litre Vantage and was the successor to the 4.3-litre N400. It provided buyers with a motor sport-inspired edition of the V8 Vantage that was less of a raw racer than the GT4.

Available as a coupé or roadster, the N420 had a subtly different appearance to the standard car thanks to a new carbon-fibre splitter and wider sills. It had a carbon diffuser at the back, and ten-spoke gloss black alloy wheels with diamond-turned faces, also black grilles, black strakes across the wing vents and 'Graphitic' tailpipe finishers. A range of two-colour 'Race Collection' paint schemes was available, including replicas of Aston Martin's Vantage N24 racing liveries.

Inside, the N420 had the Iridium package, which included graphite instruments, a leather or Alcantara steering wheel, special sill plaques and lightweight carbon-fibre seats.

Aston Martin announced no mechanical modifications over the standard car, so the N420 had the 4.7-litre, 420bhp engine, and it was available with either the manual or Sportshift transmission. However, although the engine was standard, it was slightly quicker than the regular 4.7-litre Vantage as it was 27kg (60lb) lighter.

■ 2010 V8 VANTAGE N420

Engine	V8, fuel injection
Valvegear	Twin overhead cam per bank, 4 valves per cylinder
Bore and stroke	91 × 91mm
Capacity	4735cc
Power	420bhp @ 7,000rpm
Transmission	Six-speed manual transaxle, Sportshift automatic optional, limited slip differential, rear-wheel drive
Chassis/body	Extruded aluminium 'VH' structure with steel, aluminium alloy and composite panels
Suspension	Double wishbones, coil springs, anti-roll bar and monotube dampers front and rear
Brakes	Ventilated discs all round, with anti-lock
Performance	Top speed 180mph (290km/h), 0–62mph in 4.6sec (approx)

The 4.7-litre N420 of 2010 was the replacement for the 4.3-litre N400. It was available in both coupé and roadster form.

V12 VANTAGE

THE VANTAGE RS concept of 2007 took what was then Aston Martin's smallest car and inserted one of its most powerful engines – a 600bhp 5.9-litre V12. This started the debate about what a V12 Vantage production car should be, and the result was finally launched at the Geneva show in 2009.

The production V12 Vantage was a much more civilized machine. The revised front-end structure held a 510bhp V12, essentially the DBS engine, which drove through a carbon-fibre propshaft to the six-speed manual gearbox at the rear (there was no automatic option). A 'Sport' button on the dash selected a more aggressive throttle response and a louder exhaust note.

The suspension was lowered and stiffened, and redesigned at the rear with more compact dual-rate springs, which provided space for larger wheels and tyres within the existing bodywork. Carbon ceramic brakes, like those on the DBS, were standard fit. The body itself was reshaped, using the experience gained from racing the Vantage, with revised aerodynamics including bonnet vents to allow hot air to escape from the packed engine bay.

Just 50kg (110lb) heavier than the V8 Vantage, and much more powerful, the V12 was an extraordinarily potent road car, which still offered refinement and docility when the driver desired.

The V12 Vantage RS concept combined what were then Aston Martin's smallest car and biggest engine.

The production V12 Vantage was powered by a 510bhp V12 engine, driving through a six-speed manual gearbox.

■ 2010 V12 VANTAGE

Engine	V12, fuel injection
Valvegear	Twin overhead cam per bank, 4 valves per cylinder
Bore and stroke	89 × 79.5mm
Capacity	5935cc
Power	510bhp @ 6,000rpm
Transmission	Six-speed manual transmission or six-speed Touchtronic automatic, limited slip differential, rear-wheel drive
Chassis/body	Extruded aluminium 'VH' structure with aluminium alloy and composite panels
Suspension	Double wishbones, coil springs, anti-roll bar and monotube dampers front and rear
Brakes	Ventilated discs all round, with anti-lock
Performance	Top speed 190mph (306km/h), 0–60mph in 4.1sec

LAGONDA CONCEPT

THE LAGONDA NAME returned in 2009 with this car, simply called the Lagonda Concept. According to Aston Martin it was 'an avant-garde luxury vehicle...a four-seater car that will satisfy the most discerning and demanding owner.' Lagonda was intended to become 'the pre-eminent long-distance automobile, a vehicle that combines cosseting luxury with extreme functionality and technological innovation.' Controversially, the new Lagonda was a kind of vehicle that neither Aston Martin nor Lagonda had ever built before – an SUV.

Designed by a team led by Aston Martin design director Marek Reichman, the new car was said to draw inspiration from past Lagondas, particularly the LG6 V12, and also from high-end speedboat design. It had enormous presence but not a great deal of subtlety.

A massive chromed grille dominated the nose, flanked by relatively small headlamps which stretched sideways to meet a crisp feature line running the length of the car. Above the high waistline there was a low-rise cabin with black A and B pillars and a cap roof. At the rear the Lagonda had neither a typical

SUV-style vertical tail nor a three-box saloon shape, being somewhere in between.

Four individual seats were provided inside, the interior being visually divided into front and rear zones using colour – the front seats were dark grey, the rear ones a light grey. High quality leather dominated the cabin, as might be expected. More surprising was the combination of curves and angles inside, which gave the interior an edgy, busy feel – when perhaps a calmer, more classical style might have better suited the Lagonda's remit as a luxury vehicle for long-distance travel.

Aston Martin said the Lagonda had four-wheel drive and was based on an advanced platform that was tailored to accommodate a wide range of powertrains – including flex fuel, diesel and hybrid systems – as alternatives to the Aston Martin V12. Later it emerged that the Lagonda was based on the Mercedes-Benz GL-class platform, the first tangible evidence of a commercial link between Aston Martin and Mercedes' parent company Daimler AG, a link that had been rumoured for some time.

The Lagonda Concept was controversial because it reintroduced the Lagonda name not on a saloon car but on an SUV.

The show car, unveiled at the Geneva Salon, was said to be the start of a Lagonda revival that would see production cars available not just in the existing thirty-plus countries where Aston Martins were already sold, but in many more as well, in particular in the growth areas of the Middle East, South America, India and China. But reaction to the concept was mixed, and at one stage it was reported that the SUV project had been cancelled in favour of a more conventional saloon. Now it seems likely that Lagonda will build an SUV-type vehicle, but one which may be very different to this concept. Whatever the production-ready Lagonda looks like, it is unlikely to be unveiled before 2013.

ABOVE: **The Lagonda Concept's styling was bold, if not very elegant. Production Lagondas will follow, but are likely to be very different.**
RIGHT: **The Lagonda Concept interior was lavish, but some of the detailing was fussy.**

RAPIDE

POSITIVE RESPONSE TO the Rapide concept car (see p.179) persuaded Aston Martin's new management to put the car into production, but the definitive Rapide unveiled early in 2010 was subtly different to the concept car of 2006.

There was no change to the basic idea of a four-door, four-seat sports car. The layout remained the same as it had done on the concept, but there were detail changes to the body, which took the Rapide further away from the DB9 and made it a more individual car. Most noticeably the bi-xenon headlights were reshaped, the wheel arches reprofiled, and there was a new V8

Vantage-style crease along the doors. Less obvious was the increased opening arc of the doors to make getting in and out easier. And the concept's champagne cooler had disappeared.

The Rapide production car was given a 470bhp version of the V12 engine, the same specification as the 2009 DB9, fitted as standard with the Touchtronic 2 automatic gearbox. As with other Astons, the engine was built at the Aston Martin engine plant, situated within Ford's Cologne production facility.

For the first time on an Aston Martin road car, the Rapide featured a 'dual cast' braking system with discs combining two

ABOVE: **The Rapide production car was a subtly different shape to the 2006 concept, with new headlamps, reshaped front wings and a Vantage-style side crease.**
LEFT: **This Rapide finished a creditable second in class at the Nürburgring 24-hour race in 2010.**

The Rapide Luxe of 2010 had 20in alloy wheels, a bespoke luggage set and improvements inside.

materials: iron and aluminium alloy. Using this system the Rapide's brakes were 15 to 20 per cent lighter than conventional steel brakes, but still provided excellent heat resistance and wear properties. The Rapide was also given a brake-assist function to ensure that maximum brake effort was provided during emergency stops. Running gear upgrades also included the fitment of the adaptive damping first seen on the DBS, which preserved the Rapide's ride quality while sharpening the handling response when the car was driven hard.

The most unusual aspect to the Rapide was not its four-door design but the location of manufacture. Gaydon was already working at full capacity building V8 Vantages, DB9s and DBSs, so Aston Martin had contracted out Rapide production to a specialist company, Magna Steyr. A new 23,000sq ft (2,137sq m) plant was established at Magna Steyr's production facility in Graz, Austria, to build up to 2,000 Rapides a year, making it the first Aston Martin to be built outside the UK. The Aston Martin Rapide Plant (AMRP) was open to Rapide customers, and specialist staff would assist customers to choose from the 2.5 million option combinations available.

Keen to show that the Rapide was as much a genuine Aston as any of the coupés and roadsters, Aston Martin entered a Rapide in the Nürburgring 24-hour race in 2010. The car was deliberately kept as standard as possible. Inevitably the interior was stripped out and the car gained a full roll cage, slick tyres and lowered suspension, and there were polycarbonate windows to help cut the Rapide's weight by nearly 400kg (882lb)

– but the engine and transmission were standard, and all four doors still functioned (four-door race cars usually have the rear doors welded shut). The Rapide finished the race thirty-fourth overall and a fine second in its class.

Late in 2010 Aston Martin unveiled a Rapide Luxe, which added a number of extras to the standard specification, including 20in twenty-spoke alloy wheels, glass gear selector switches, a bespoke luggage set and upgraded in-car entertainment.

■ 2010 RAPIDE

Engine	V12, fuel injection
Valvegear	Twin overhead cam per bank, 4 valves per cylinder
Bore and stroke	89×79.5mm
Capacity	5935cc
Power	470bhp @ 6,000rpm
Transmission	Six-speed manual transmission or six-speed Touchtronic automatic, limited slip differential, rear-wheel drive
Chassis/body	Extruded aluminium 'VH' structure with aluminium alloy and composite panels
Suspension	Double wishbones, coil springs, anti-roll bar and adaptive dampers front and rear
Brakes	Ventilated iron/aluminium discs all round, with anti-lock
Performance	Top speed 190mph (306km/h), 0–60mph in 5sec

ONE-77

THE ONE-77 IS the ultimate Aston Martin: it is the fastest, the most powerful, and the most expensive production car the company has ever built.

In the summer of 2008 Aston Martin released a single image of the One-77 and a few scant details, but they were enough to set pulses racing: this was to be a 7.3-litre V12 supercar with a carbon-fibre chassis. A mock-up appeared at the Paris show a few weeks later but remained mostly hidden under dust covers, so the first time the car was revealed in public was at the Geneva Salon early in 2009. Customers were invited to put down a deposit of £200,000 against the full price of £1 million – plus taxes.

In December 2009 Aston Martin revealed that a One-77 development car had exceeded 220mph in testing. The exact top speed was unclear: Aston Martin claimed it was '220.007mph (354.86km/h)', but the presence of those famous 007 digits looked fishy, and in any case 354.86km/h is actually 220.500mph... Whatever the reality, the One-77 was certainly destined to be the fastest production Aston ever made, substantially faster than either the DBS (the fastest of the current range) or the Vanquish S (the previous fastest ever). Its top speed even exceeded that of the AMR1 Le Mans racer.

The immense power output required to achieve these very high speeds was produced by a comprehensively redeveloped version of the V12 engine, which had been reworked in conjunction with engine specialists Cosworth. With a capacity of 7.3 litres and a power output in excess of 750bhp, the new V12 was the most powerful naturally aspirated (that is, non-turbo) engine on the planet. Like the V8 in the Vantage, the engine was fitted in a front-mid position, several inches behind the front axle line, and it fed its prodigious output to a rear-mounted six-speed automated manual transmission.

To control all the power the One-77 was fitted with carbon ceramic brakes like those on the DBS, and there were electronic stability control and traction control systems. The suspension was unusual for a road car, as the spring and damper units were mounted horizontally and actuated by pushrods – a system more usually seen on racing cars – and the ride height varied depending on the driving conditions.

The bodywork was hand-crafted aluminium, a curious choice given that the chassis underneath was moulded from carbon-fibre reinforced composites, and that Aston Martin had plenty of experience with carbon-fibre bodywork on the DBS. Perhaps it had something to do with designer Marek Reichman's stated aim of building a car 'closer to art than the automobile'. Certainly the One-77's shape was breathtaking, with a muscularity and athleticism that was a step beyond any of the existing range.

As the name suggests, each One-77 was one of just seventy-seven customer cars, and the first of them was seen in Monaco early in 2011.

The One-77 is the ultimate road-going Aston Martin. Just seventy-seven of these 7.3-litre V12 supercars will be built.

RIGHT: **The One-77 was breathtaking, inside and out. Carbon-fibre featured inside and was used to construct the chassis, but the bodywork was aluminium.**

BELOW: **During testing a One-77 exceeded 220mph (354km/h), making it the fastest Aston Martin ever built.**

■ 2011 ONE-77

Engine	V12, fuel injection
Valvegear	Twin overhead cam per bank, 4 valves per cylinder
Bore and stroke	Not quoted
Capacity	7300cc (approx)
Power	750bhp
Transmission	Six-speed sequential manual transmission, limited slip differential, rear-wheel drive
Chassis/body	Carbon-fibre composite structure with aluminium alloy panels
Suspension	Double wishbones, pushrods, coil spring/damper units, anti-roll bar front and rear
Brakes	Carbon ceramic discs all round, with anti-lock
Performance	Top speed 220mph (354km/h), 0–60mph in 3.5sec

DB9 SPECIAL EDITIONS

ABOVE: **Late in 2010 Aston Martin released three special edition DB9s. The ones pictured are the Carbon Black (*left*) and Morning Frost cars; the third one was Quantum Silver.**

LEFT: **The Morning Frost limited edition featured bronze leather, and piano black facia and door trims.**

JUST AS THE DB7 six-cylinder and V12 models spawned a series of special edition models towards the end of their production run, so the DB9 provided the basis for special edition cars, including three limited run versions announced just before Christmas 2010. These cars emphasized the DB9's luxury and performance qualities.

The luxury version was the Morning Frost edition, which featured pearlescent white paint and the same sort of bronze leather interior trim that had been fitted to the DBS UB2010 special edition earlier in the year. The interior of the Morning Frost DB9 also incorporated a piano black centre console and door trims. On the outside it was recognizable by 19in ten-spoke diamond-turned wheels, silver brake calipers and silver grilles. Volantes were available with brown or black roofs, with ivory headlinings. Mechanically the car was exactly the same as the standard-spec DB9, as were all three special editions.

The other two were the Carbon Black and Quantum Silver editions, the former sharing the black exterior colour scheme of the V12 Vantage Carbon Black, the latter taking its exterior colour from the *Quantum of Solace* DBS. Both had what Aston Martin described rather floridly as 'menacing sport specifications': that meant a remapped sports exhaust system which provided 'an even more evocative sound', 19in gloss black diamond-turned wheels, black grilles and graphite tail pipes. Inside there was Obsidian black leather with perforated seat facings, semi-aniline leather roof lining, coarse silver stitching, and even polished glass switchgear. As with Morning Frost, both Carbon Black and Quantum Silver were available in Volante form, with a grey-lined black hood.

All these DB9 specials were fitted with automatic gearboxes and Touchtronic 2 gear selection systems, and all had sill plaques laser-etched with the Aston Martin logo and the edition name.

LOLA-ASTON MARTIN B08/60 AND B09/60 LMP1

ASTON MARTIN MOVED up from GT1 racing to the big league – the LMP1 class – in 2008. The car was a Lola, but its power came from a revised version of the DBR9's production-based V12 engine. The Lola was run by the Czech team Charouz Racing System. Driven by Jan Charouz, Tomas Enge and Stefan Mücke, it finished a fine ninth overall at Le Mans. The best result of the year was second place in the 1,000km of Silverstone.

For 2009 the team had the new Lola B09/60 chassis – which Aston Martin liked to refer to as the DBR1-2, though Lola weren't so keen on that idea – and an evocative new Gulf Oil livery. The season started well when Charouz, Enge and Mücke won the 1,000km of Catalunya in April in their 007-numbered Lola, and at Le Mans they achieved an excellent fourth place overall and top petrol-powered car behind three diesel cars, which were favoured by the regulations. There was a second win at the Nürburgring 1,000km in August, Lola-Astons filling

Aston Martin returned to top-level sports car racing in 2008 with a Lola chassis and a development of the V12 engine.

the first three places. As a result the 007 Lola won the Le Mans Series.

The Lola-Astons competed in some of the Le Mans Series events in 2010, with a best finish of second at Paul Ricard. At Le Mans the Lolas could do no better than sixth.

2010 LOLA-ASTON MARTIN B09/60

Engine	V12, fuel injection with Pectel engine management
Valvegear	Twin overhead cam per bank, 4 valves per cylinder
Bore and stroke	Not quoted
Capacity	6000cc (approx)
Power	650bhp @ 7,500rpm
Transmission	Xtrac transverse six-speed sequential manual gearbox with triple-plate carbon clutch
Chassis/body	Carbon-fibre monocoque
Suspension	Double wishbone front and rear with Koni adjustable dampers
Brakes	Ventilated carbon discs all round, Brembo six-pot calipers
Performance	Top speed 210mph (337km/h), 0–60mph in 3.5sec (approx)

CYGNET

NO ASTON MARTIN has ever created such debate and controversy as the Cygnet – not even the leap into the crisp-creased, digital future that was the 1976 Lagonda. Cygnet represents not just a new model for Aston Martin, but a journey into territory not only new to the brand, but unknown in the history of the manufacture of bespoke cars.

The Cygnet is, simply, a Toyota iQ city car, reskinned with an Aston Martin grille and retrimmed with the kind of materials and craftsmanship that would be seen in any other modern Aston. With a list price of £30,995 it costs a third as much as any other Aston Martin, and with a 1.3-litre engine and just 97bhp it has nothing like the pace associated with the brand. What it does do is offer the kind of ambience and exclusivity that are essential features of any Aston, and it means that city-bound Aston owners can drive a practical, economical runabout without sacrificing their loyalty to their favourite automotive brand.

Production of the Cygnet began in April 2011 with two limited edition models, White and Black, available with the choice of a six-speed manual gearbox or MultiDrive continuously variable transmission. An electric version seems likely in the future.

Whether the car proves to be a success or not – and whether it enhances or hinders the marque – remains to be seen. Either way the Cygnet will certainly be an Aston Martin that admirers of the brand will be talking about for many years to come.

◼ 2011 CYGNET

Engine	In-line four, fuel injection
Valvegear	Twin overhead cam, 4 valves per cylinder
Bore and stroke	72.5 × 80.5mm
Capacity	1329cc
Power	97bhp @ 7,200rpm
Transmission	Six-speed manual gearbox or MultiDrive CVT, front-wheel drive
Chassis/body	Steel monocoque
Suspension	MacPherson strut front, torsion beam rear
Brakes	Discs all round, ventilated front, with anti-lock
Performance	Top speed 106mph (171km/h), 0–60mph in 11.6sec (approx)

Inside, the Cygnet has the quality of fixtures and fittings associated with a modern Aston.

The Toyota iQ-based Cygnet was the most controversial Aston Martin ever made.

V8 VANTAGE S

THE V8 VANTAGE S, unveiled in January 2011, was the first Aston Martin to use a new seven-speed Sportshift II semi-automatic transmission, fitted as standard, which could be operated by magnesium-alloy paddles behind the steering wheel. This new automated manual transmission was said to shift 20 per cent faster than the original six-speed Sportshift, introduced on the V8 Vantage at the Paris show in 2006. The new transmission was also lighter than the old six-speeder, and according to Aston Martin it was around 50kg (110lb) lighter than the dual-clutch gearboxes being used by rival sports-car manufacturers. In the Vantage S, shorter gear ratios and a shorter final-drive ratio of 4.182:1 were used to maximize acceleration.

In addition to the new transmission, the V8 Vantage S was given a revised version of the 4.7-litre V8 engine producing 430bhp and 361lb ft (an increase of 10bhp and 15lb ft, respectively over the existing 4.7 litre car). The steering was given a faster ratio, the front brakes were enlarged and the rear tyres were wider. Visual changes included a larger air intake at the front, a new rear bumper and sill extensions.

The Vantage S was available as either a coupé or a roadster, and Aston Martin revealed that each one took 185 man hours to build – including fifty hours to paint and seventy to trim the leather-clad interior.

ABOVE: **Aston Martin said the Vantage S took 185 man hours to build, including fifty hours to paint and seventy hours to trim.**
BELOW: **The Vantage S had more power and a quicker shifting automated transmission.**

▪ 2011 V8 VANTAGE

Engine	V8, fuel injection
Valvegear	Twin overhead cam per bank, 4 valves per cylinder
Bore and stroke	91 × 91mm
Capacity	4735cc
Power	420bhp @ 7,200rpm
Transmission	Seven-speed automated manual transmission, limited slip differential, rear-wheel drive
Chassis/body	Extruded aluminium 'VH' structure with aluminium alloy, magnesium alloy and composite panels
Suspension	Double wishbones, coil springs, anti-roll bar a nd monotube dampers front and rear
Brakes	Ventilated discs all round, with anti-lock
Performance	Top speed 189mph (305km/h), 0–60mph in 4.5sec (approx)

VIRAGE

A NEW ASTON Martin was spotted testing at the Nürburgring in 2010. Clearly the new car was another variation on the DB9 theme, but opinion was divided over whether this new machine was an updated DB9 or a restyled DBS. It proved to be neither of those things, and was instead a brand new model that was designed to sit between those existing cars. Unveiled a week ahead of the Geneva Motor Show, the new car carried a familiar name from Aston Martin's past: Virage.

According to Aston Martin, the Virage combined outright sports-car performance with the highest levels of luxury and refinement. The V12 engine in the Virage, identified by its black plenum chamber, provided up to 490bhp – which made it exactly mid-way between the 470bhp DB9 and 510bhp DBS in power

terms. The plenum itself was redesigned to improve its rigidity, which improved the engine note. The Touchtronic 2 automatic transmission was fitted as standard. Also included in the standard specification was a Bilstein adaptive damping system similar to the one introduced on the DBS, though with softer basic settings. The system firmed up the dampers during spirited driving to sharpen the Virage's handling responses. Changes to the suspension bushes and solidly mounted subframes improved handling precision and cut noise and vibration. Another DBS-style feature to make it into the Virage spec was fade-resistant carbon ceramic brakes.

Although the Virage was obviously related to the DB9 it had its own individual style, with revised Rapide-style bi-xenon headlamps and a five-bar grille similar to that of the One-77. Underneath there was a wide air intake and angled sides to the front valance, which led visually into wider sill panels and directed air around the front wheels. Pirelli P-Zero tyres wrapped the 20in twenty-spoke alloys, with five-spoke and ten-spoke wheels available as options.

Inside, the Virage had a revised Garmin satnav system, unique seat stitching and polished glass selector switches for the transmission.

The Virage and Virage Volante provided a further variation on the theme of Aston Martin's popular DB9, giving Gaydon's customers another attractive V12 car to consider.

■ 2011 VIRAGE

Engine	V12, fuel injection
Valvegear	Twin overhead cam per bank, 4 valves per cylinder
Bore and stroke	89 × 79.5mm
Capacity	5935cc
Power	470bhp @ 6,500rpm
Transmission	Six-speed Touchtronic 2 automatic, limited slip differential, rear-wheel drive
Chassis/body	Extruded aluminium 'VH' structure with aluminium alloy and composite panels
Suspension	Double wishbones, coil springs, anti-roll bar and monotube dampers front and rear
Brakes	Ventilated discs all round, with anti-lock
Performance	Top speed 186mph (299km/h), 0–62mph in 4.6sec

Early in 2011 Aston Martin plugged the gap between the DB9 and DBS with the Virage.

AMR-ONE

AFTER THREE YEARS of racing in LMP1 with Lola-based cars, Aston Martin Racing switched to its own purpose-built chassis, announcing that an initial run of six cars would be built. All were to be powered by a completely new Aston Martin racing engine.

Preliminary design work on the new car began at the end of 2009, but progress was relatively slow until the Le Mans organizers, the Automobile Club de l'Ouest (ACO), confirmed a new equivalence formula designed to balance up the performance of petrol and diesel cars. In previous years diesel cars had always had the upper hand because they were favoured by the regulations, but that was set to change under the new formula, giving a petrol-powered Aston a genuine chance of outright victory.

At the 1,000km of Silverstone in September 2010 Aston Martin Racing announced its new LMP1 programme; in the words of Aston Martin chairman David Richards:

> I personally believe Le Mans is the greatest motor race in the world and it has always been not just a personal ambition of mine, but also that of Aston Martin, to come back and try and win it outright. To do that we need a specially built car, we need a special chassis, we need our own engine.

The team confirmed that it would be building an open car, to be powered by an all-new petrol engine. Team principal George Howard-Chappell revealed that the new regulations were

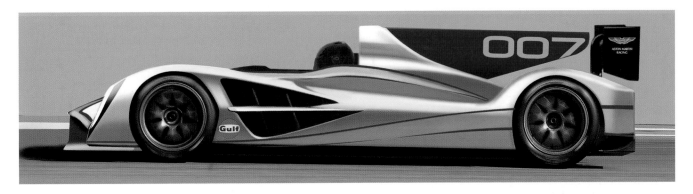

ABOVE: **Early sketches for the AMR-One included a DBR1-style side vent that did not appear on the final car.**

BELOW: **Aston Martin's 2011 challenger in LMP1 racing was the AMR-One, powered by a brand new 6-cylinder turbocharged engine.**

ABOVE: **The 'office' of the AMR-One. Three drivers share the cockpit over the course of twenty-four hours at Le Mans.**
LEFT: **With just 100 days between the public announcement of AMR-One and the start of the Le Mans 24-hour race, the team had no great expectations of success.**

crucial in making the decision to build the new car: 'The thing that really swung it for us was the introduction of Article 19 in the new regulations which assures us of a balance between fuel types and engine technologies.'

Said ACO sporting director Vincent Beaumesnil, speaking alongside Richards at the Aston Martin press conference:

> Looking for equilibrium of performance is a very complex thing – you have to consider many factors. It's not just the lap time. Performance is conditioned by the driver, the tyres, the aerodynamics, and so many other factors. Our purpose is to identify the right regulation to make equal two different technologies. We are committed to work on this and we will work in an open way with constructors on this subject.

The new engine was run on the Prodrive dynamometer in January 2011, and the new car – named AMR-One – was tested in the spring. Just 100 days after the public launch of the project the AMR-Ones were at Le Mans for the 24-hour race, but they were dogged by engine problems and could not match the speed of the diesel Audis and Peugeots. Both AMR-Ones were out of the race early, just six laps completed between them.

It was a huge disappointment for the team and for Aston Martin fans across the world. But the AMR-One will be back at Le Mans in 2012 with much more development behind them, and perhaps a further rethink of the petrol/diesel equivalence formula so they can compete on level terms with the diesel cars.

■ 2011 AMR-ONE

Engine	In-line six, turbocharged, direct fuel injection with Cosworth engine management
Valvegear	Twin overhead cam per bank, 4 valves per cylinder
Bore and stroke	Not quoted
Capacity	2000cc (approx)
Power	540bhp (approx)
Transmission	Six-speed Xtrac transverse semi-automatic gearbox with pneumatic shift
Chassis/body	Carbon-fibre monocoque with steel engine subframe
Suspension	Double wishbones, coil springs, anti-roll bar and monotube dampers front and rear
Brakes	Carbon discs and pads with six-pot Brembo calipers
Performance	Top speed 179mph (288km/h)

V12 VANTAGE ZAGATO

ASTON MARTIN'S LINKS with the Italian styling house Zagato were re-established in 2011 with the announcement of the V12 Vantage Zagato. Previous Zagato Astons were styled in Italy, but this time the project was much more of a collaboration between the Italian designers and Aston Martin's own design studio at Gaydon.

The shape of the new Zagato Aston was developed using both the latest computer-aided modelling techniques and traditional clay models, the aim being to combine styling cues from both Aston Martin and Zagato in a single, cohesive shape. Aston Martin design director Marek Reichman called it 'elegant yet brutal', a description that encapsulated a design that was muscular and aggressive, yet still had the grace of a modern Aston. Under the hand-made aluminium skin, the new Zagato shared its mechanicals with the V12 Vantage.

The Zagato made its debut at the Villa d'Este concours in May 2011, where it won Concorso d'Eleganza award. Two endurance racing versions then finished fifth and sixth overall in the Nürburgring 24-hours in June. As with Aston Martin's previous entries in the famous German event, the driver team was led by Dr Ulrich Bez.

▪ 2011 V12 VANTAGE ZAGATO

Engine	V12, fuel injection
Valvegear	Twin overhead cam per bank, 4 valves per cylinder
Bore and stroke	89 × 79.5mm
Capacity	5935cc
Power	510bhp @ 6,000rpm
Transmission	Six-speed automated manual transmission, limited slip differential, rear-wheel drive
Chassis/body	Extruded aluminium 'VH' structure with aluminium alloy panels
Suspension	Double wishbones, coil springs, anti-roll bar and monotube dampers front and rear
Brakes	Ventilated discs all round, with anti-lock
Performance	Top speed 190mph (306km/h), 0–60mph in 4.1sec

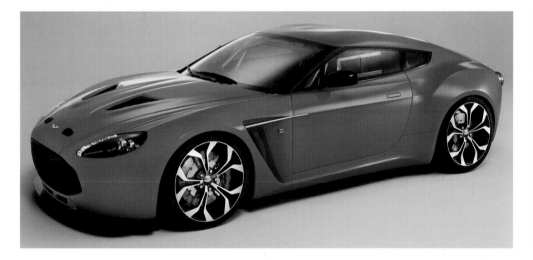

ABOVE: **In May 2011 Aston Martin unveiled what Ulrich Bez called a 'natural successor' to the Zagato Astons of the past: the Aston Martin V12 Vantage Zagato.**
ABOVE RIGHT: **Bold front wing vents carry Zagato 'Z' badges.**
LEFT: **The latest Zagato carries forward ideas from previous cars, such as the double-bubble roof and short overhangs.**

INDEX